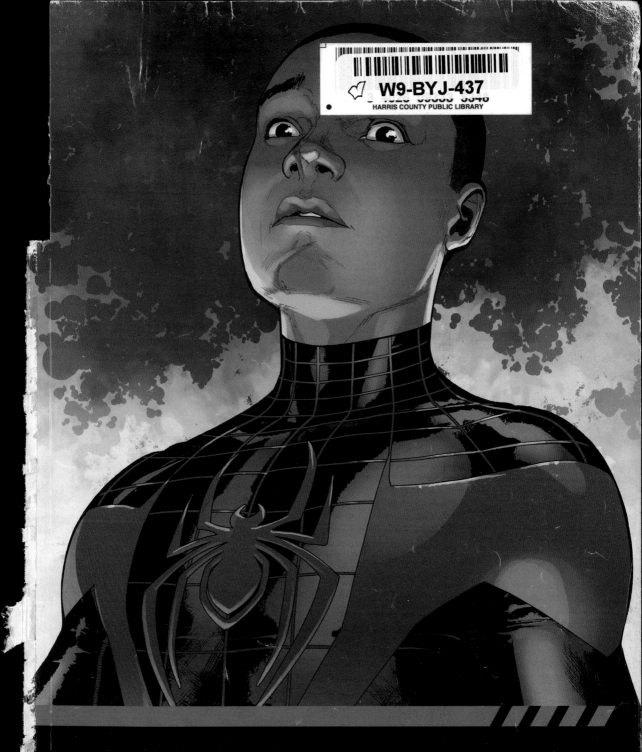

MILES MORALES: THE ULTIMATE
# SPIDER-MAN

REVELATIONS

COLLECTION EDITOR: JENNIFER GRÜNWALD
ASSISTANT EDITOR: SARAH BRUNSTAD
ASSOCIATE MANAGING EDITOR: ALEX STARBUCK
EDITOR, SPECIAL PROJECTS: MARK D. BEAZLEY
SENIOR EDITOR, SPECIAL PROJECTS: JEFF YOUNGQUIST
SVP PRINT, SALES & MARKETING: DAVID GABRIEL

EDITOR IN CHIEF: AXEL ALONSO
CHIEF CREATIVE OFFICER: JOE QUESADA
PUBLISHER: DAN BUCKLEY
EXECUTIVE PRODUCER: ALAN FINE

**MILES MORALES: ULTIMATE SPIDER-MAN VOL. 2 — REVELATIONS.** Contains material originally published in magazine form as MILES MORALES: ULTIMATE SPIDER-MAN #6-12. First printing 2015. ISBN# 978-0-785 5418-1. Published by MARVEL WORLDWIDE, INC., a subsidiary of MARVEL ENTERTAINMENT, LLC. OFFICE OF PUBLICATION: 135 West 50th Street, New York, NY 10020.  **Printed the U.S.A.** ALAN FINE, President, Marvel Entertainment; DAN BUCKLEY, President, TV, Publishing and Brand Management; JOE QUESADA, Chief Creative Officer; TOM BREVOORT, SVP of Publishing; DAVID BOGART, S of Operations & Procurement, Publishing; C.B. CEBULSKI, VP of International Development & Brand Management; DAVID GABRIEL, SVP Print, Sales & Marketing; JIM O'KEEFE, VP of Operations & Logistics; DAN CA Executive Director of Publishing Technology; SUSAN CRESPI, Editorial Operations Manager; ALEX MORALES, Publishing Operations Manager; STAN LEE, Chairman Emeritus. For information regarding advertising in Marvel Comics or on Marvel.com, please contact Jonathan Rheingold, VP of Custom Solutions & Ad Sales, at jrheingold@marvel.com. For Marvel subscription inquiries, please call 800-217-9158. **Manufactured between 4/17/2015 and 5/25/2015 by R.R. DONNELLEY, INC., SALEM, VA, USA.**

10 9 8 7 6 5 4 3 2 1

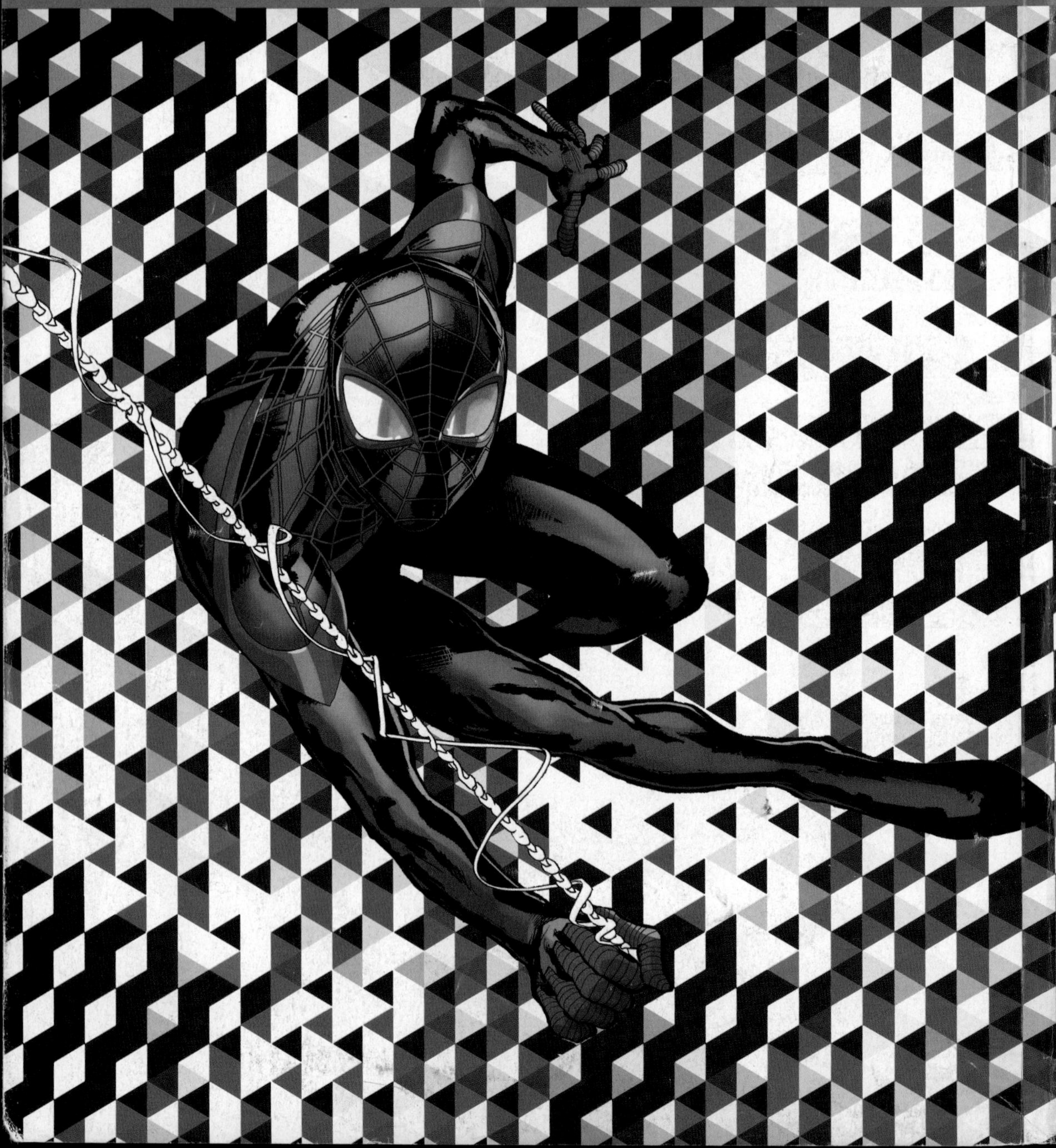

# MILES MORALES: THE ULTIMATE
# SPIDER-MAN

## REVELATIONS

WRITER:
**BRIAN MICHAEL BENDIS**

ARTIST:
**DAVID MARQUEZ**

COLOR ARTIST:
**JUSTIN PONSOR**
WITH **JASON KEITH** (#6)

LETTERER:
**VC'S CORY PETIT**

COVER ART:
**DAVID MARQUEZ** &
**JUSTIN PONSOR**

ASSISTANT EDITORS:
**EMILY SHAW** &
**CHRIS ROBINSON**

EDITOR:
**MARK
PANICCIA**

In an act of desperation, Miles Morales revealed his secret identity to his father. That was the last time Miles ever saw him. All this and Miles was shocked to discover that long-thought-dead Peter Parker is alive, as is his killer, Norman Osborn, the Green Goblin, who had escaped S.H.I.E.L.D. custody.

Peter and Miles both fought the Green Goblin, but Osborn managed to escape. After the fight, the Spider-Men were surrounded by the NYPD and broadcast all over the news.

Detective Maria Hill found Miles and together they decided to figure out the real story behind Peter's return. They discovered Peter at the house of ex-girlfriend Mary Jane Watson.

Meanwhile, publisher J. Jonah Jameson got a home visit from Norman Osborn, who wanted to put his story on the record. But before he could finish his tale, Jameson shot Norman Osborn point blank!

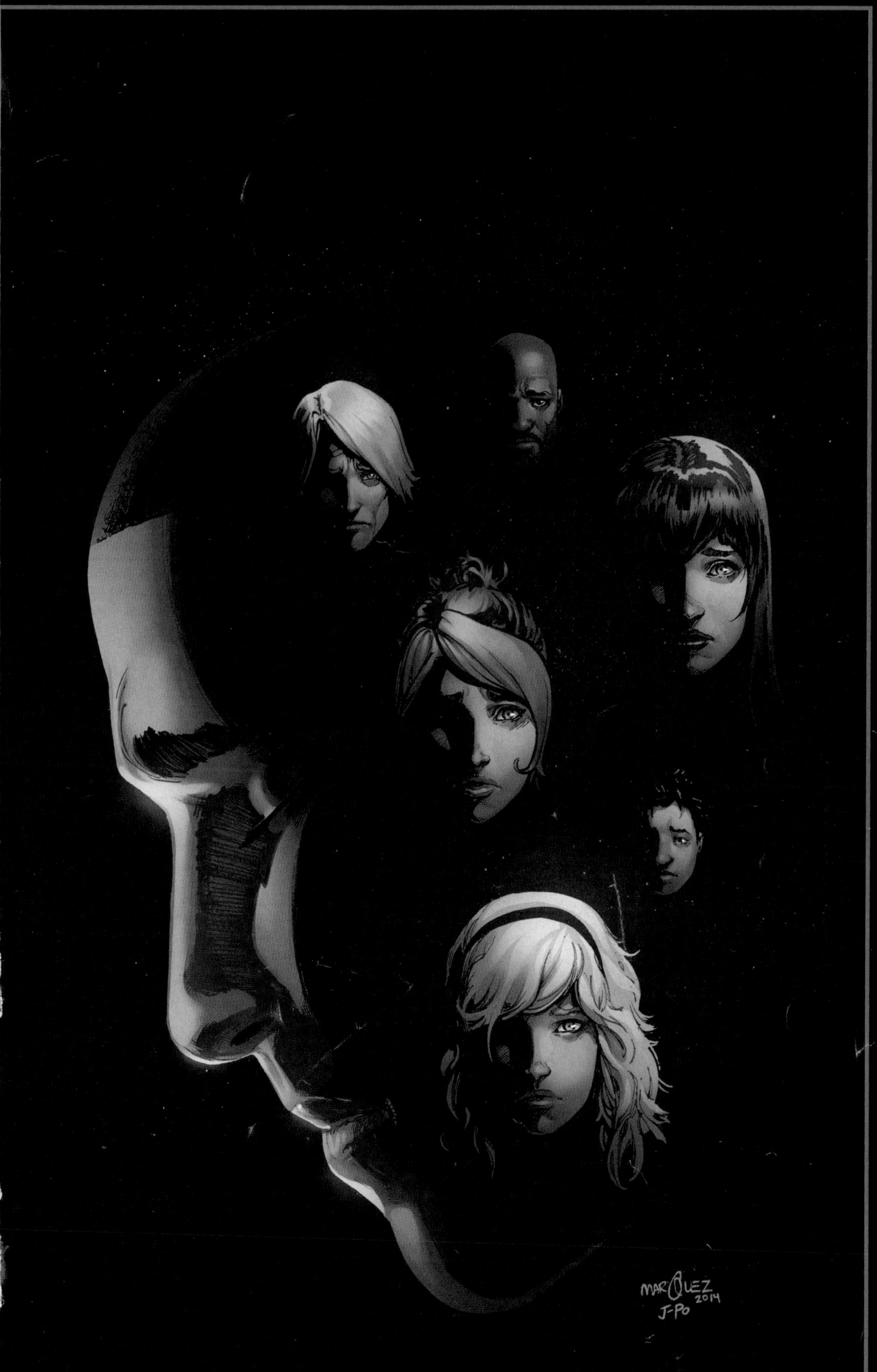
MARQUEZ 2014
J-Po

6

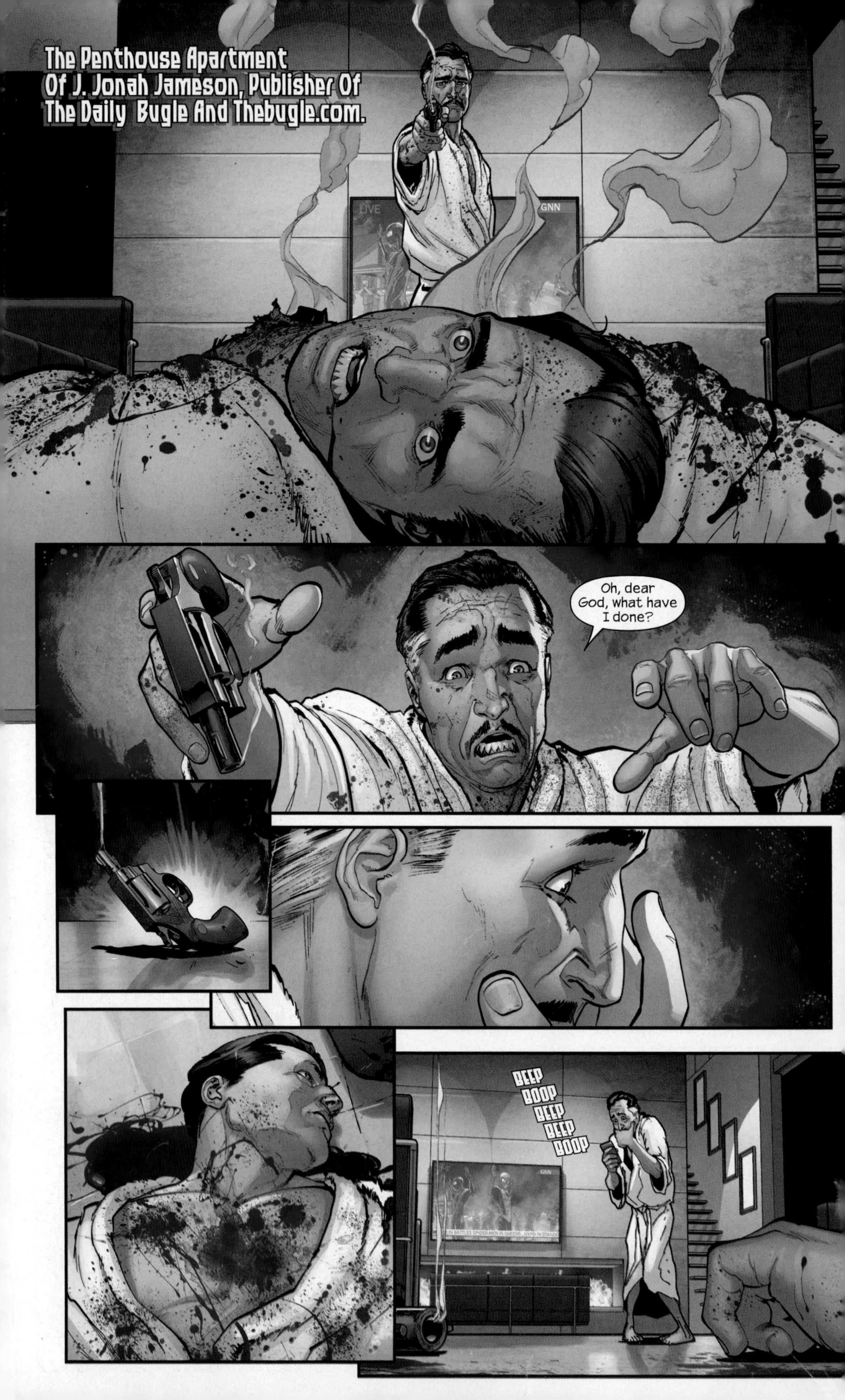
The Penthouse Apartment
Of J. Jonah Jameson, Publisher Of
The Daily Bugle And Thebugle.com.
Oh, dear
God, what have
I done?
BEEP
BOOP
BEEP
BEEP
BOOP

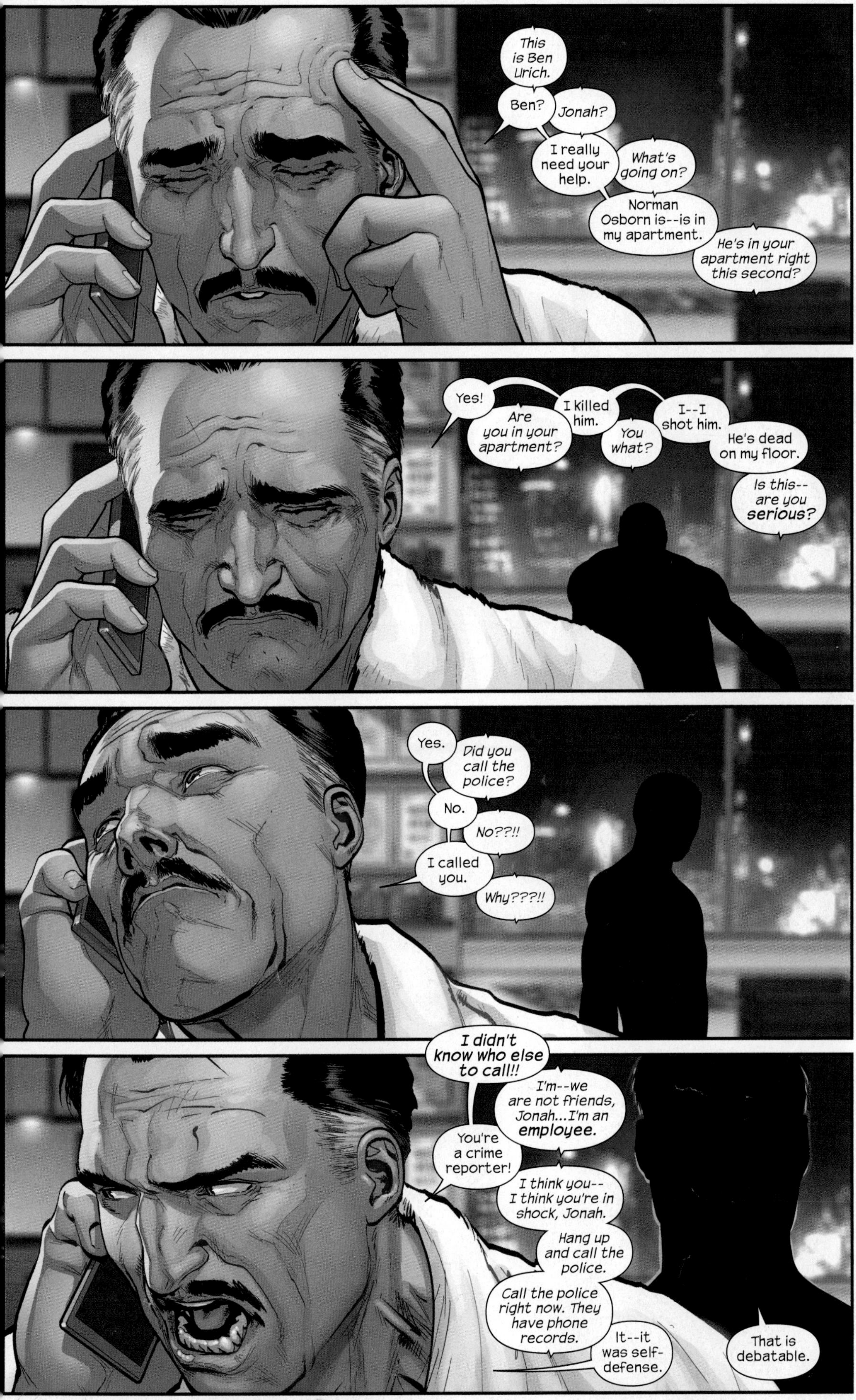
This is Ben Urich.
Ben?
Jonah?
I really need your help.
What's going on?
Norman Osborn is--is in my apartment.
He's in your apartment right this second?
Yes!
Are you in your apartment?
I killed him.
You what?
I--I shot him.
He's dead on my floor.
Is this--are you serious?
Yes.
Did you call the police?
No.
No??!!
I called you.
Why???!!
I didn't know who else to call!!
I'm--we are not friends, Jonah...I'm an employee.
You're a crime reporter!
I think you--I think you're in shock, Jonah.
Hang up and call the police.
Call the police right now. They have phone records.
It--it was self-defense.
That is debatable.

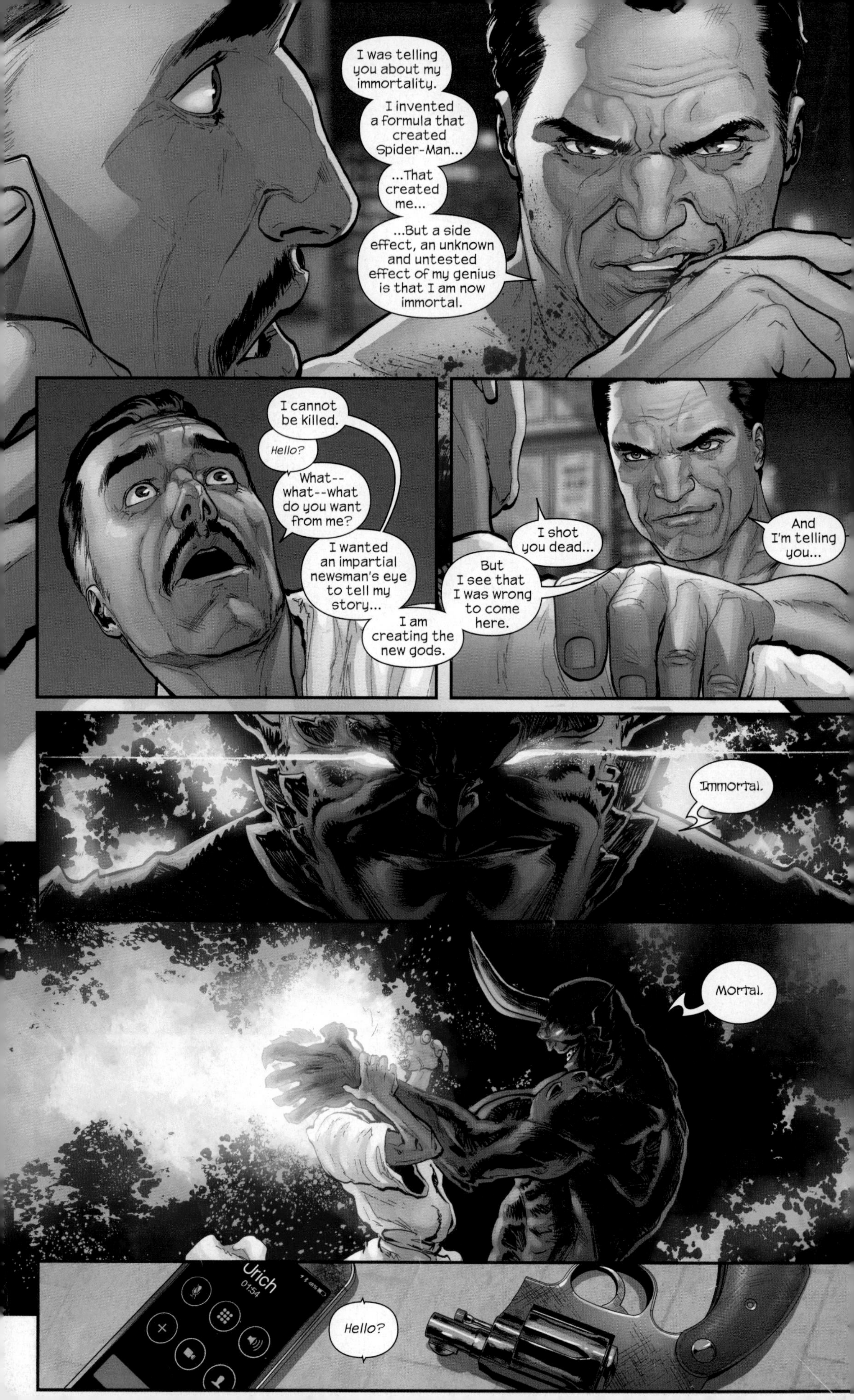
I was telling you about my immortality.
I invented a formula that created Spider-Man...
...That created me...
...But a side effect, an unknown and untested effect of my genius is that I am now immortal.
I cannot be killed.
Hello?
What--what--what do you want from me?
I wanted an impartial newsman's eye to tell my story...
I am creating the new gods.
I shot you dead...
But I see that I was wrong to come here.
And I'm telling you...
Immortal.
Mortal.
Urich
01:54
Hello?

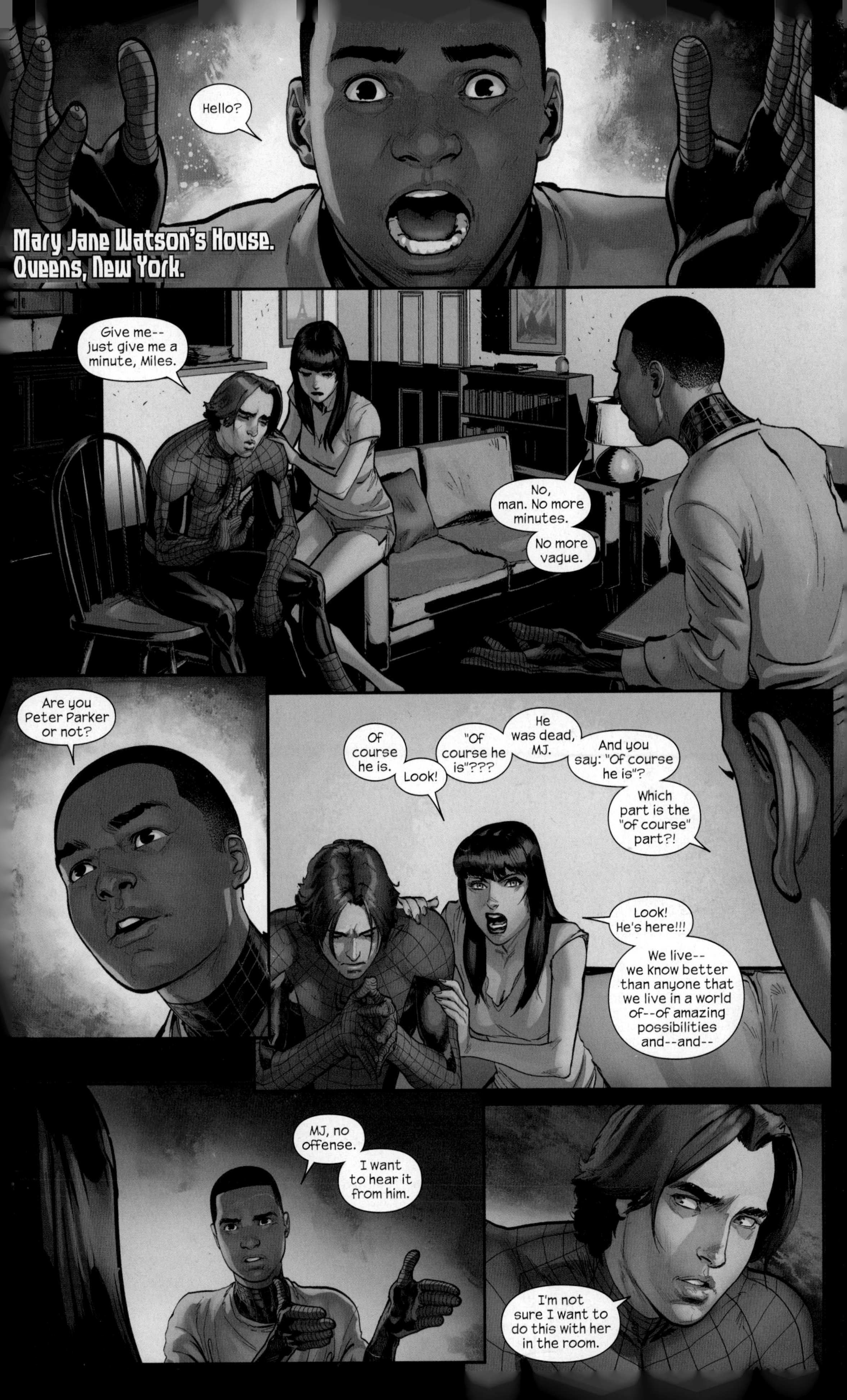

Hello?
Mary Jane Watson's House.
Queens, New York.
Give me-- just give me a minute, Miles.
No, man. No more minutes.
No more vague.
Are you Peter Parker or not?
Of course he is.
Look!
"Of course he is"???
He was dead, MJ.
And you say: "Of course he is"?
Which part is the "of course" part?!
Look! He's here!!!
We live-- we know better than anyone that we live in a world of--of amazing possibilities and--and--
MJ, no offense.
I want to hear it from him.
I'm not sure I want to do this with her in the room.

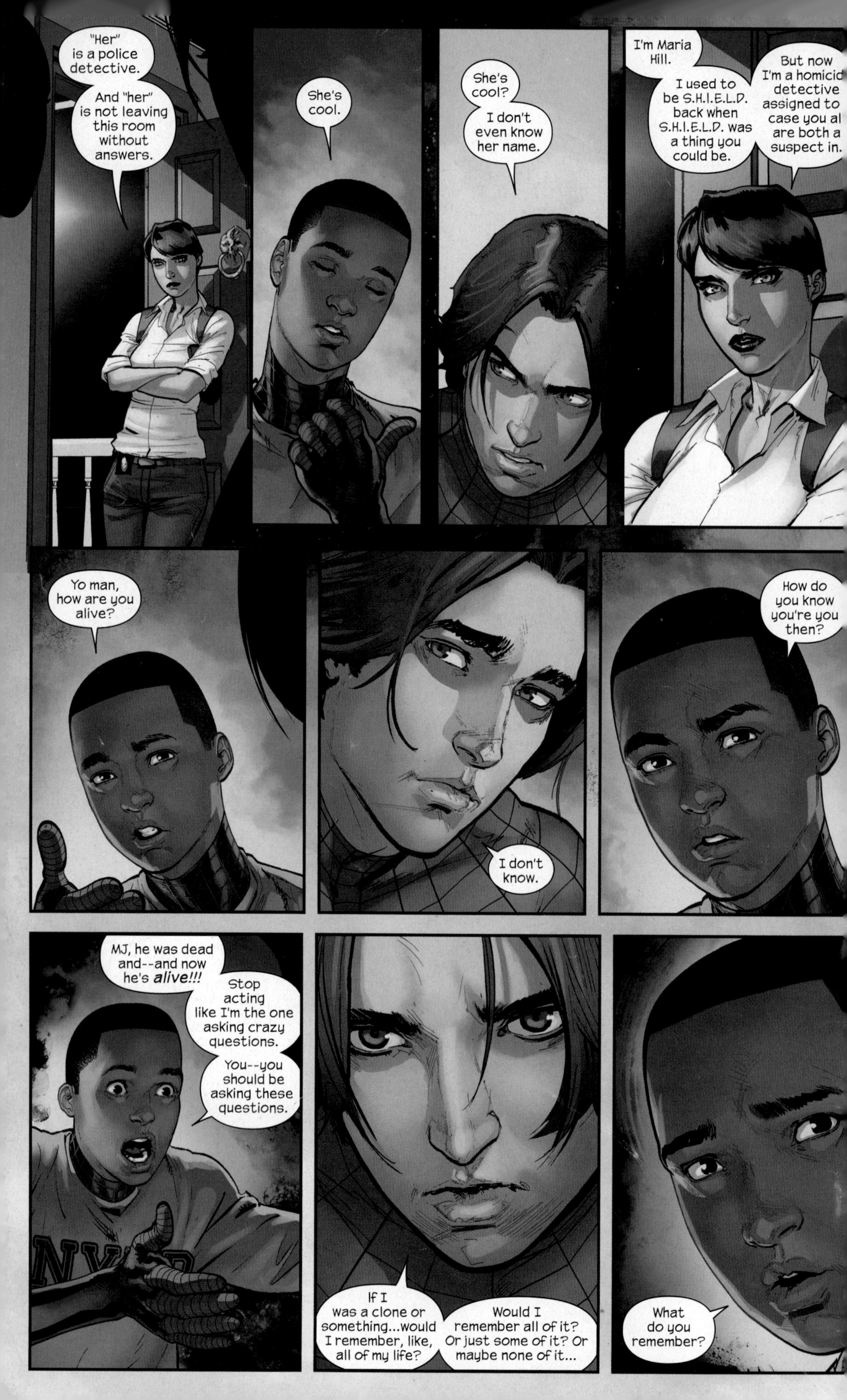
"Her" is a police detective.
And "her" is not leaving this room without answers.
She's cool.
She's cool?
I don't even know her name.
I'm Maria Hill.
I used to be S.H.I.E.L.D. back when S.H.I.E.L.D. was a thing you could be.
But now I'm a homicid detective assigned to case you al are both a suspect in.
Yo man, how are you alive?
I don't know.
How do you know you're you then?
MJ, he was dead and--and now he's *alive!!!*
Stop acting like I'm the one asking crazy questions.
You--you should be asking these questions.
If I was a clone or something...would I remember, like, all of my life?
Would I remember all of it? Or just some of it? Or maybe none of it...
What do you remember?

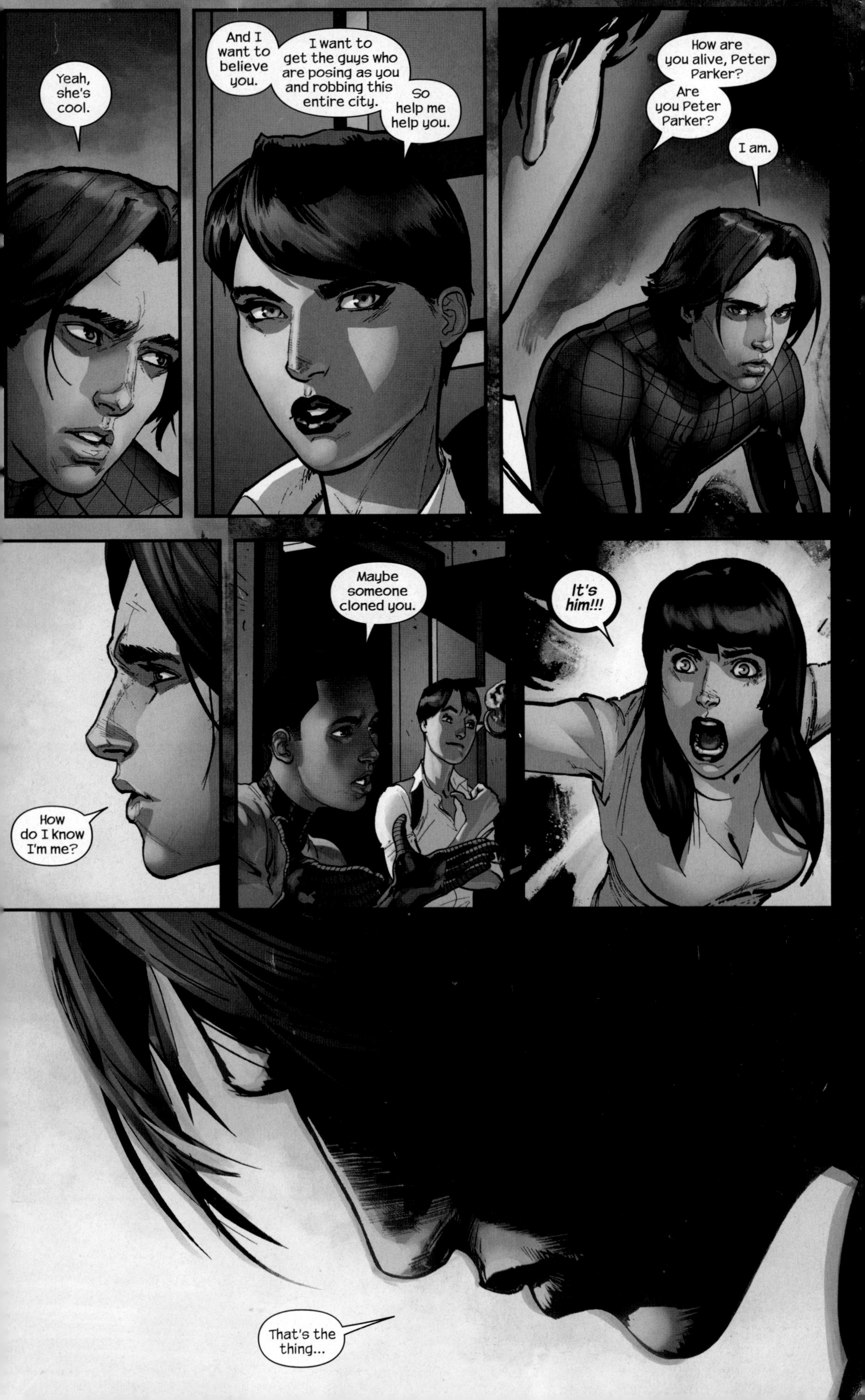
Yeah, she's cool.
And I want to believe you.
I want to get the guys who are posing as you and robbing this entire city.
So help me help you.
How are you alive, Peter Parker?
Are you Peter Parker?
I am.
How do I know I'm me?
Maybe someone cloned you.
It's him!!!
That's the thing...

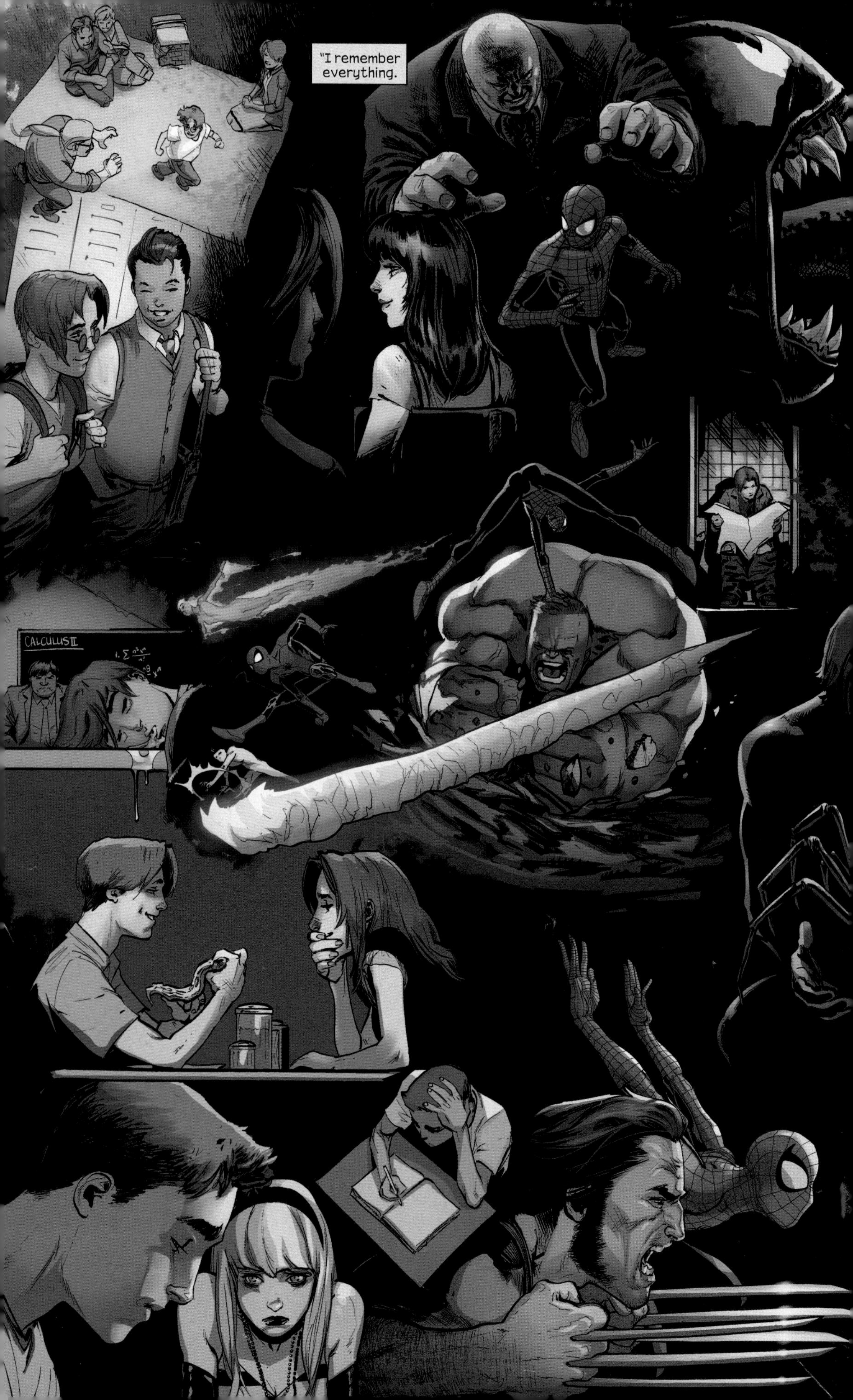
"I remember everything.
CALCULUS II

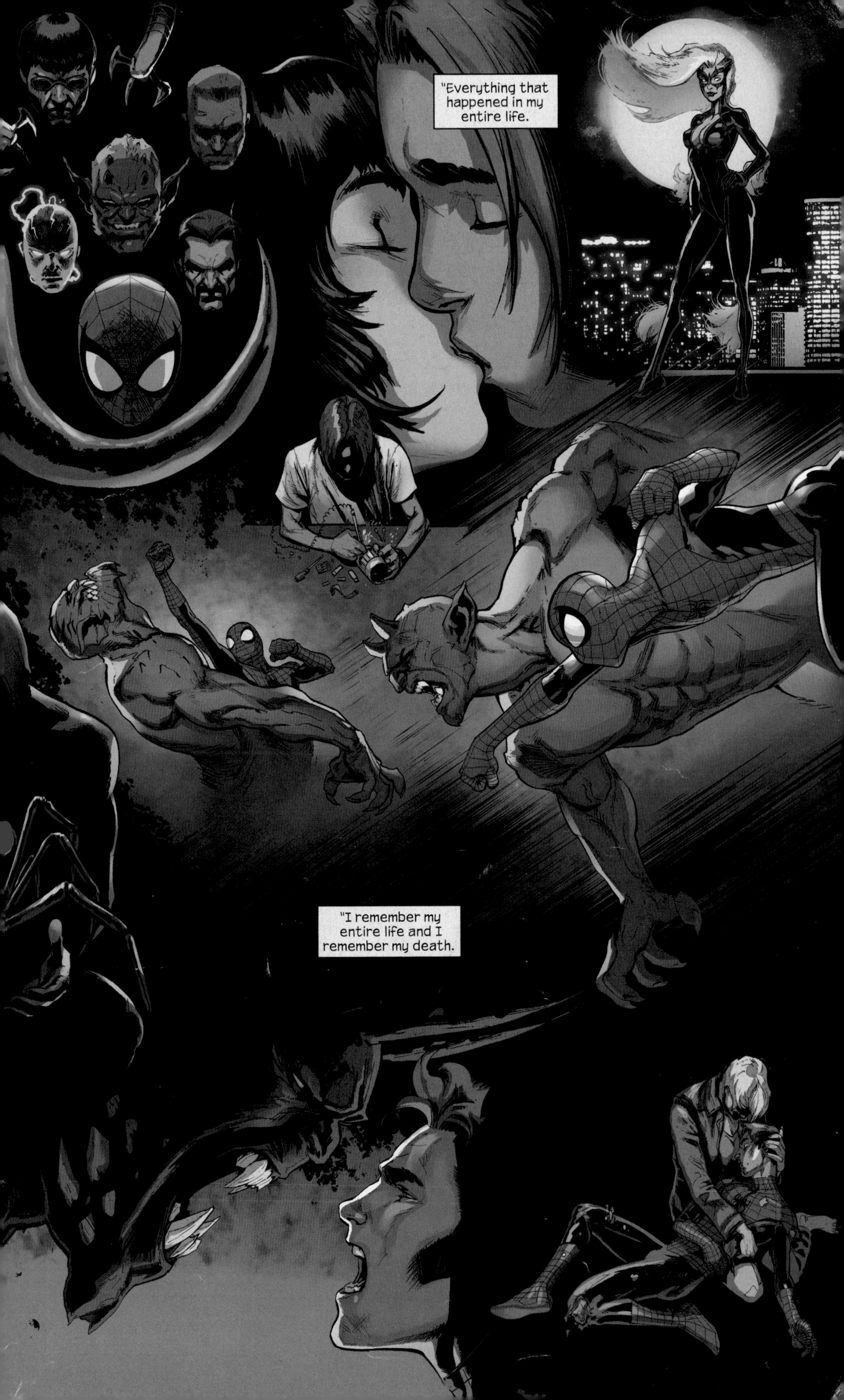
"Everything that happened in my entire life.
"I remember my entire life and I remember my death.

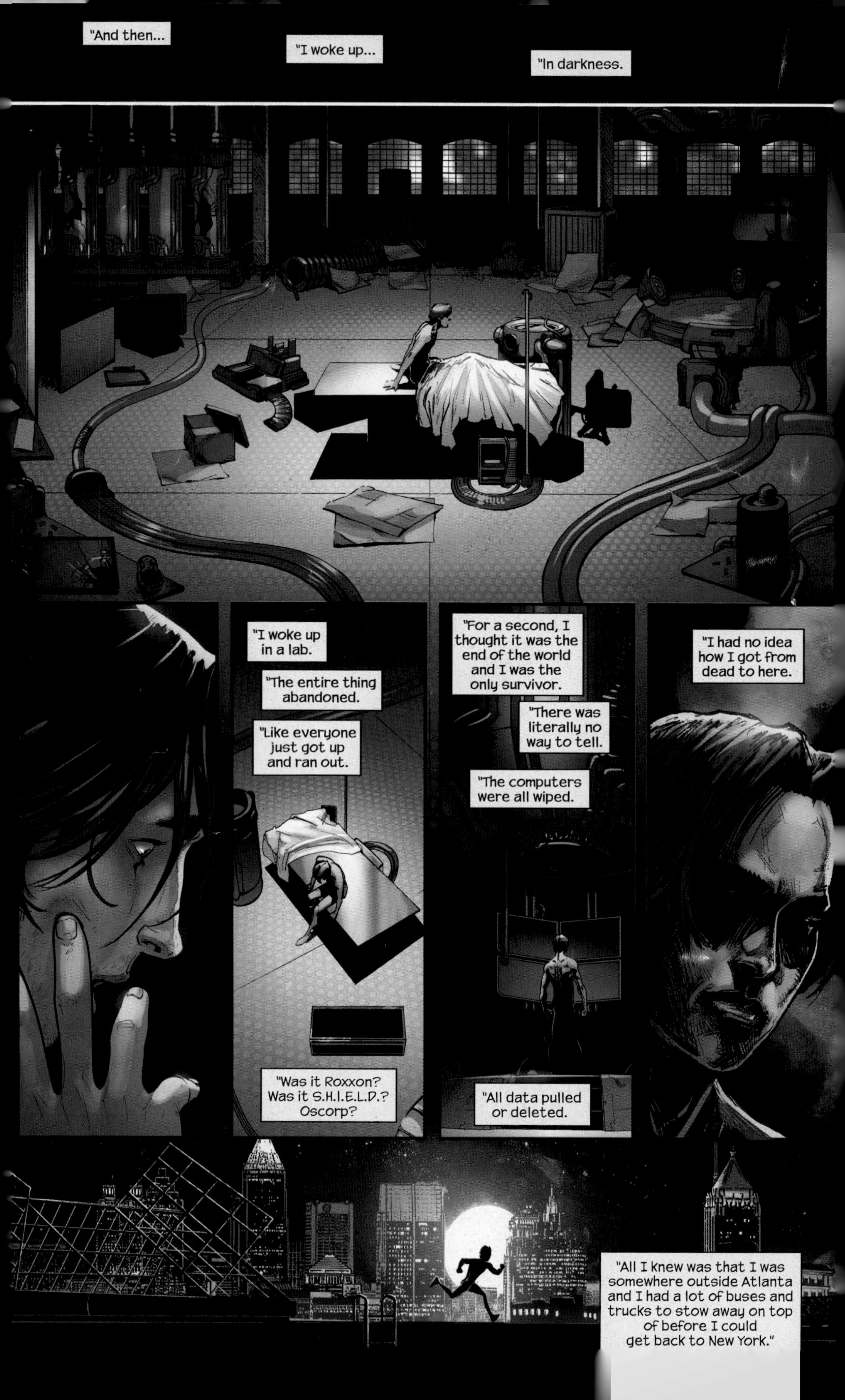
"And then...
"I woke up...
"In darkness.
"I woke up in a lab.
"The entire thing abandoned.
"Like everyone just got up and ran out.
"Was it Roxxon? Was it S.H.I.E.L.D.? Oscorp?
"For a second, I thought it was the end of the world and I was the only survivor.
"There was literally no way to tell.
"The computers were all wiped.
"All data pulled or deleted.
"I had no idea how I got from dead to here.
"All I knew was that I was somewhere outside Atlanta and I had a lot of buses and trucks to stow away on top of before I could get back to New York."

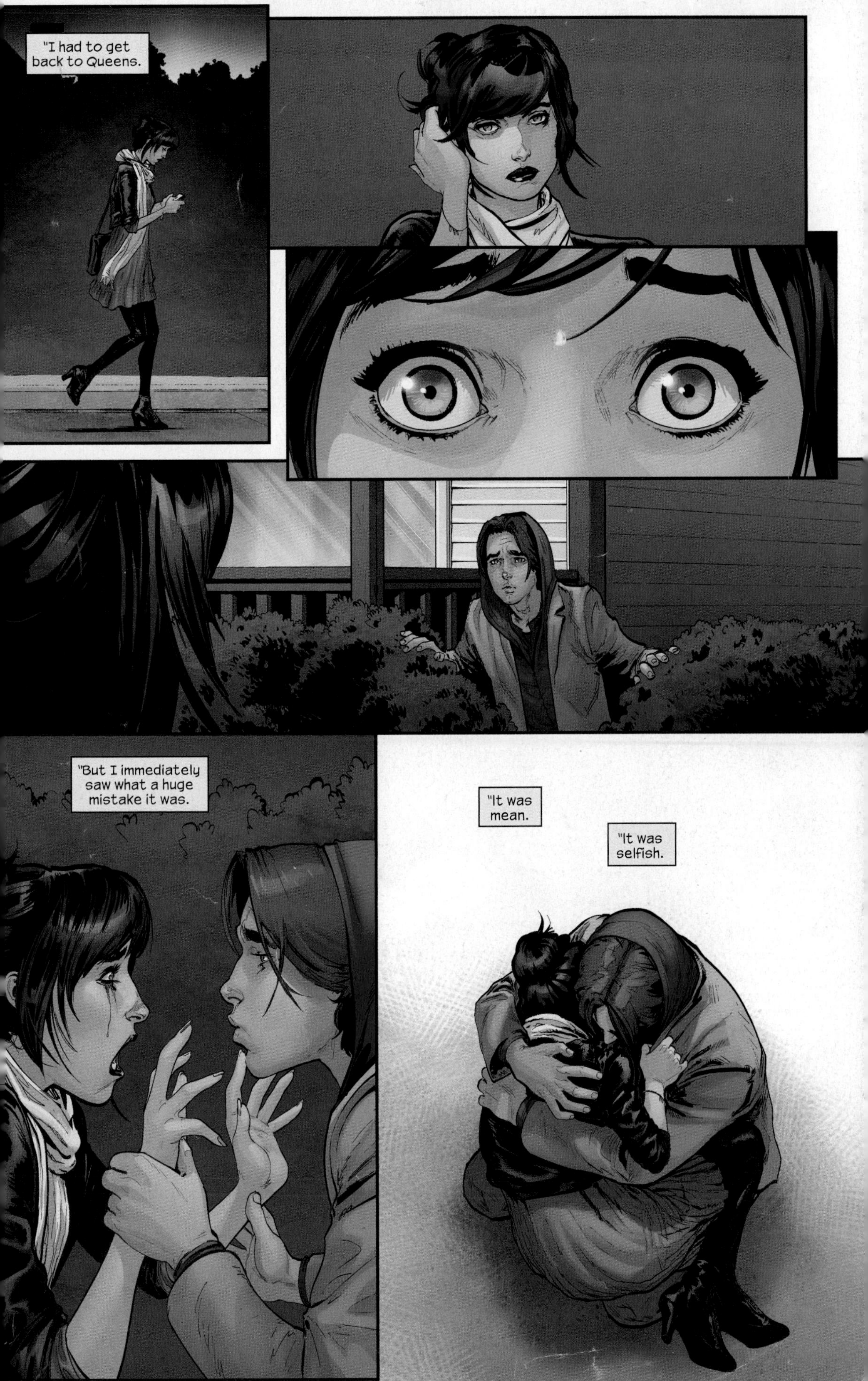
"I had to get back to Queens.
"But I immediately saw what a huge mistake it was.
"It was mean.
"It was selfish.

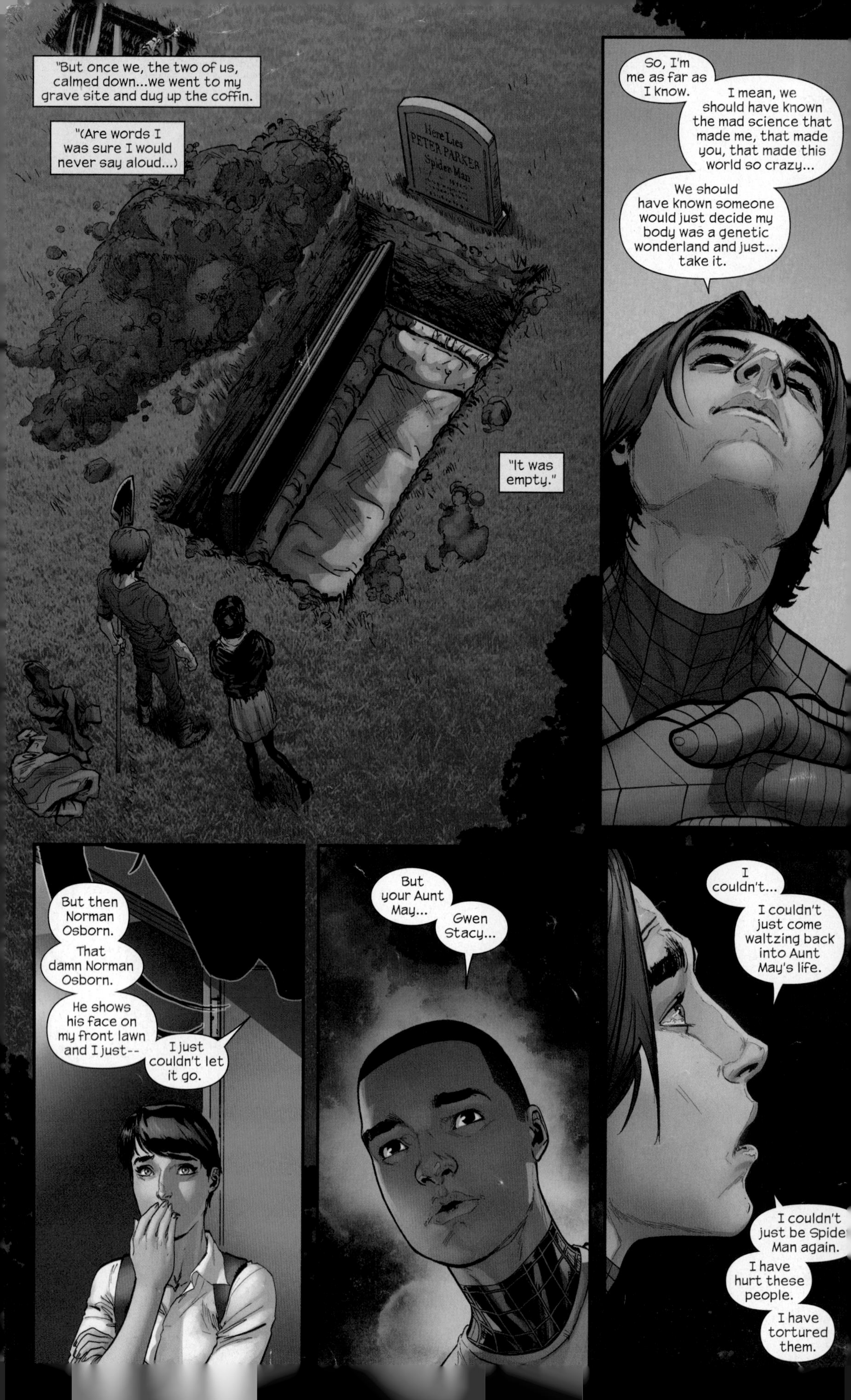

"But once we, the two of us, calmed down...we went to my grave site and dug up the coffin.
"(Are words I was sure I would never say aloud...)
Here Lies PETER PARKER Spider-Man
"It was empty."
So, I'm me as far as I know.
I mean, we should have known the mad science that made me, that made you, that made this world so crazy...
We should have known someone would just decide my body was a genetic wonderland and just... take it.
But then Norman Osborn.
That damn Norman Osborn.
He shows his face on my front lawn and I just--
I just couldn't let it go.
But your Aunt May...
Gwen Stacy...
I couldn't...
I couldn't just come waltzing back into Aunt May's life.
I couldn't just be Spide Man again.
I have hurt these people.
I have tortured them.

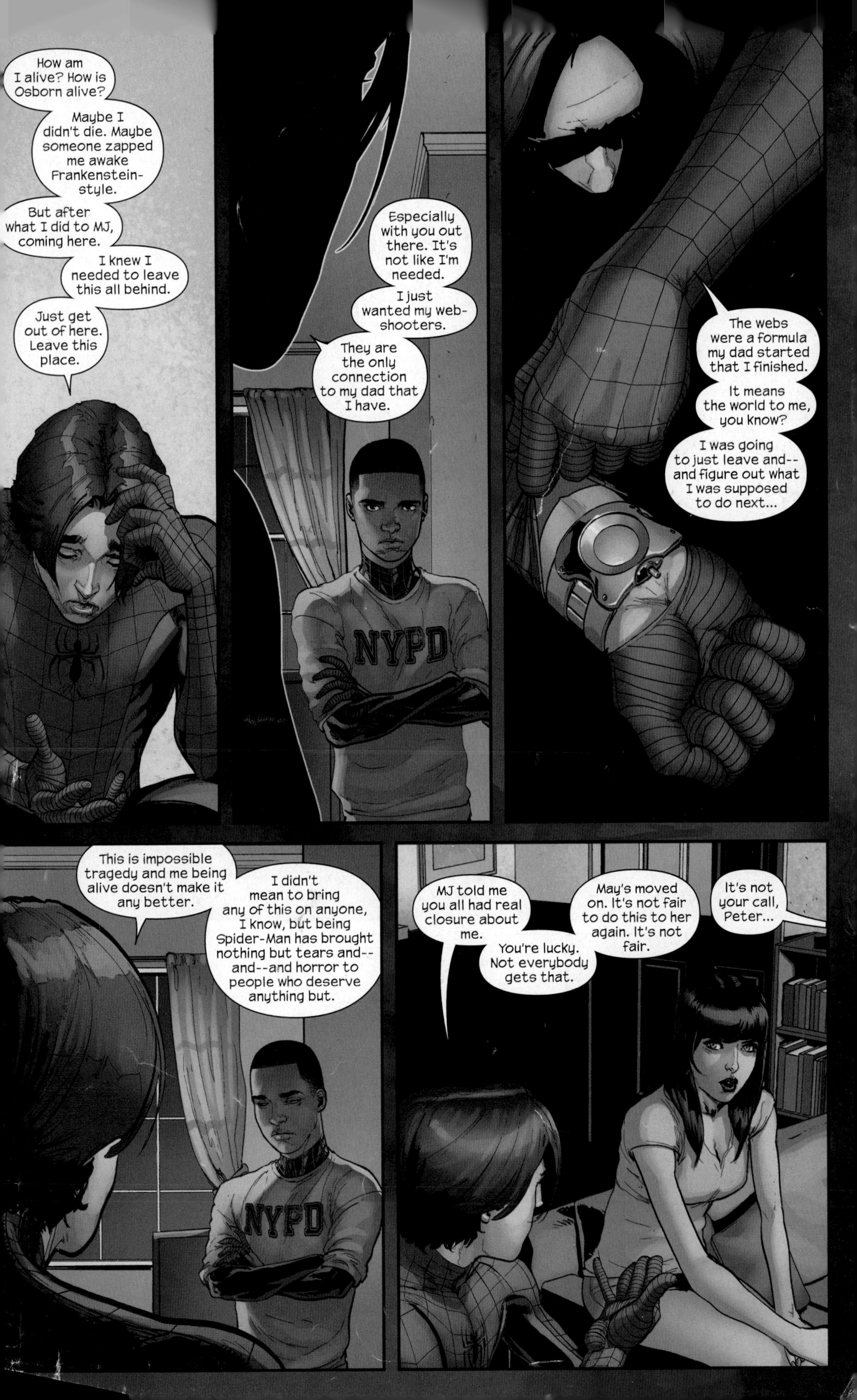
How am I alive? How is Osborn alive?
Maybe I didn't die. Maybe someone zapped me awake Frankenstein-style.
But after what I did to MJ, coming here.
I knew I needed to leave this all behind.
Just get out of here. Leave this place.
Especially with you out there. It's not like I'm needed.
I just wanted my web-shooters.
They are the only connection to my dad that I have.
NYPD
The webs were a formula my dad started that I finished.
It means the world to me, you know?
I was going to just leave and-- and figure out what I was supposed to do next...
This is impossible tragedy and me being alive doesn't make it any better.
I didn't mean to bring any of this on anyone, I know, but being Spider-Man has brought nothing but tears and-- and--and horror to people who deserve anything but.
NYPD
MJ told me you all had real closure about me.
You're lucky. Not everybody gets that.
May's moved on. It's not fair to do this to her again. It's not fair.
It's not your call, Peter...

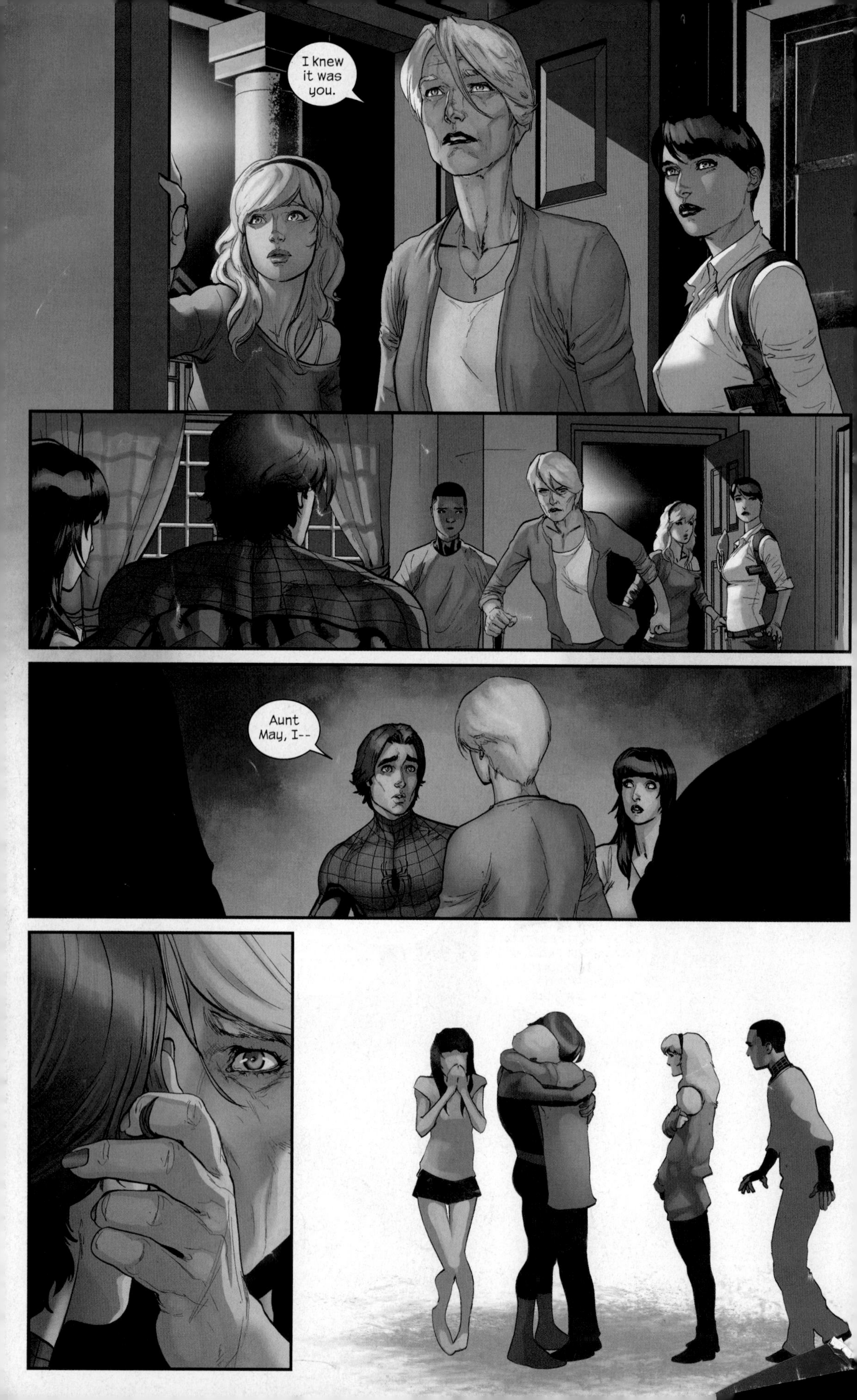
I knew it was you.
Aunt May, I--

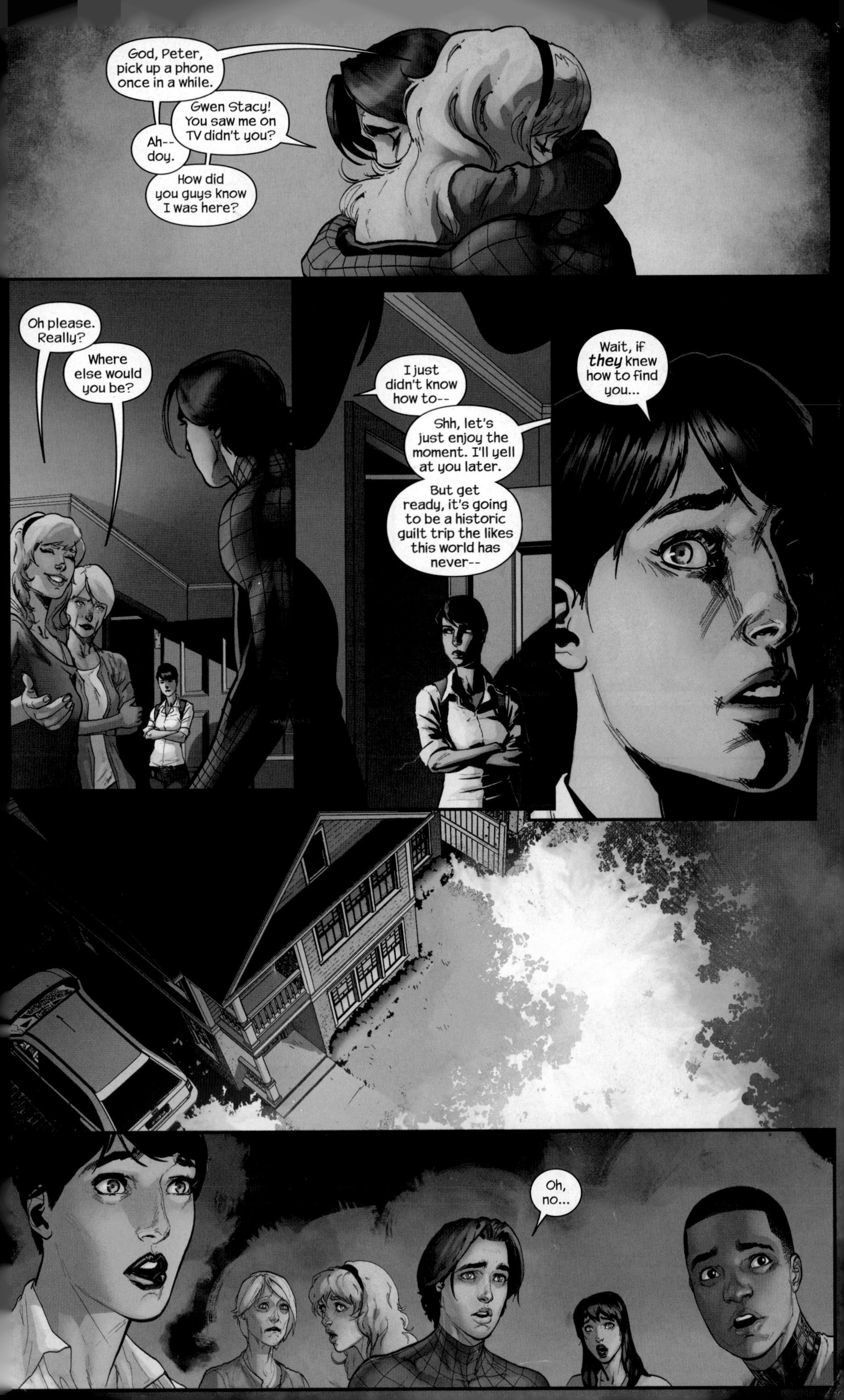
God, Peter, pick up a phone once in a while.
Gwen Stacy! You saw me on TV didn't you?
Ah-- doy.
How did you guys know I was here?
Oh please. Really?
Where else would you be?
I just didn't know how to--
Shh, let's just enjoy the moment. I'll yell at you later.
But get ready, it's going to be a historic guilt trip the likes this world has never--
Wait, if *they* knew how to find you...
Oh, no...

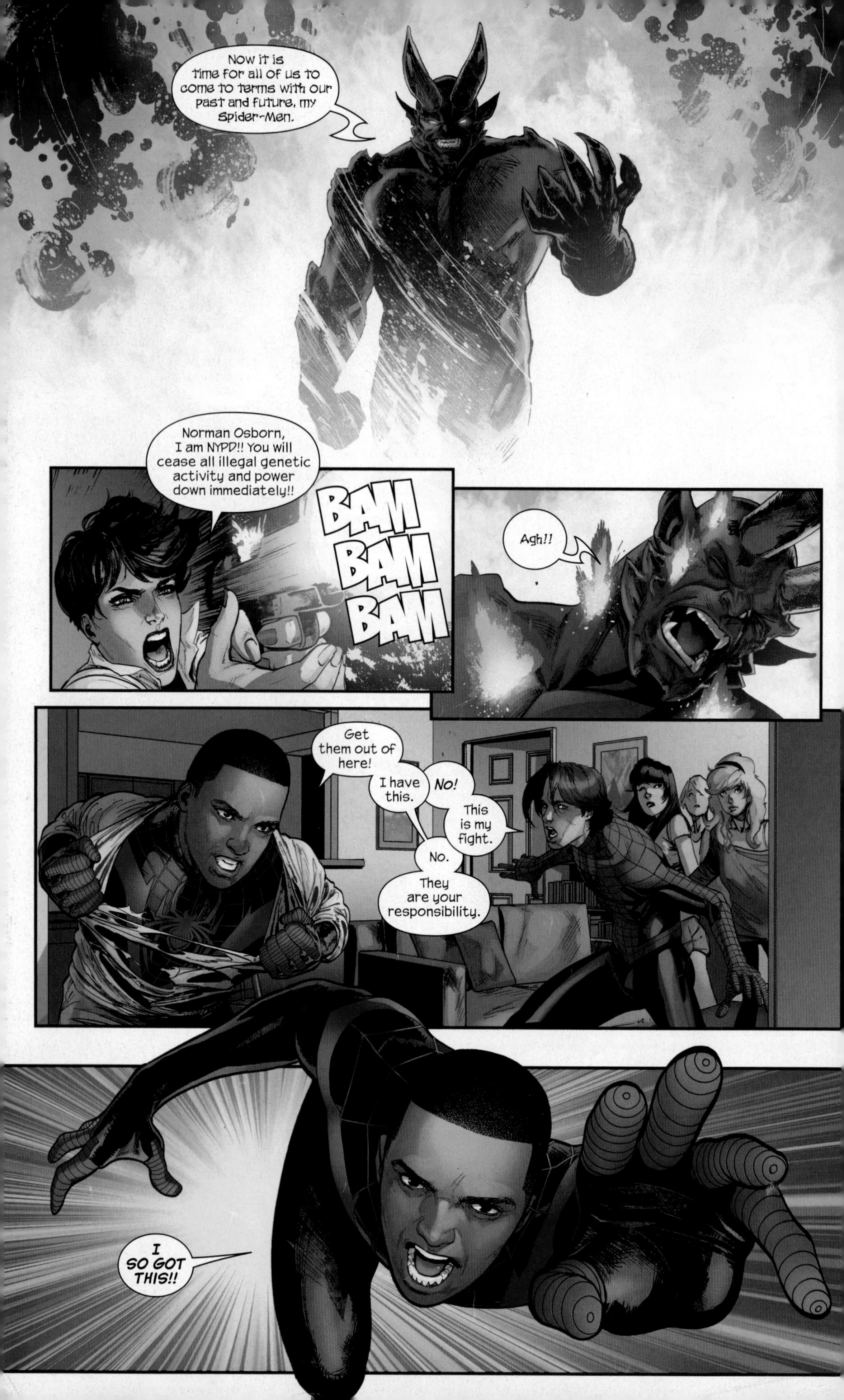
Now it is time for all of us to come to terms with our past and future, my Spider-Men.
Norman Osborn, I am NYPD!! You will cease all illegal genetic activity and power down immediately!!
BAM BAM BAM
Agh!!
Get them out of here!
I have this.
No!
This is my fight.
No.
They are your responsibility.
I SO GOT THIS!!

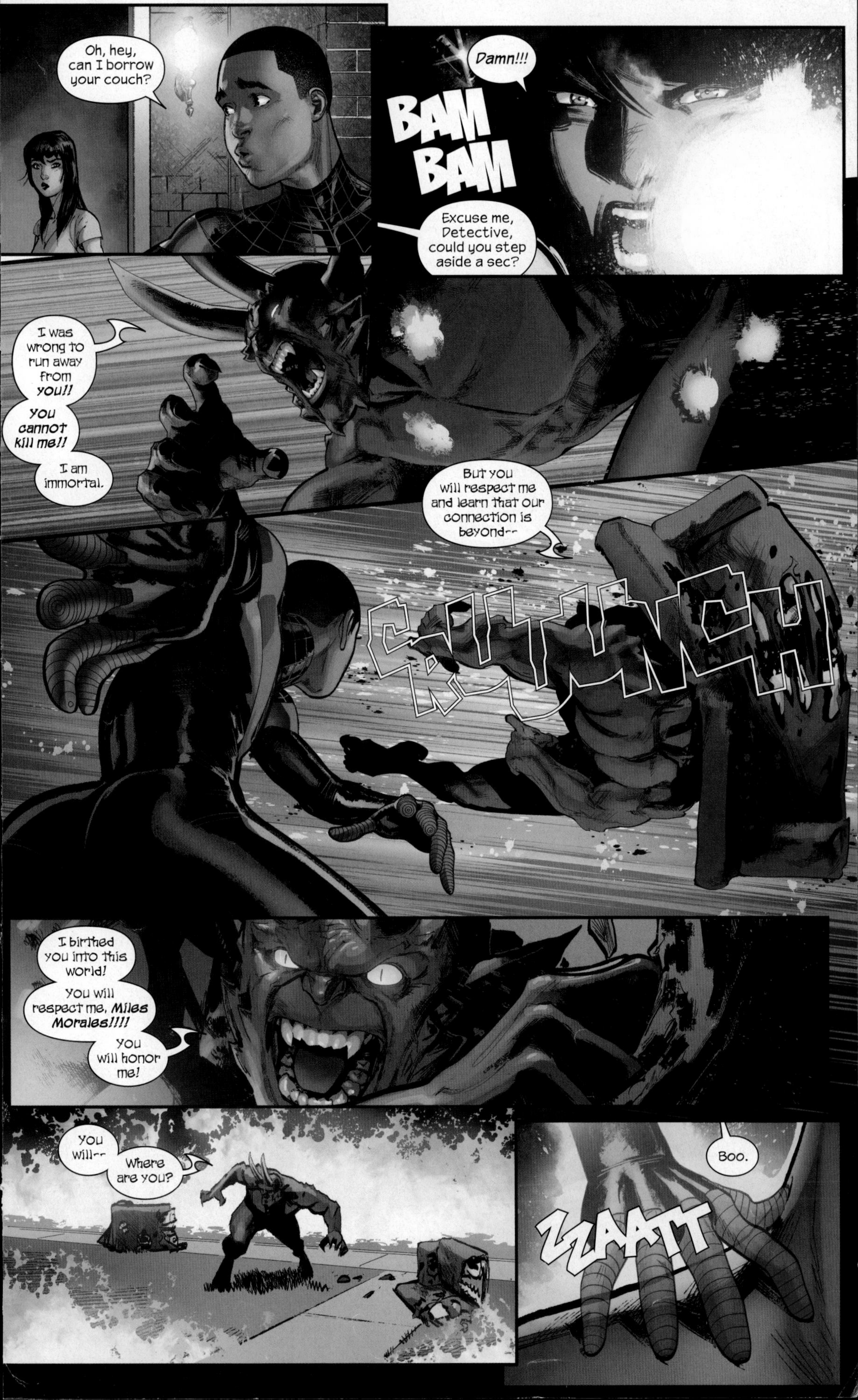

Oh, hey, can I borrow your couch?
Damn!!!
BAM BAM
Excuse me, Detective, could you step aside a sec?
I was wrong to run away from *you!!*
*You cannot kill me!!*
I am immortal.
But you will respect me and learn that our connection is beyond--
CRUNCH
I birthed you into this world!
You will respect me, *Miles Morales!!!!*
You will honor me!
You will--
Where are you?
Boo.
ZZAATT

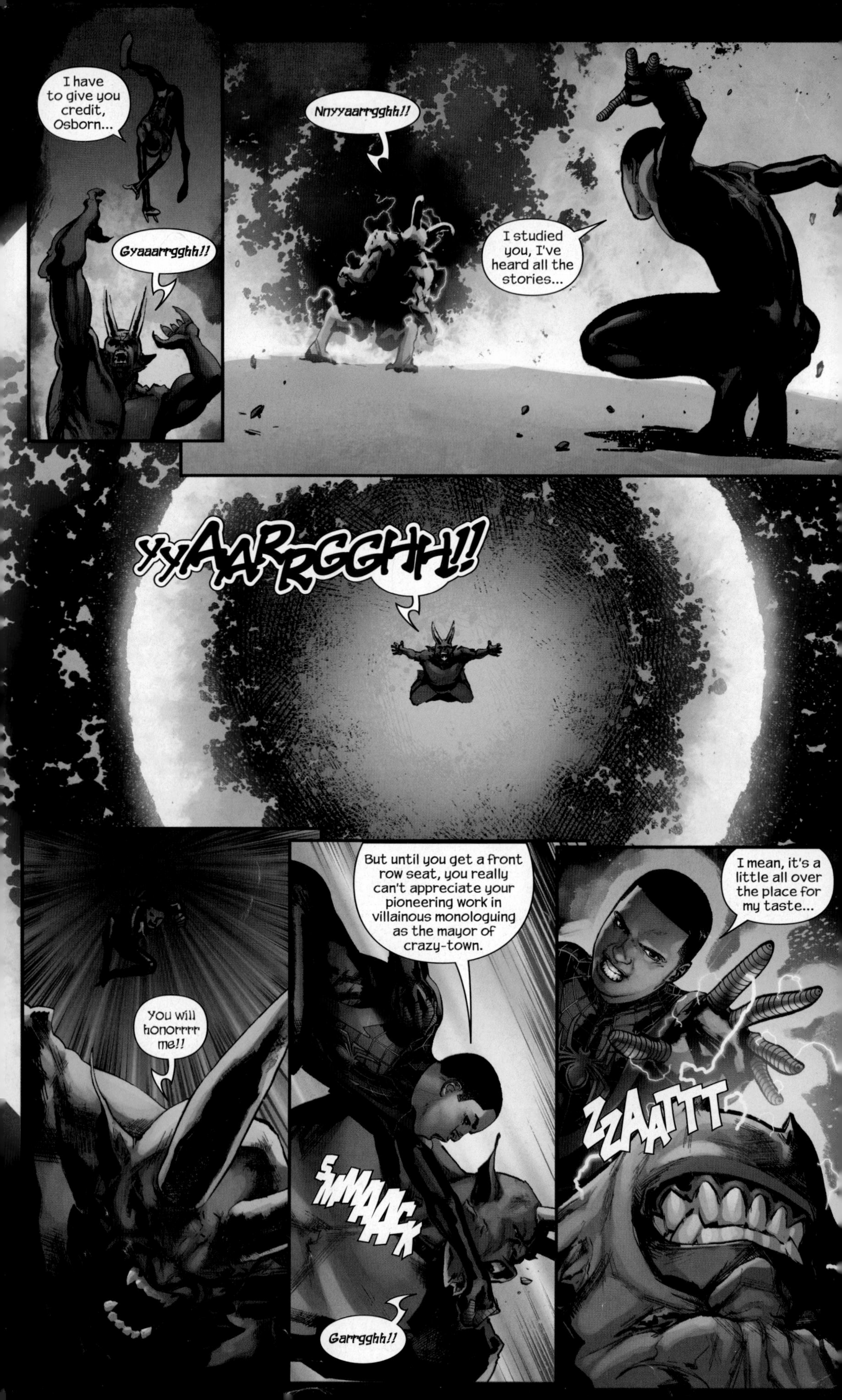
I have to give you credit, Osborn...
Gyaaarrgghh!!
Nnyyaarrggghh!!
I studied you, I've heard all the stories...
YYAARRGGHH!!
You will honorrrr me!!
But until you get a front row seat, you really can't appreciate your pioneering work in villainous monologuing as the mayor of crazy-town.
SMMAACK
Garrgghh!!
I mean, it's a little all over the place for my taste...
ZZAATTT

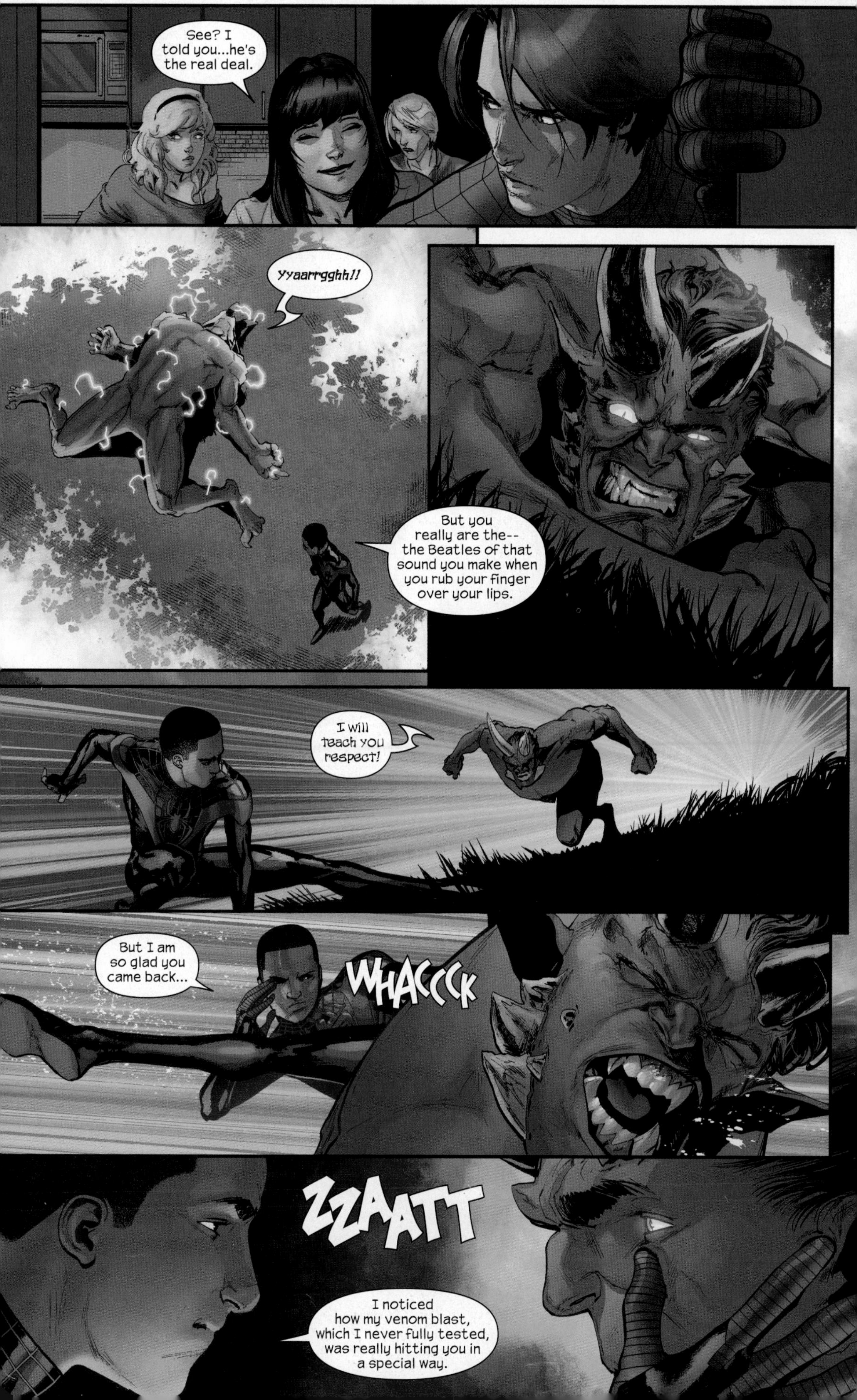
See? I told you...he's the real deal.
Yyaarrgghh!!
But you really are the-- the Beatles of that sound you make when you rub your finger over your lips.
I will teach you respect!
But I am so glad you came back...
WHACCCK
ZZAATT
I noticed how my venom blast, which I never fully tested, was really hitting you in a special way.

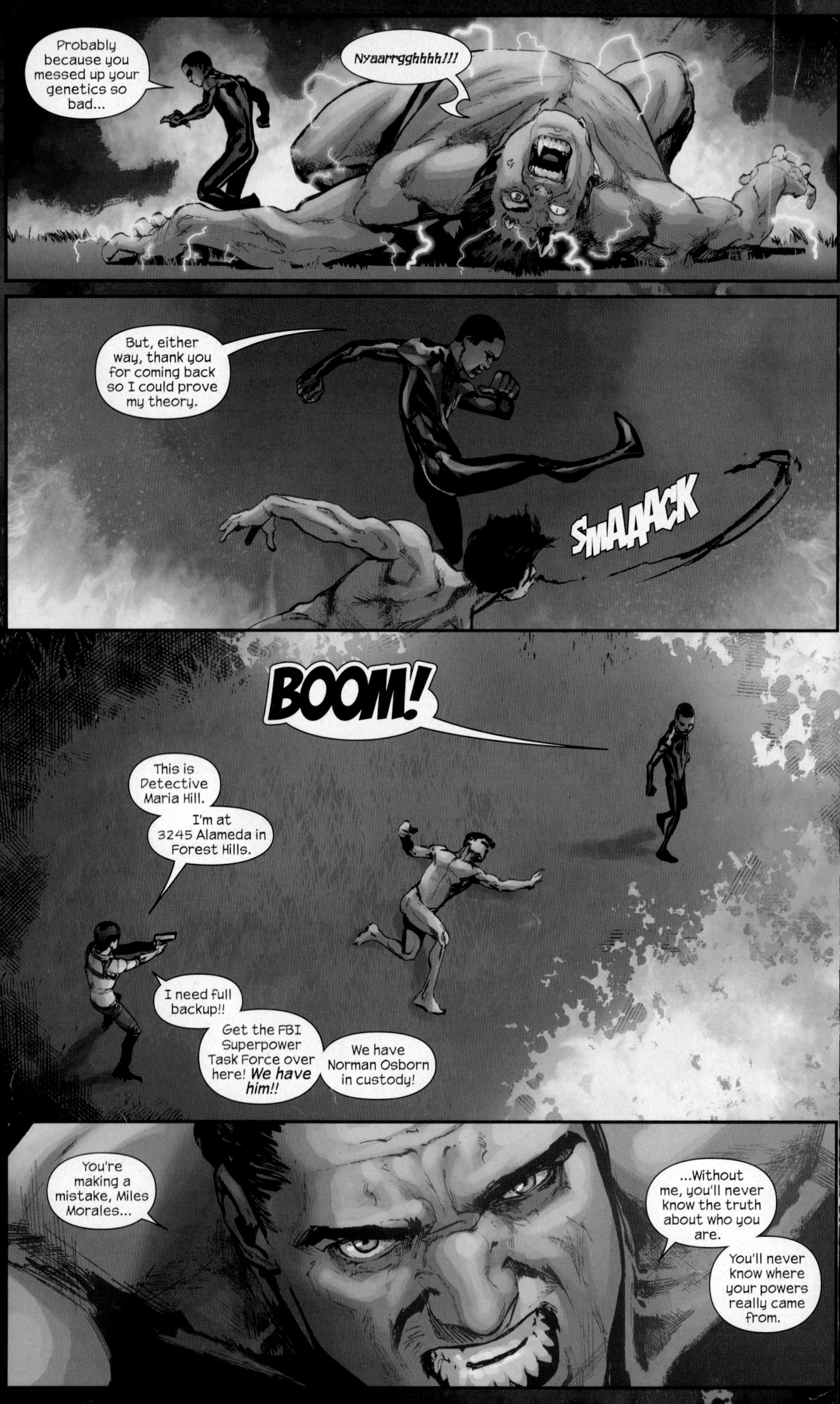
Probably because you messed up your genetics so bad...
Nyaarrgghhhh!!!
But, either way, thank you for coming back so I could prove my theory.
SMAAACK
BOOM!
This is Detective Maria Hill.
I'm at 3245 Alameda in Forest Hills.
I need full backup!!
Get the FBI Superpower Task Force over here! We have him!!
We have Norman Osborn in custody!
You're making a mistake, Miles Morales...
...Without me, you'll never know the truth about who you are.
You'll never know where your powers really came from.

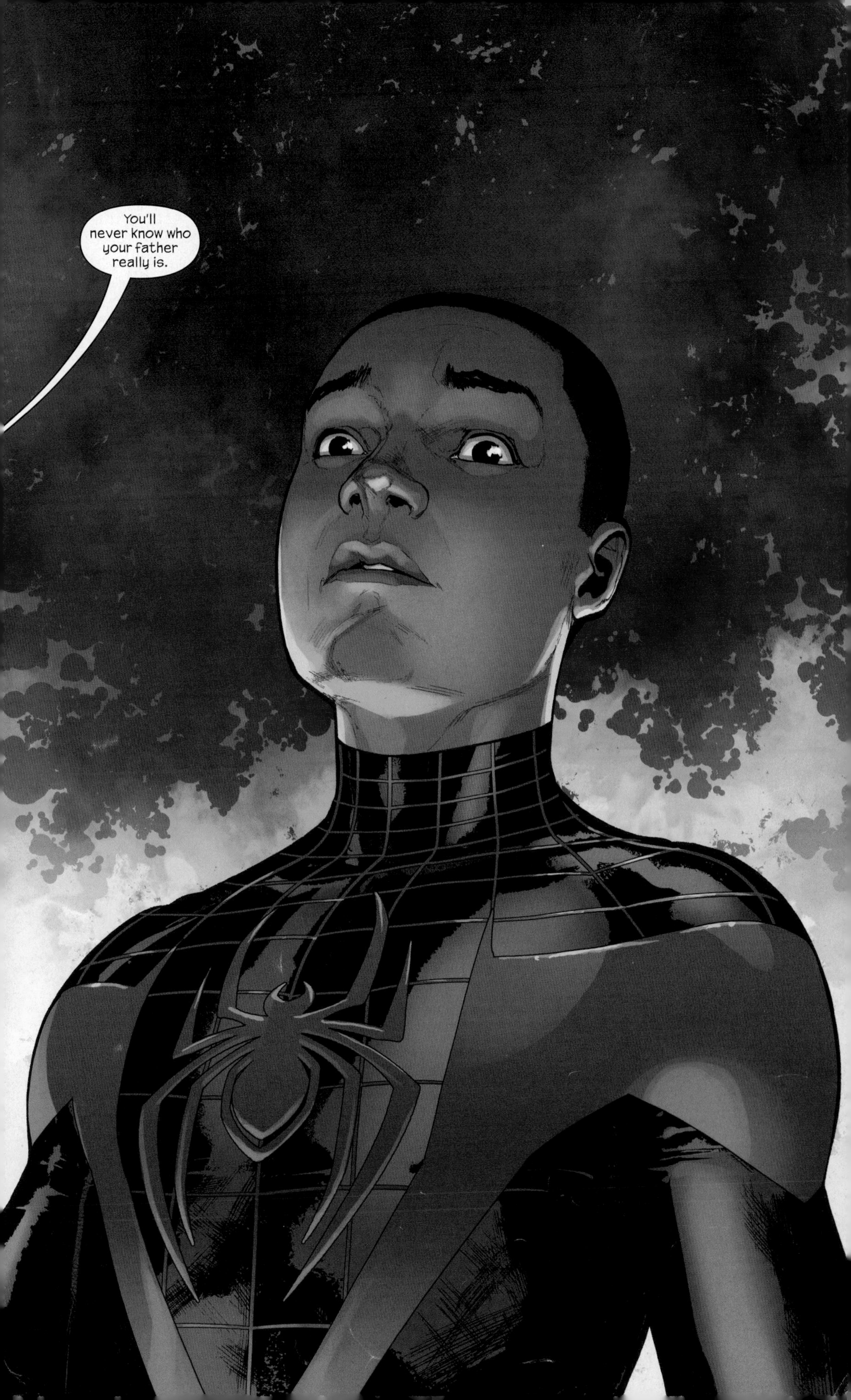
You'll never know who your father really is.

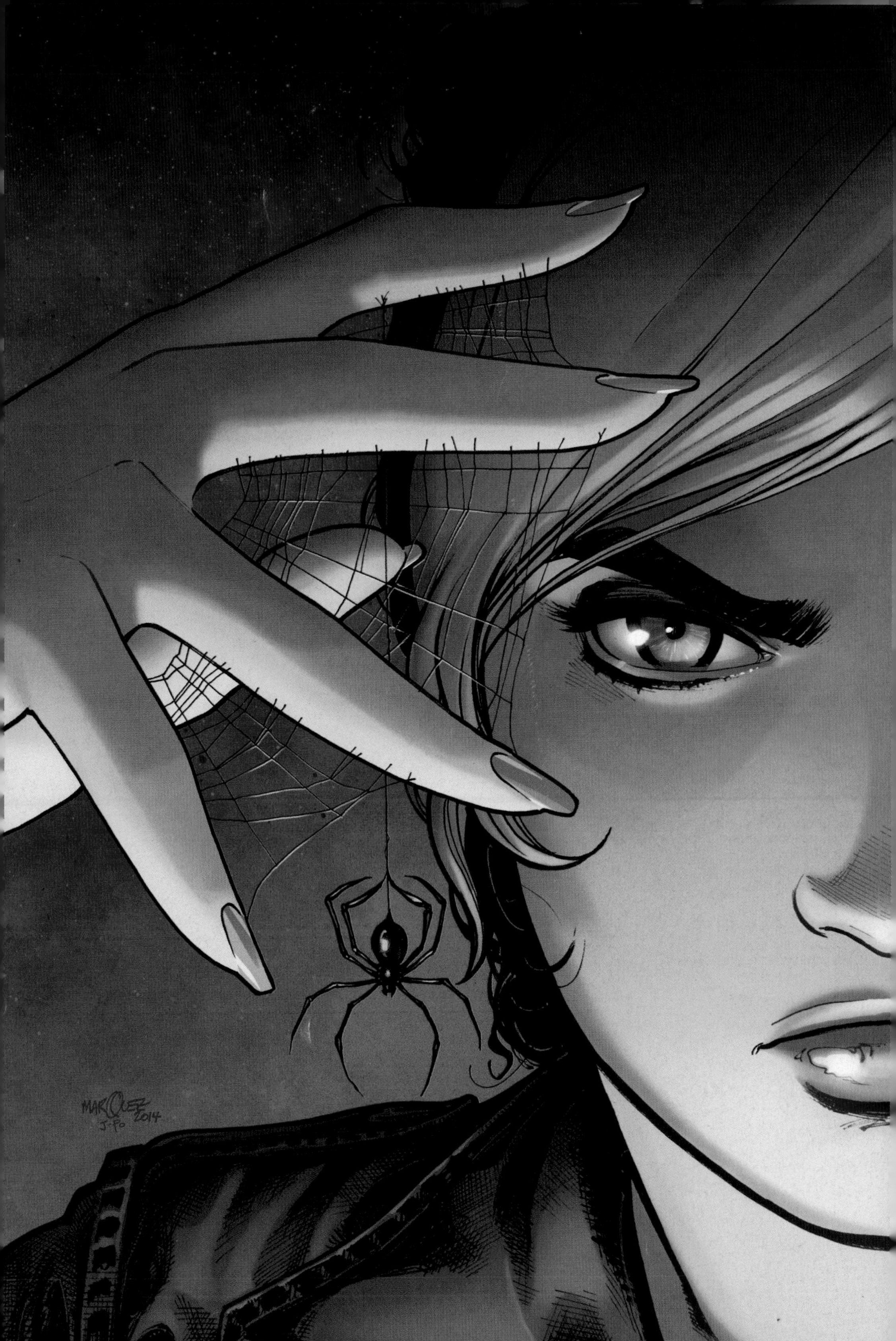
MARQUEZ 2014
J-Po

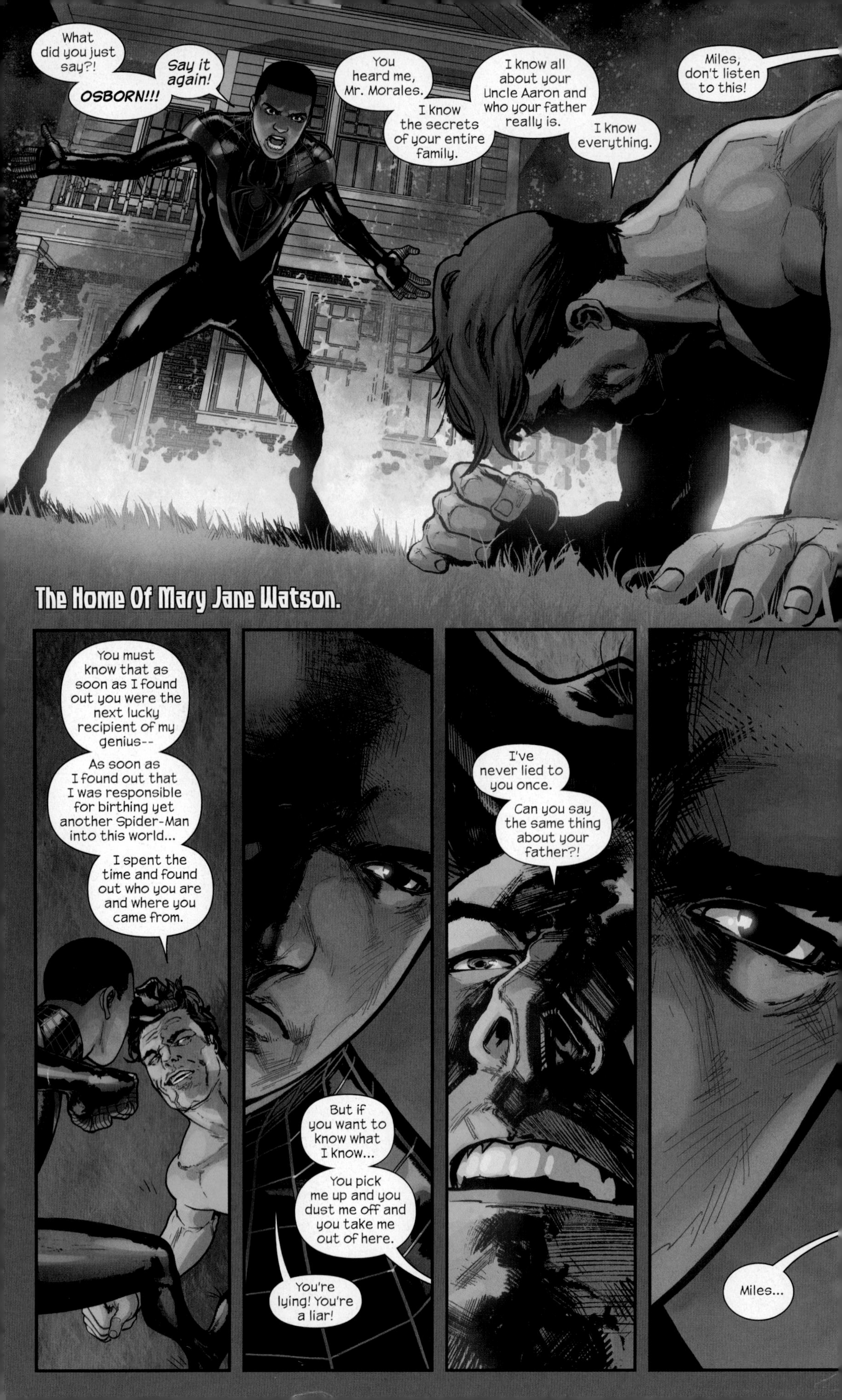

What did you just say?!
Say it again!
OSBORN!!!
You heard me, Mr. Morales.
I know the secrets of your entire family.
I know all about your Uncle Aaron and who your father really is.
I know everything.
Miles, don't listen to this!
The Home Of Mary Jane Watson.
You must know that as soon as I found out you were the next lucky recipient of my genius--
As soon as I found out that I was responsible for birthing yet another Spider-Man into this world...
I spent the time and found out who you are and where you came from.
But if you want to know what I know...
You pick me up and you dust me off and you take me out of here.
You're lying! You're a liar!
I've never lied to you once.
Can you say the same thing about your father?!
Miles...

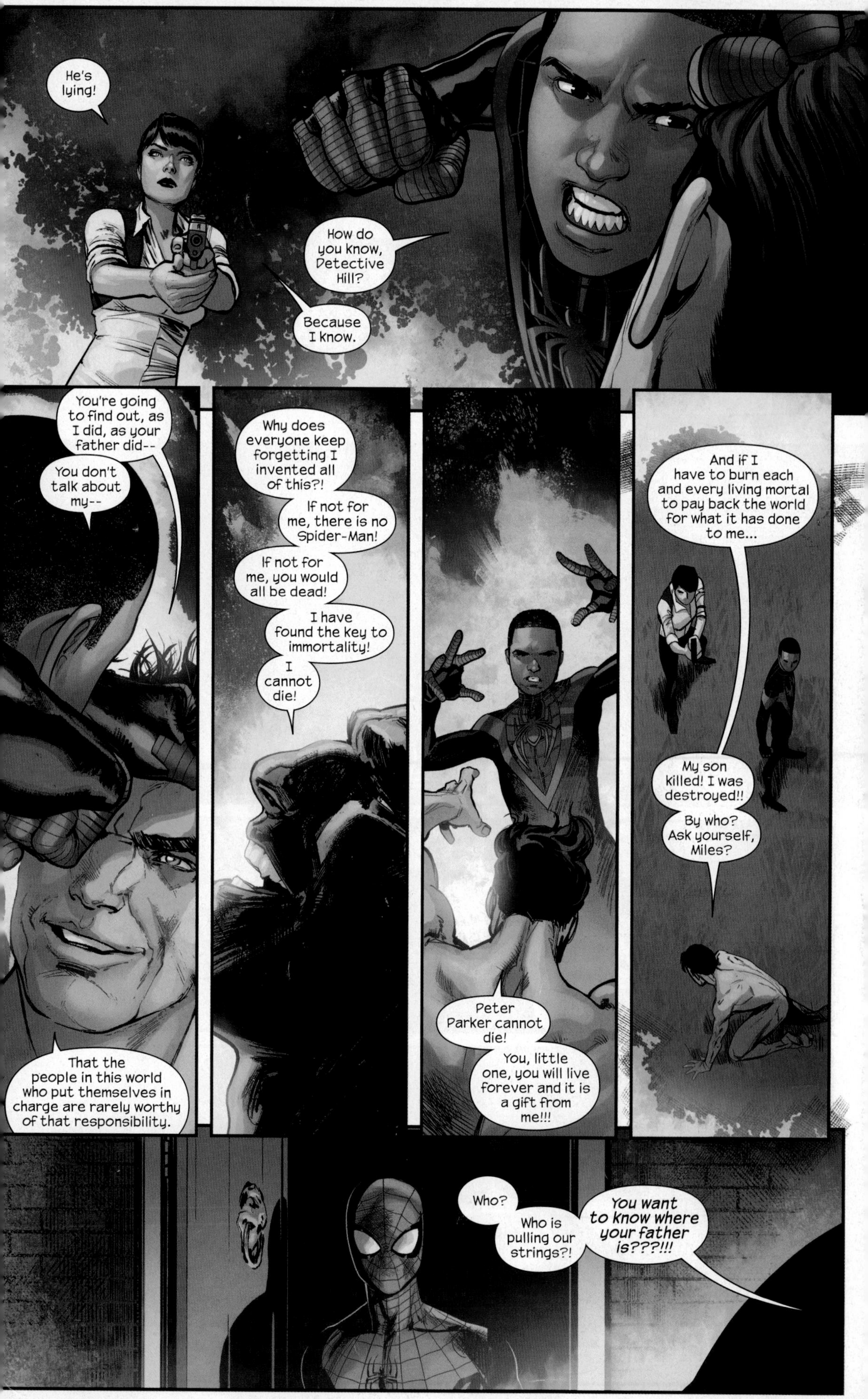
He's lying!
How do you know, Detective Hill?
Because I know.
You're going to find out, as I did, as your father did--
You don't talk about my--
That the people in this world who put themselves in charge are rarely worthy of that responsibility.
Why does everyone keep forgetting I invented all of this?!
If not for me, there is no Spider-Man!
If not for me, you would all be dead!
I have found the key to immortality!
I cannot die!
Peter Parker cannot die!
You, little one, you will live forever and it is a gift from me!!!
And if I have to burn each and every living mortal to pay back the world for what it has done to me...
My son killed! I was destroyed!!
By who? Ask yourself, Miles?
Who?
Who is pulling our strings?!
You want to know where your father is???!!!

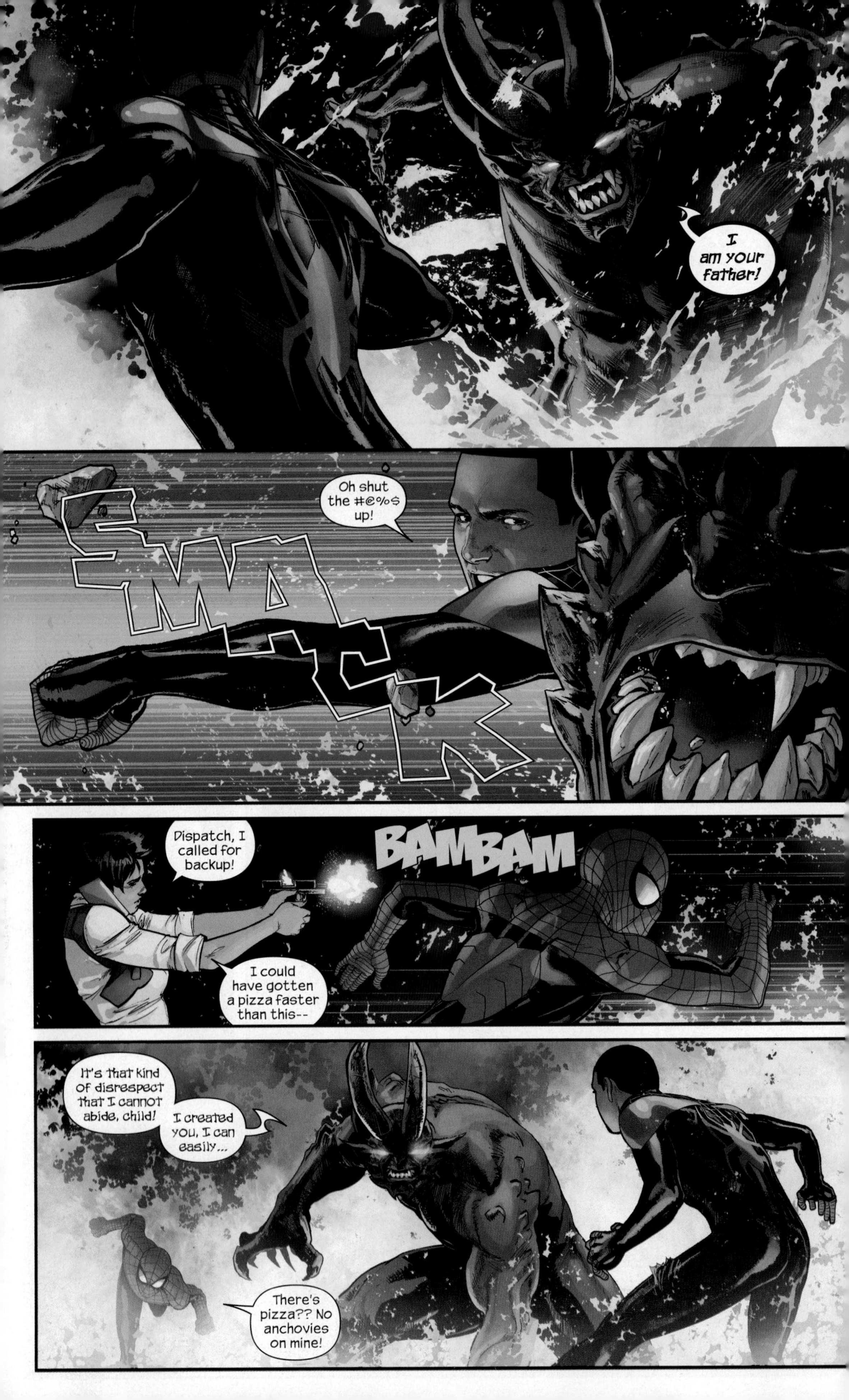
I am your father!
Oh shut the #@%$ up!
SMACK
Dispatch, I called for backup!
BAMBAM
I could have gotten a pizza faster than this--
It's that kind of disrespect that I cannot abide, child!
I created you, I can easily...
There's pizza?? No anchovies on mine!

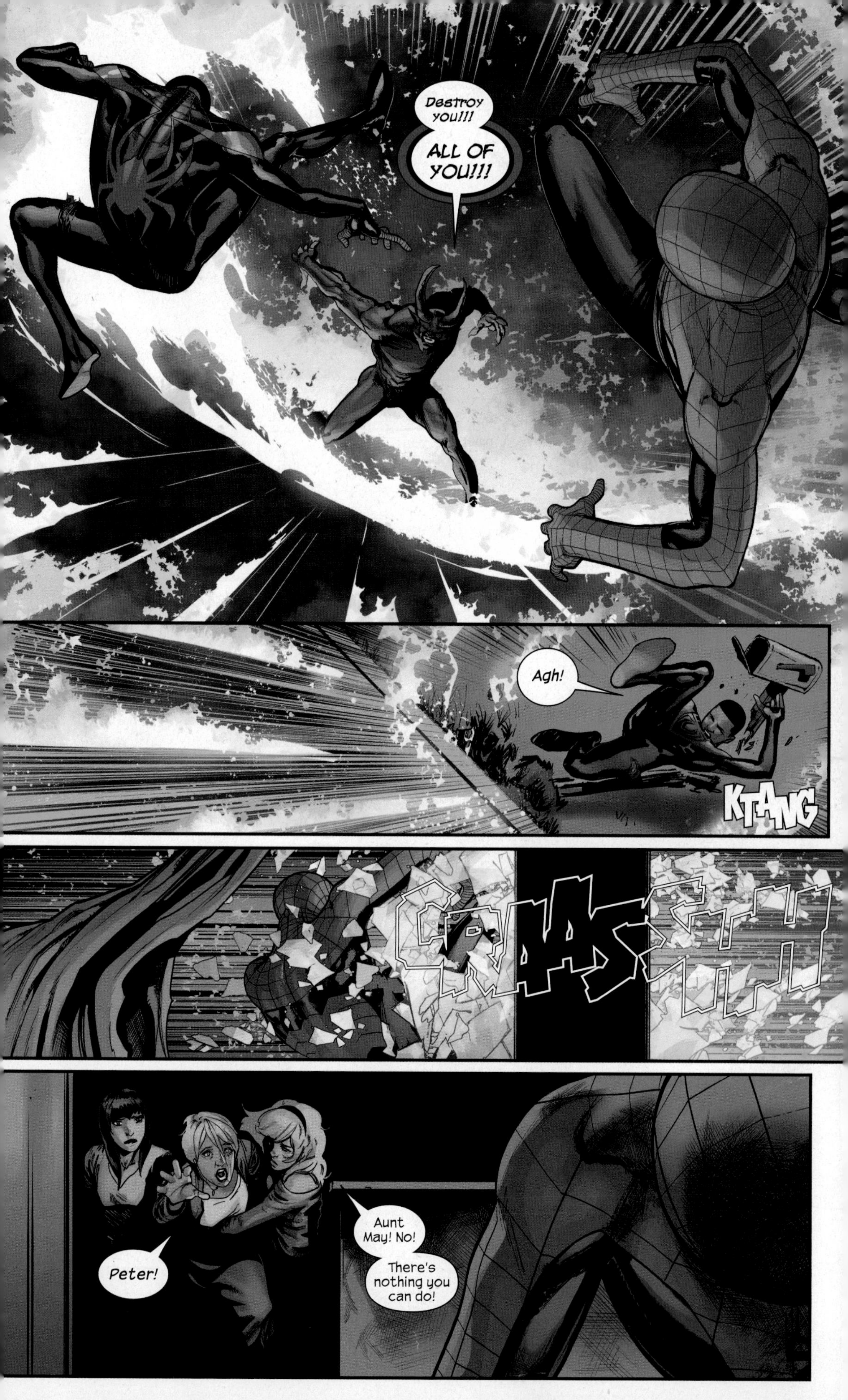
Destroy you!!!
ALL OF YOU!!!
Agh!
KTANG
Peter!
Aunt May! No!
There's nothing you can do!

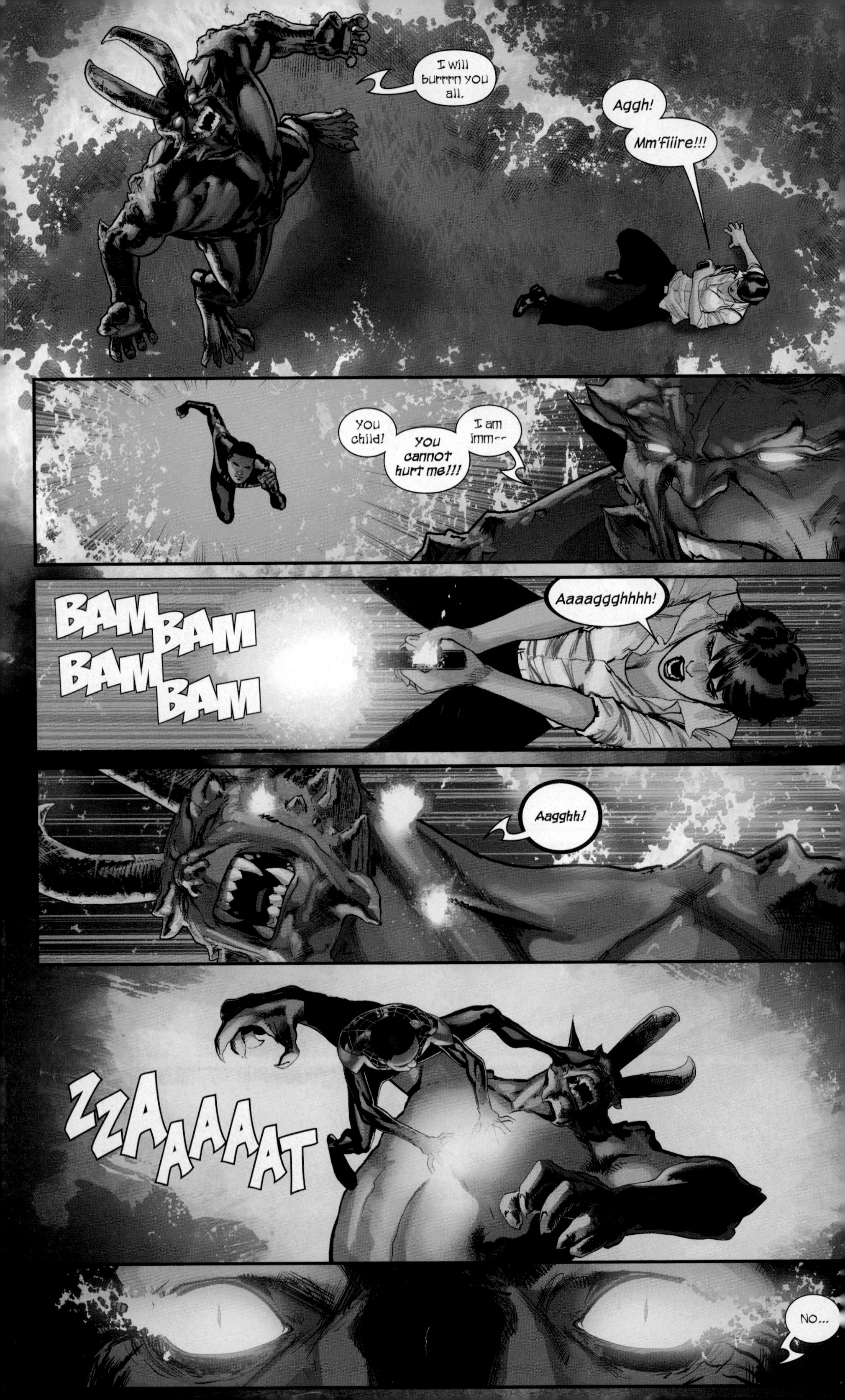
I will burrrn you all.
Aggh!
Mm'fiiire!!!
You child!
You cannot hurt me!!!
I am imm--
BAM BAM BAM BAM
Aaaaggghhhh!
Aagghh!
ZZAAAAAT
No...

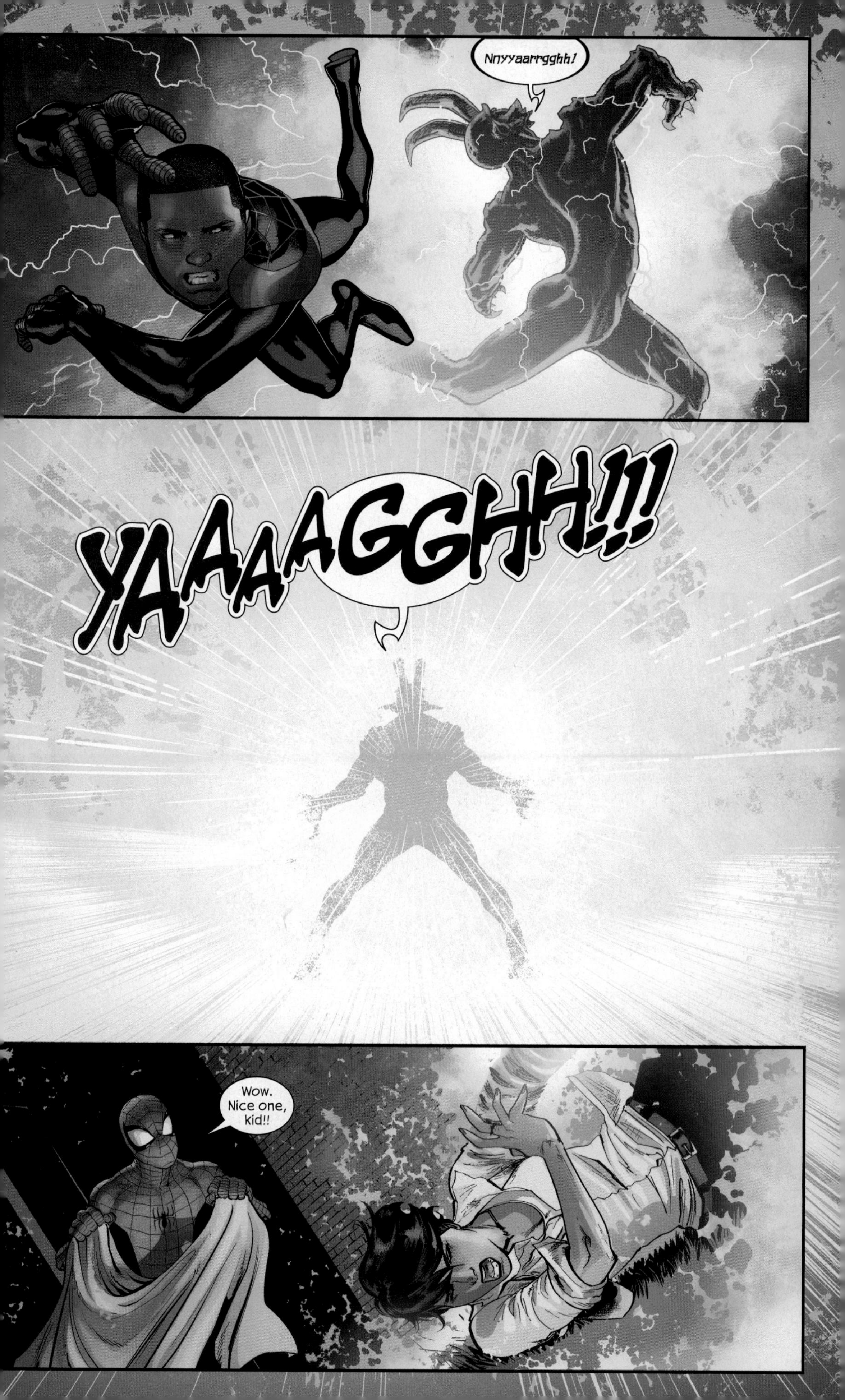
Nnyyaarrgghh!
YAAAAGGHH!!!
Wow. Nice one, kid!!

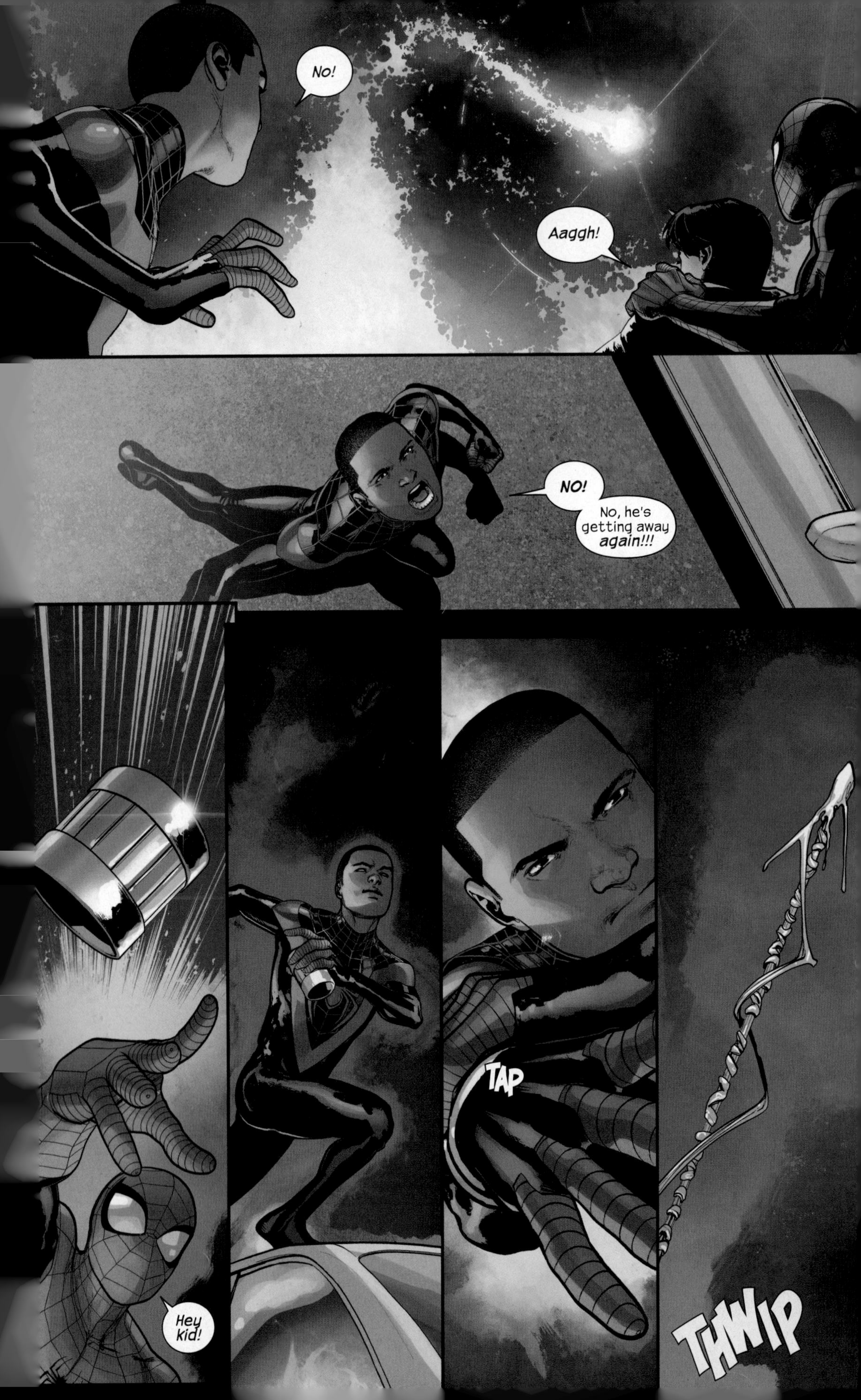
No!
Aaggh!
NO!
No, he's getting away again!!!
Hey kid!
TAP
THWIP

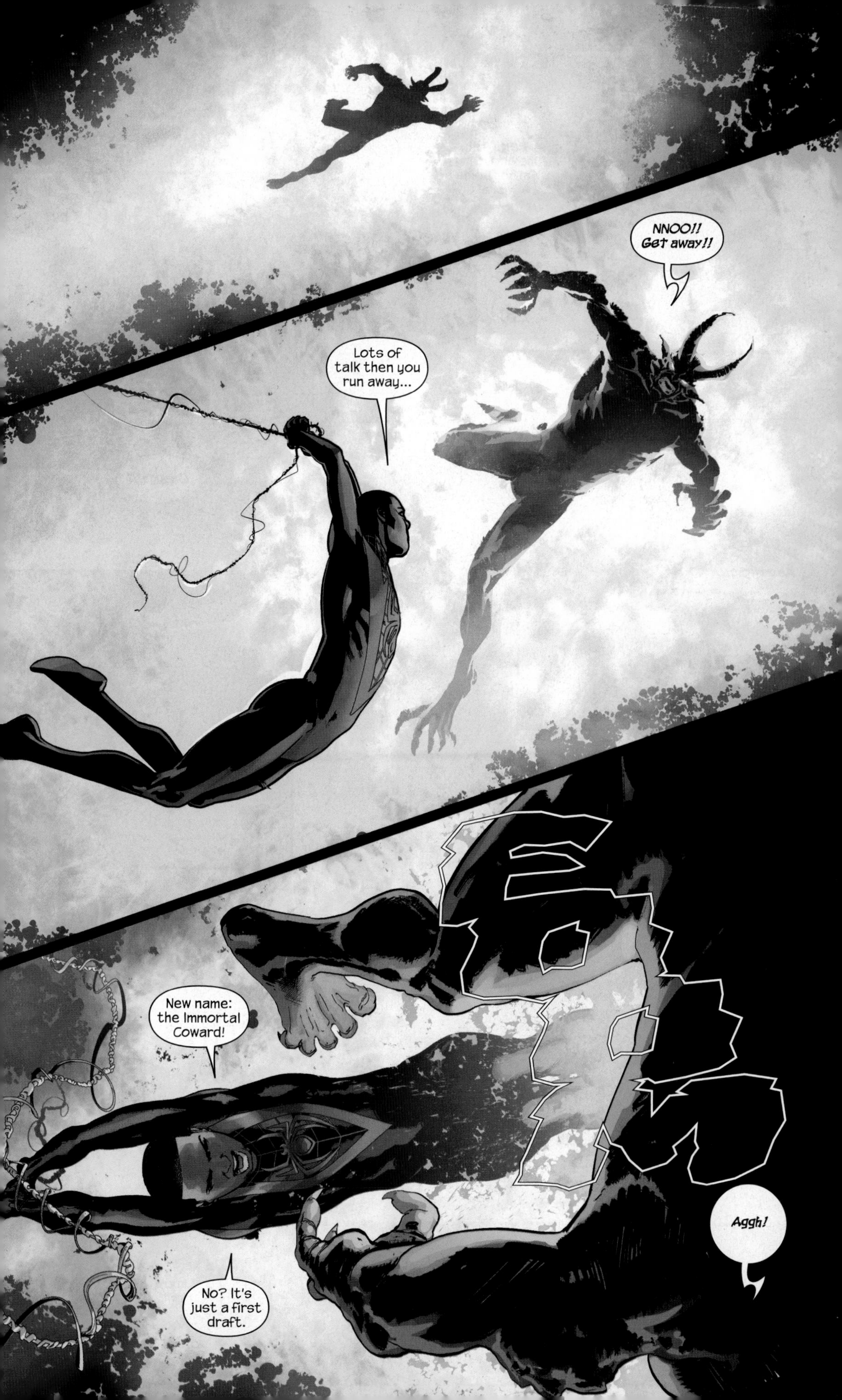

NNOO!! Get away!!
Lots of talk then you run away...
New name: the Immortal Coward!
No? It's just a first draft.
Aggh!

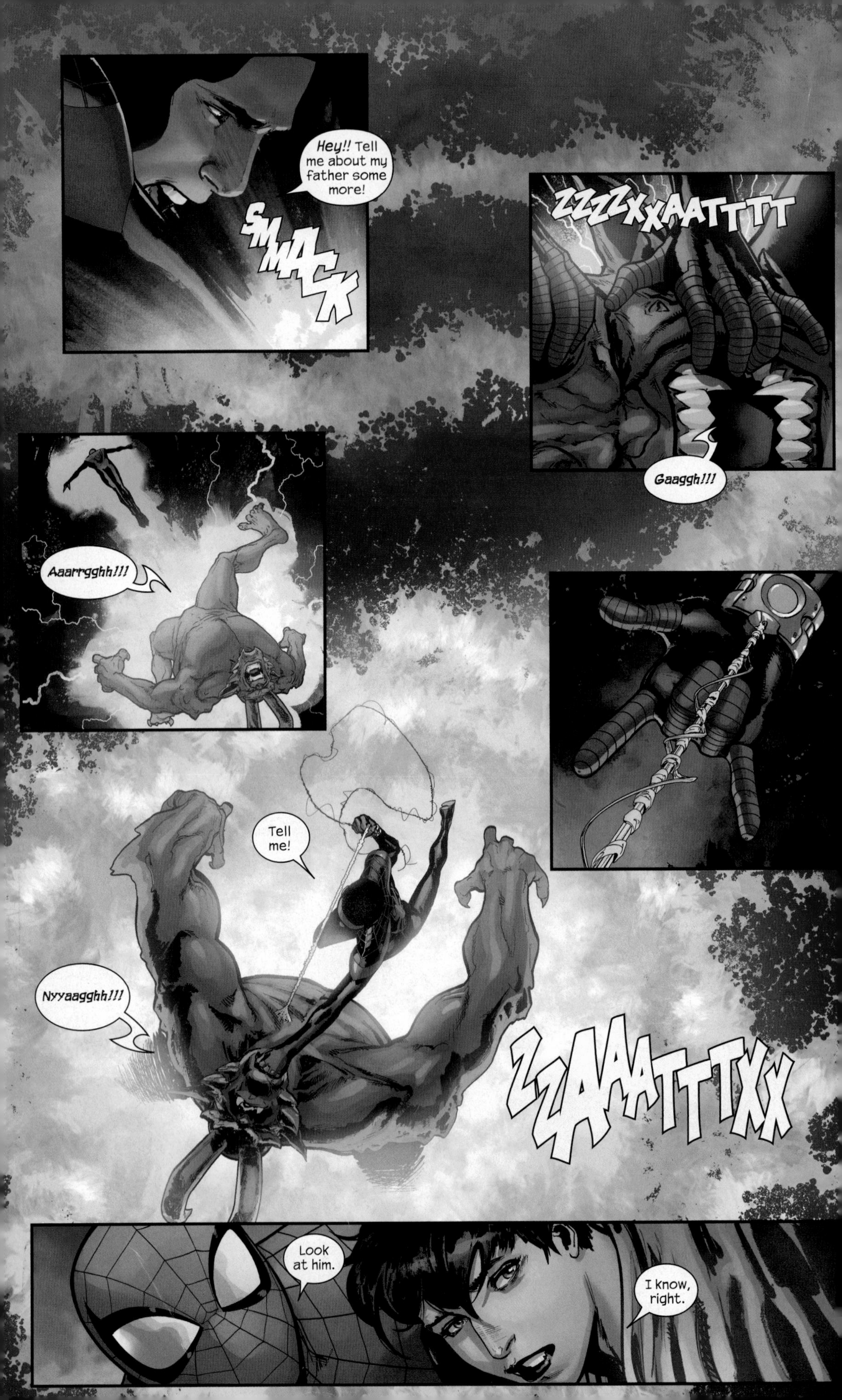
Hey!! Tell me about my father some more!
SMMACK
ZZZZXXAATTTTT
Gaaggh!!!
Aaarrgghh!!!
Tell me!
Nyyaagghh!!!
ZZAAATTTXX
Look at him.
I know, right.

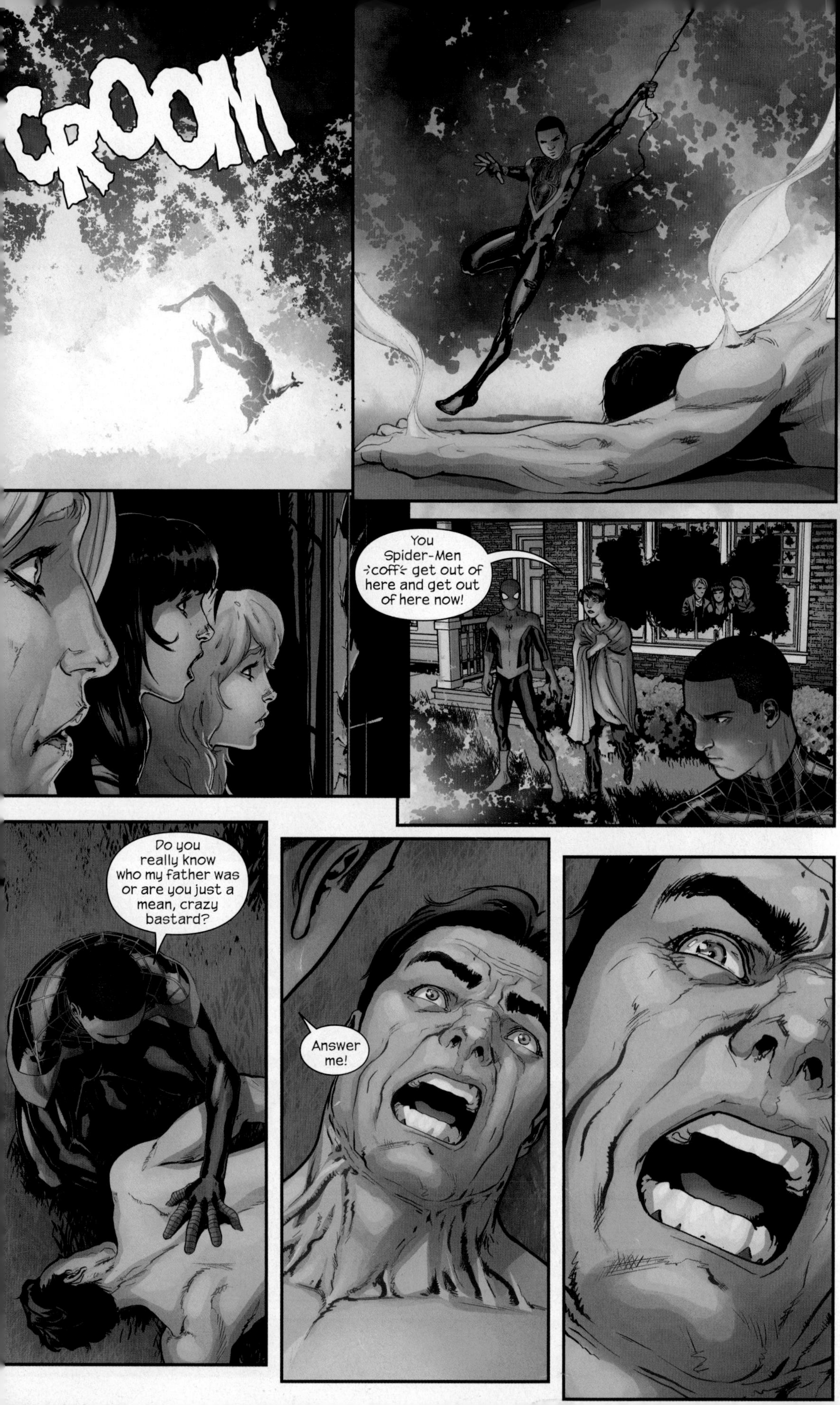
CROOM
You Spider-Men ~coff~ get out of here and get out of here now!
Do you really know who my father was or are you just a mean, crazy bastard?
Answer me!

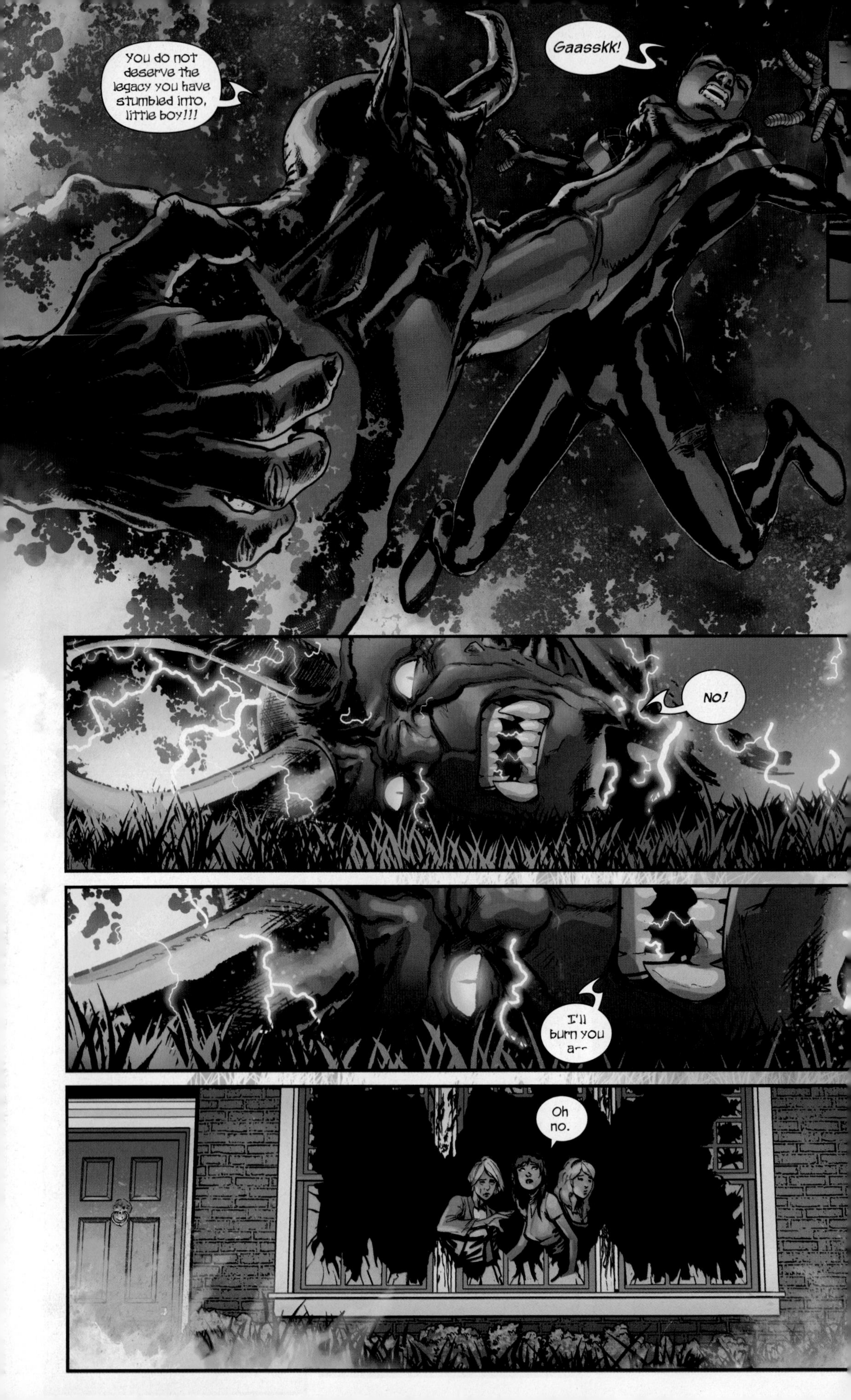
You do not deserve the legacy you have stumbled into, little boy!!!
Gaasskk!
NO!
I'll burn you a--
Oh no.

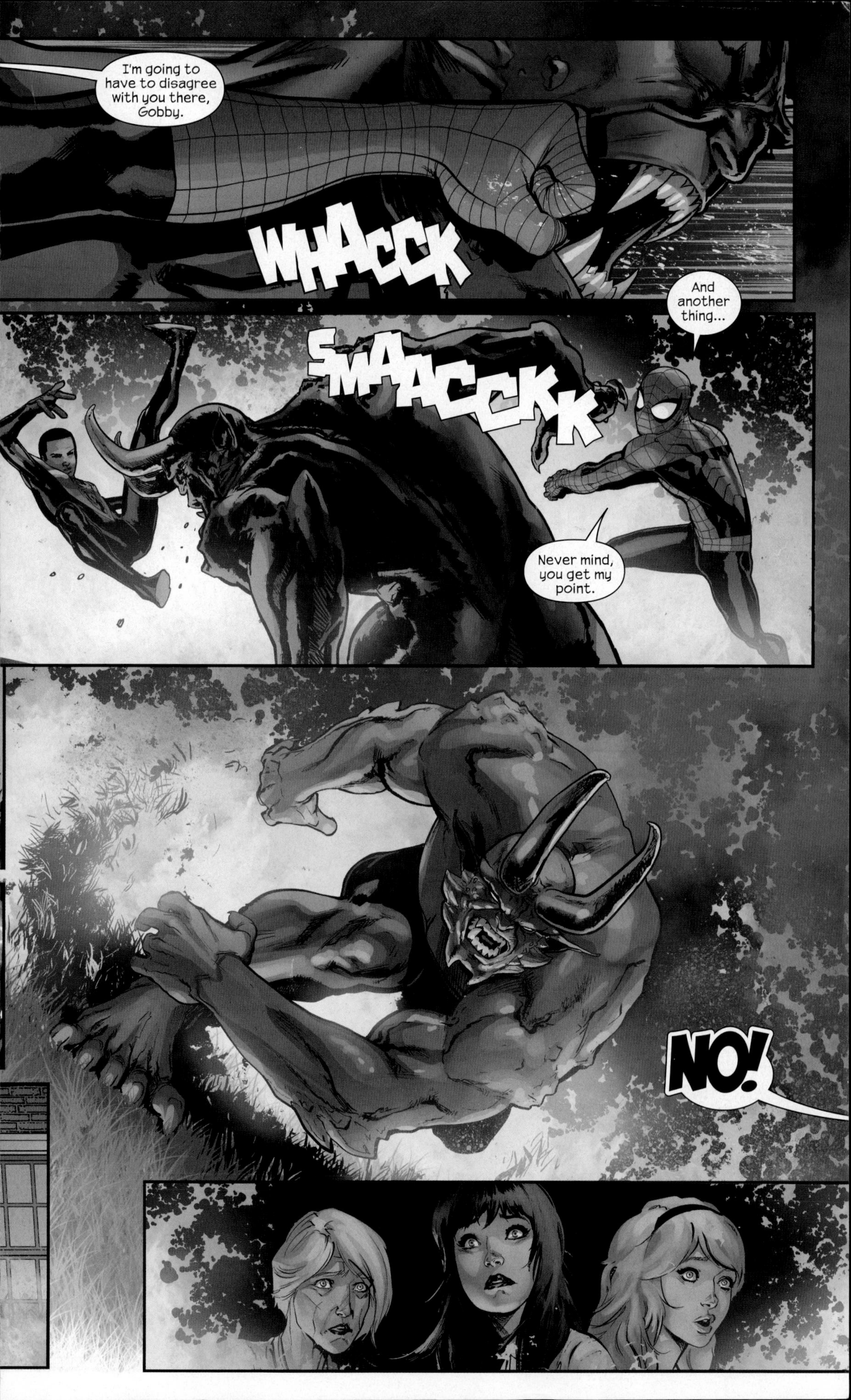
I'm going to have to disagree with you there, Gobby.
WHACCK
And another thing...
SMAACCKK
Never mind, you get my point.
NO!

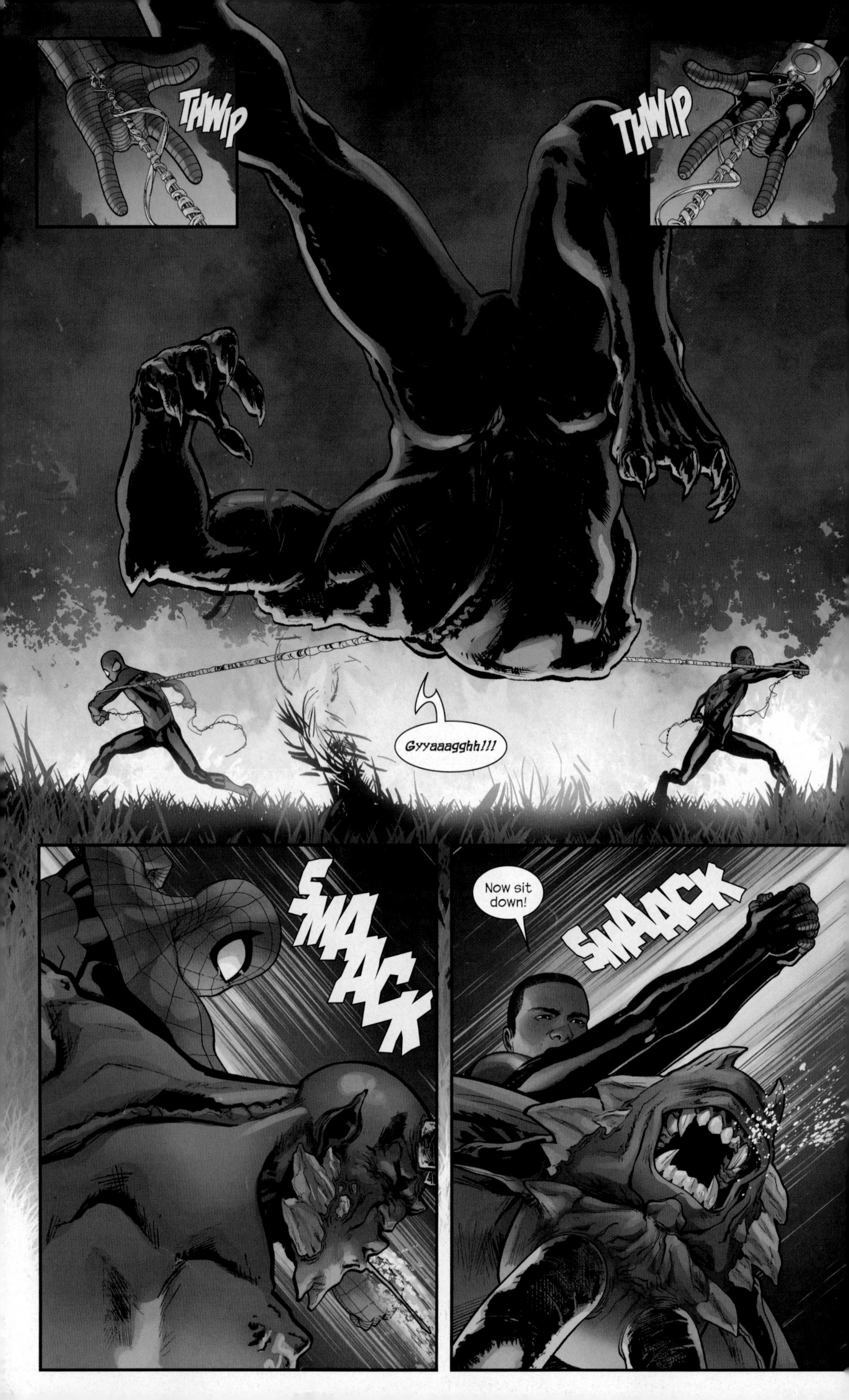
THWIP
THWIP
Gyyaaagghh!!!
SMACK
Now sit down!
SMAACK

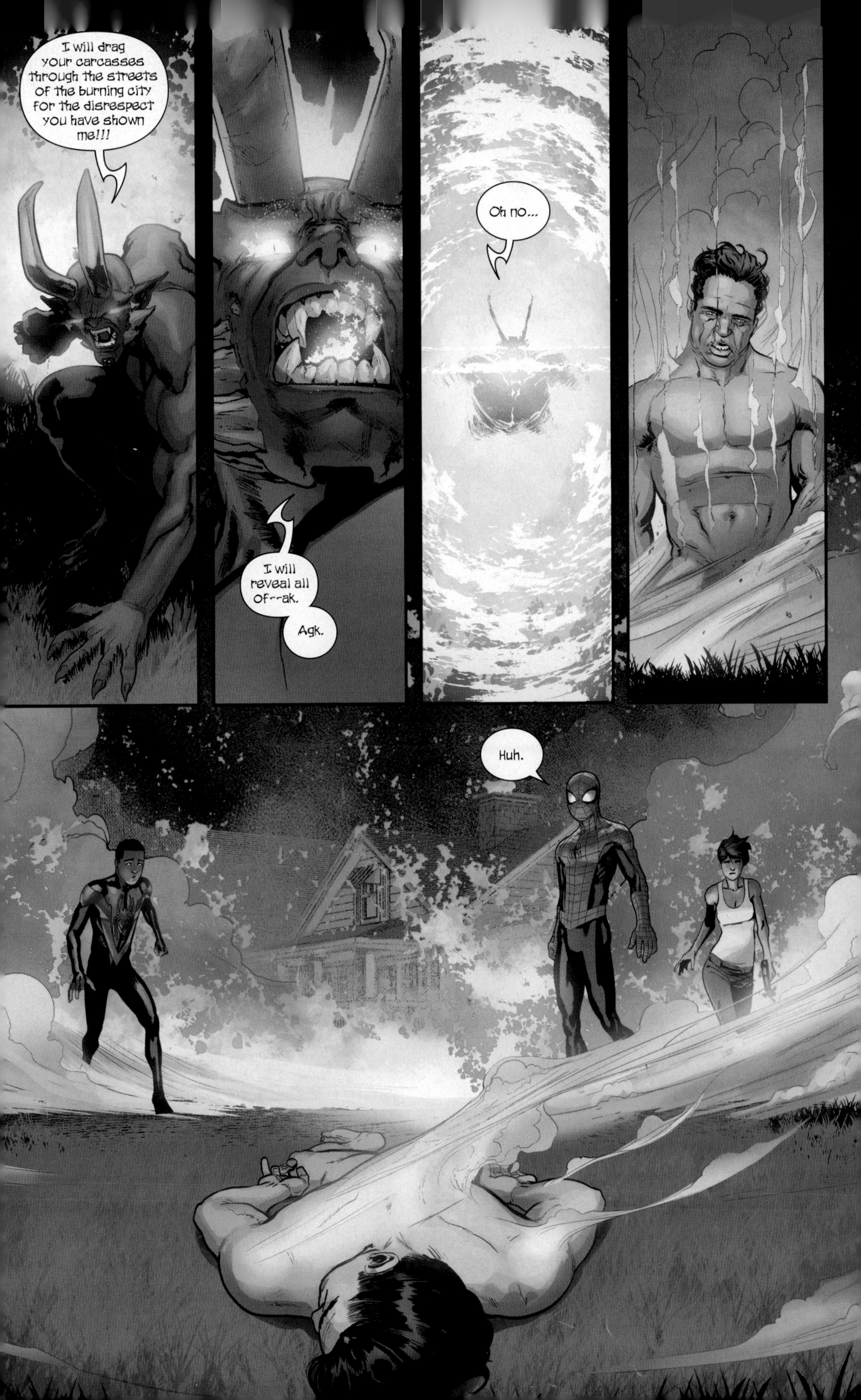
I will drag your carcasses through the streets of the burning city for the disrespect you have shown me!!!
I will reveal all of--ak.
Agk.
Oh no...
Huh.

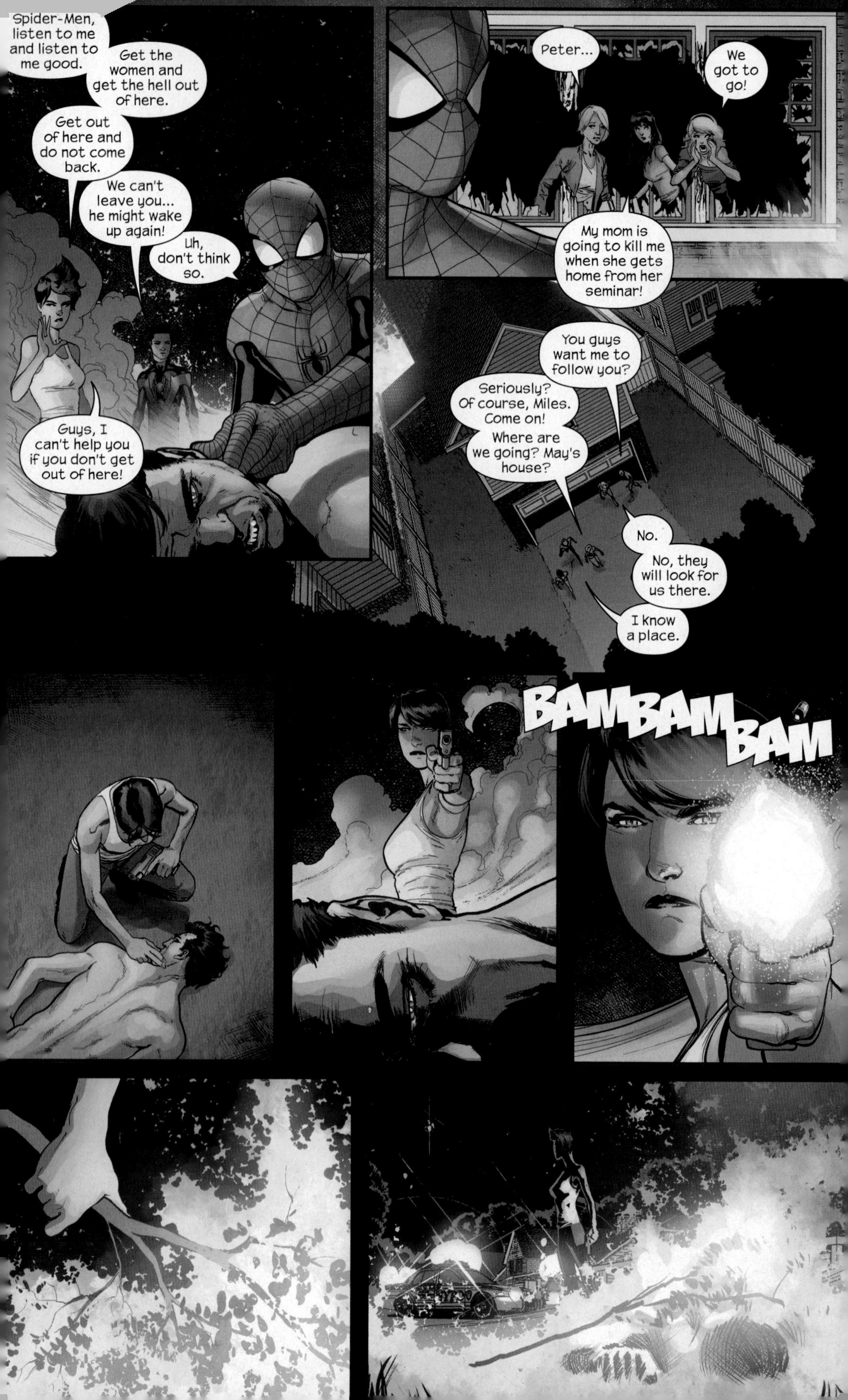
Spider-Men, listen to me and listen to me good.
Get the women and get the hell out of here.
Get out of here and do not come back.
We can't leave you... he might wake up again!
Uh, don't think so.
Guys, I can't help you if you don't get out of here!
Peter...
We got to go!
My mom is going to kill me when she gets home from her seminar!
You guys want me to follow you?
Seriously? Of course, Miles. Come on!
Where are we going? May's house?
No.
No, they will look for us there.
I know a place.
BAMBAMBAM

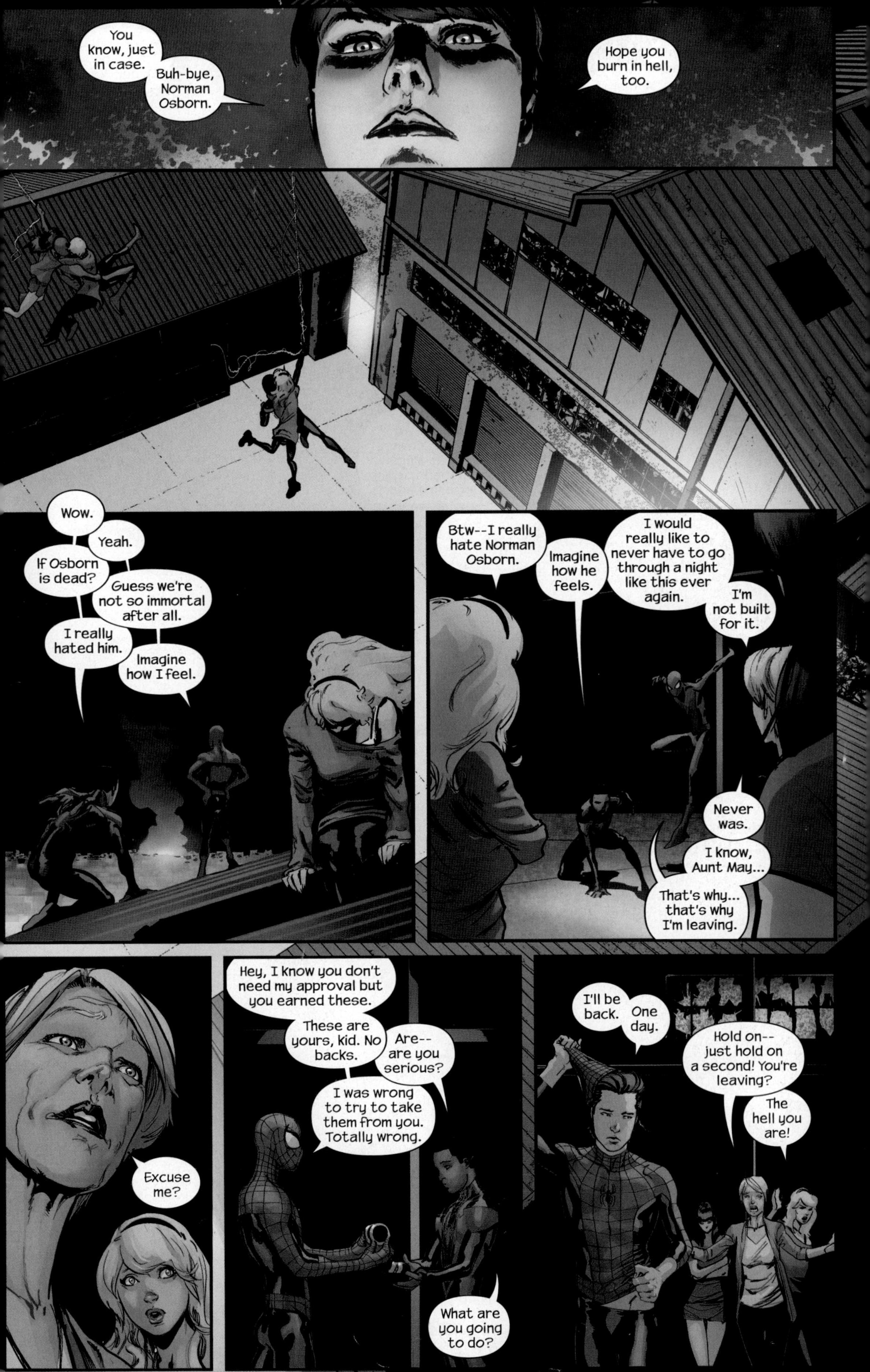
You know, just in case.
Buh-bye, Norman Osborn.
Hope you burn in hell, too.
Wow.
Yeah.
If Osborn is dead?
Guess we're not so immortal after all.
I really hated him.
Imagine how I feel.
Btw--I really hate Norman Osborn.
Imagine how he feels.
I would really like to never have to go through a night like this ever again.
I'm not built for it.
Never was.
I know, Aunt May...
That's why... that's why I'm leaving.
Excuse me?
Hey, I know you don't need my approval but you earned these.
These are yours, kid. No backs.
Are-- are you serious?
I was wrong to try to take them from you. Totally wrong.
What are you going to do?
I'll be back.
One day.
Hold on-- just hold on a second! You're leaving?
The hell you are!

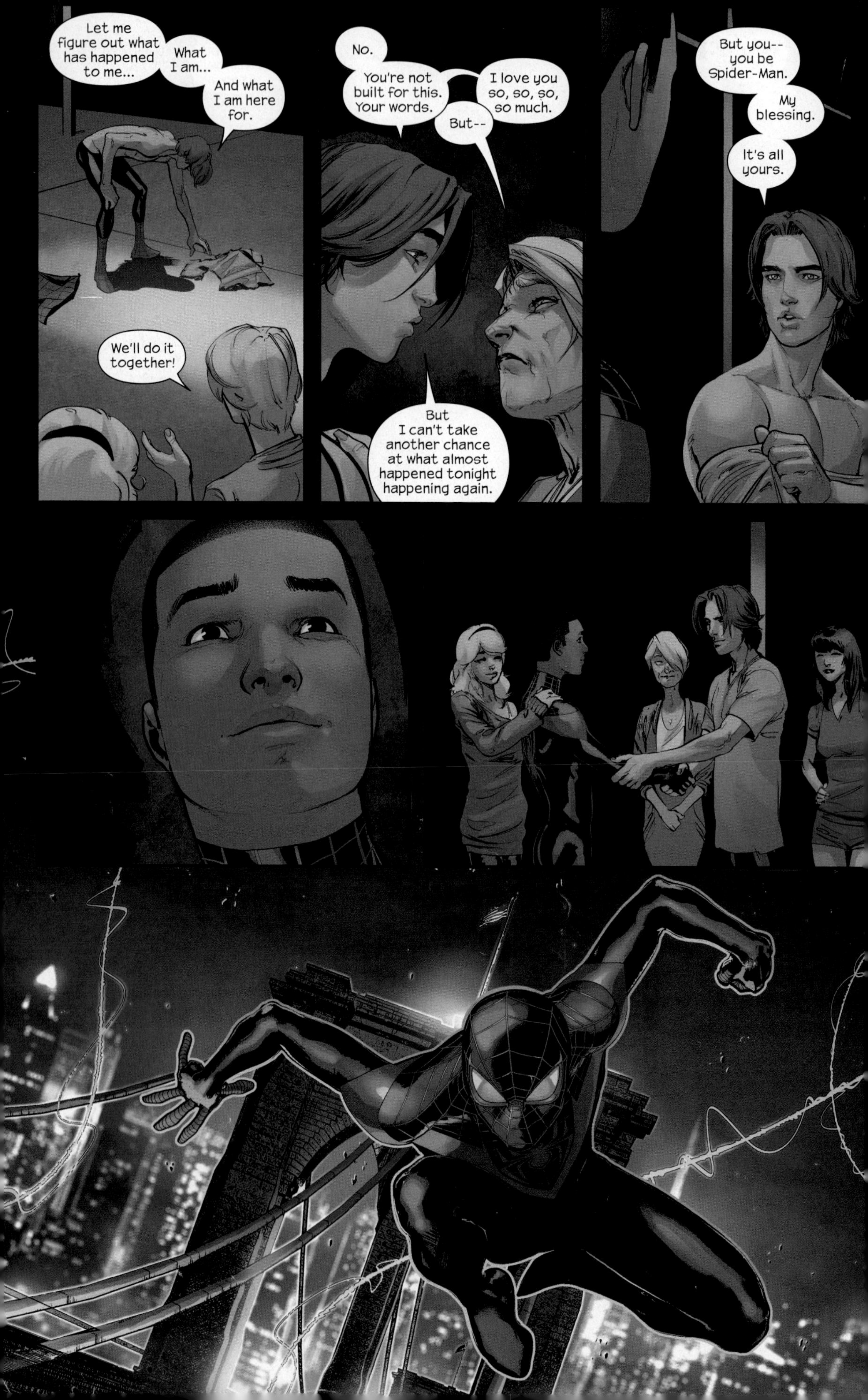
Let me figure out what has happened to me...
What I am...
And what I am here for.
We'll do it together!
No.
You're not built for this. Your words.
I love you so, so, so, so much.
But--
But I can't take another chance at what almost happened tonight happening again.
But you-- you be Spider-Man.
My blessing.
It's all yours.

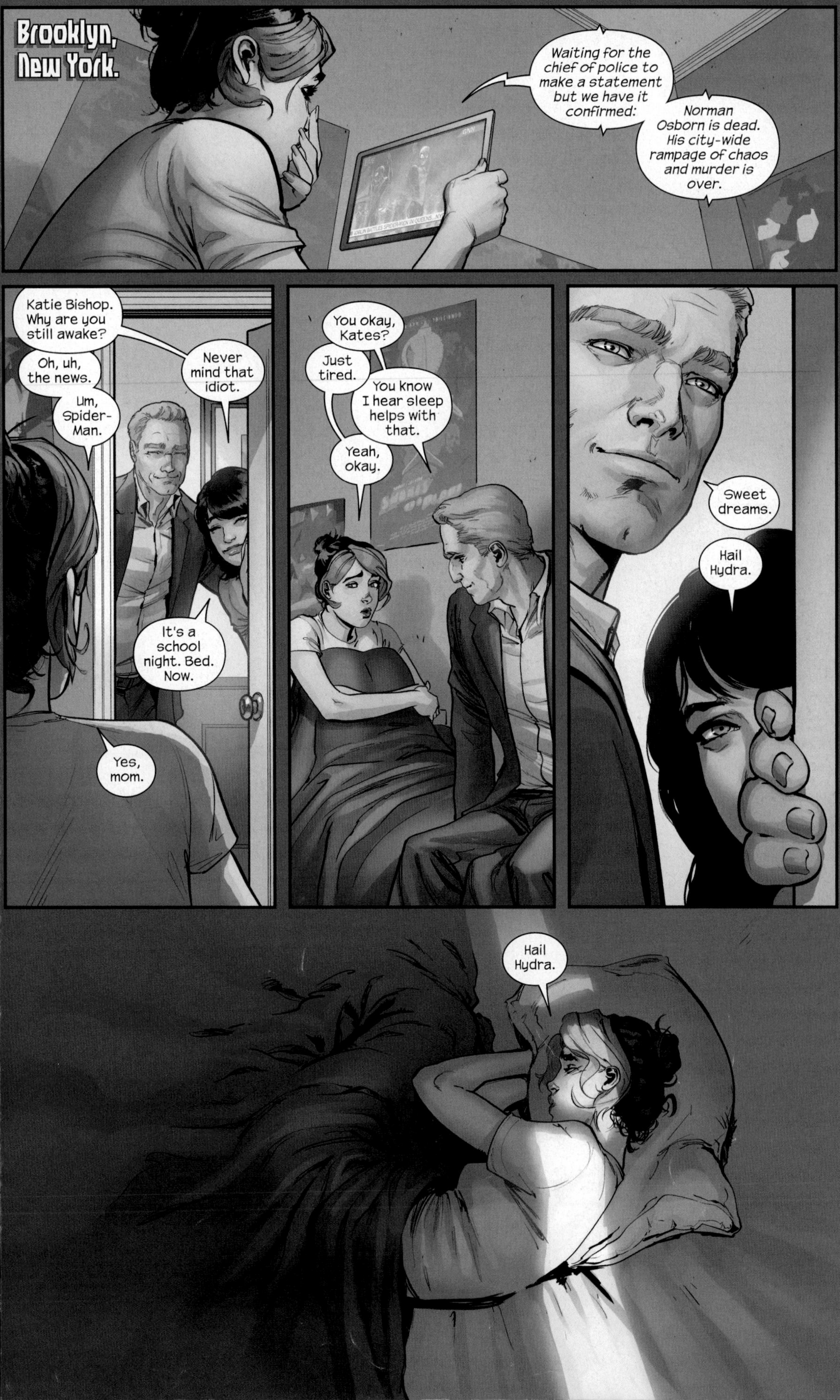
Brooklyn, New York.
Waiting for the chief of police to make a statement but we have it confirmed:
Norman Osborn is dead. His city-wide rampage of chaos and murder is over.
Katie Bishop. Why are you still awake?
Oh, uh, the news.
Um, Spider-Man.
Never mind that idiot.
It's a school night. Bed. Now.
Yes, mom.
You okay, Kates?
Just tired.
You know I hear sleep helps with that.
Yeah, okay.
Sweet dreams.
Hail Hydra.
Hail Hydra.

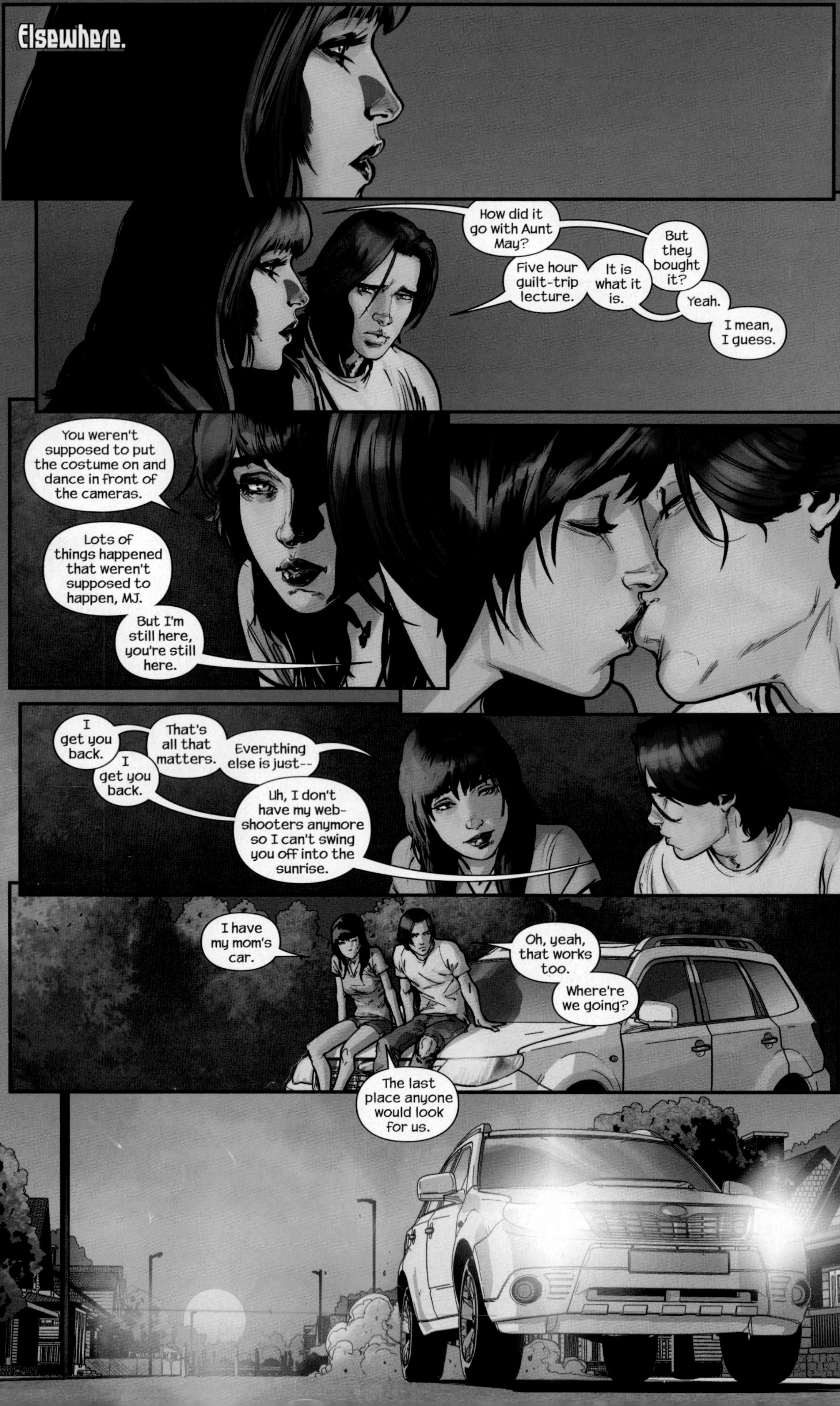
Elsewhere.
How did it go with Aunt May?
Five hour guilt-trip lecture.
It is what it is.
But they bought it?
Yeah.
I mean, I guess.
You weren't supposed to put the costume on and dance in front of the cameras.
Lots of things happened that weren't supposed to happen, MJ.
But I'm still here, you're still here.
I get you back.
That's all that matters.
I get you back.
Everything else is just--
Uh, I don't have my web-shooters anymore so I can't swing you off into the sunrise.
I have my mom's car.
Oh, yeah, that works too.
Where're we going?
The last place anyone would look for us.

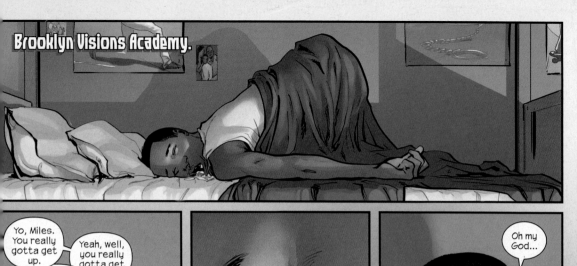

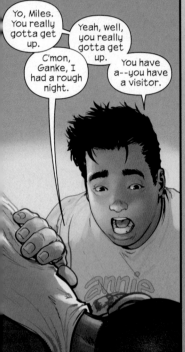

Brooklyn Visions Academy.
Yo, Miles. You really gotta get up.
C'mon, Ganke, I had a rough night.
Yeah, well, you really gotta get up.
You have a--you have a visitor.
Oh my God...
DAD!
Hey, boy...
I believe you and I need to talk.

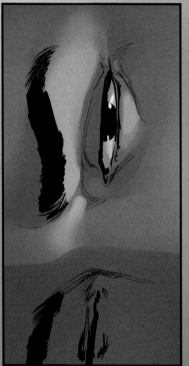

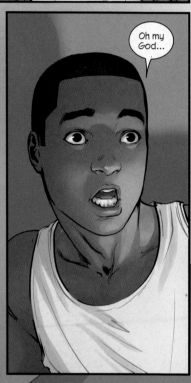

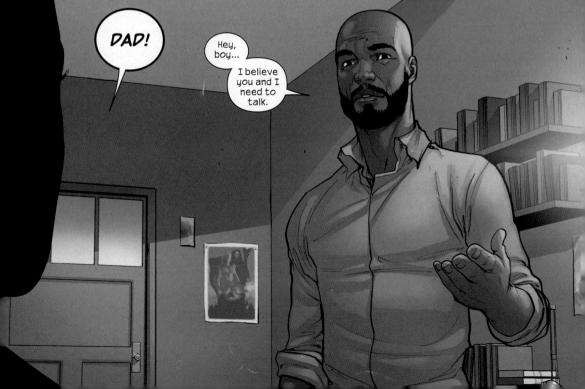

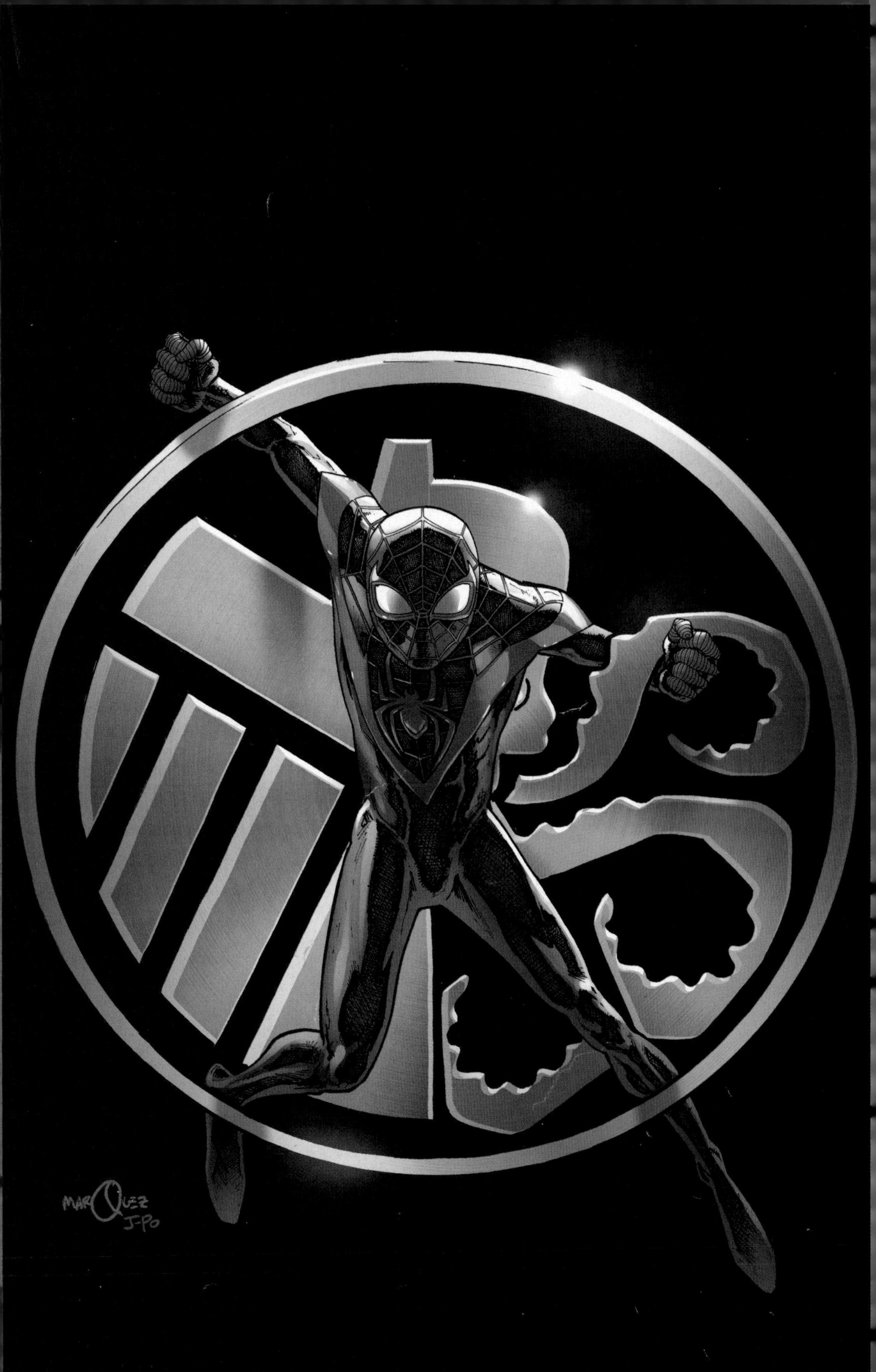
MARQUEZ
J-Po

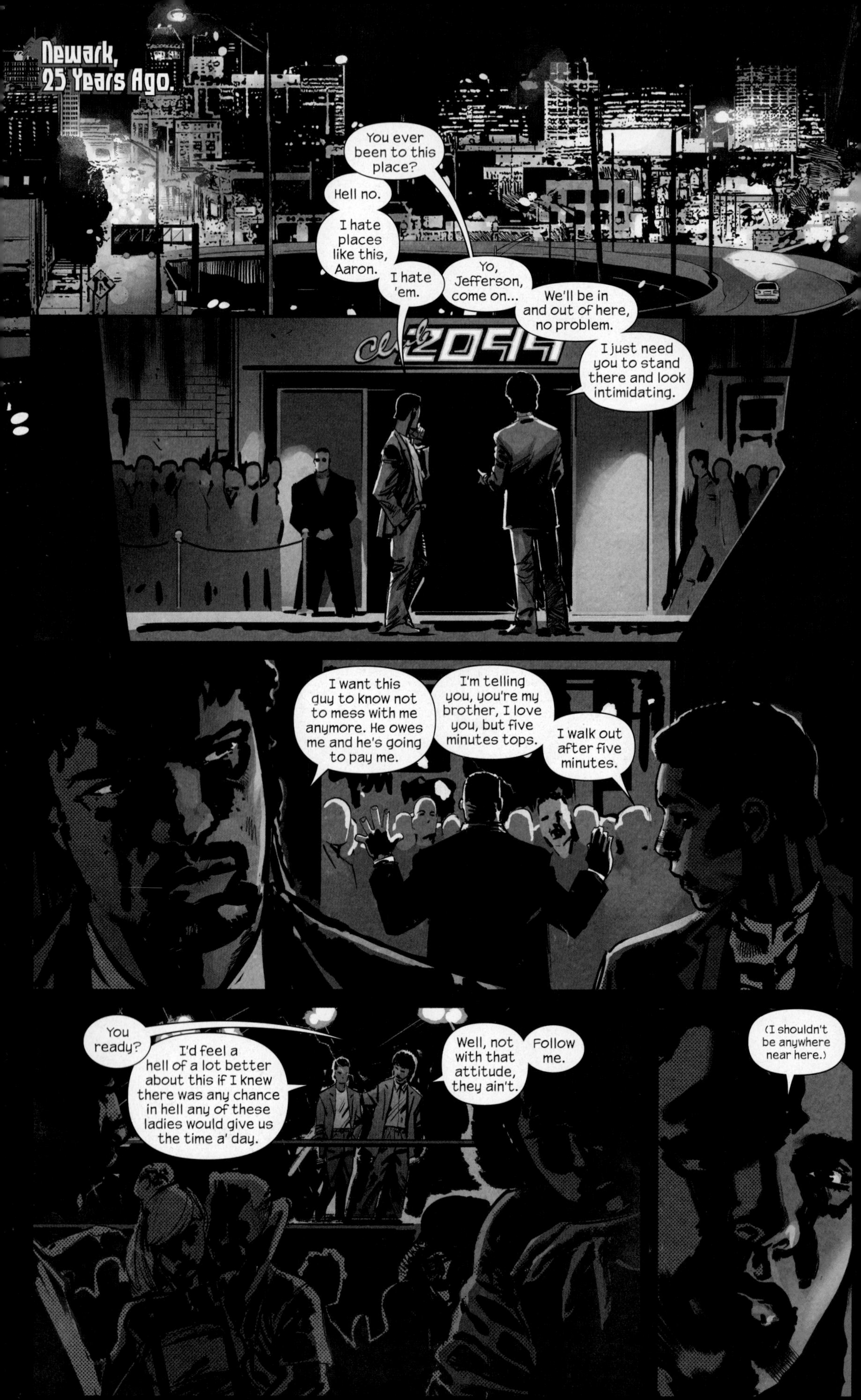
Newark, 25 Years Ago.
You ever been to this place?
Hell no.
I hate places like this, Aaron.
I hate 'em.
Yo, Jefferson, come on...
We'll be in and out of here, no problem.
I just need you to stand there and look intimidating.
I want this guy to know not to mess with me anymore. He owes me and he's going to pay me.
I'm telling you, you're my brother, I love you, but five minutes tops.
I walk out after five minutes.
You ready?
I'd feel a hell of a lot better about this if I knew there was any chance in hell any of these ladies would give us the time a' day.
Well, not with that attitude, they ain't.
Follow me.
(I shouldn't be anywhere near here.)

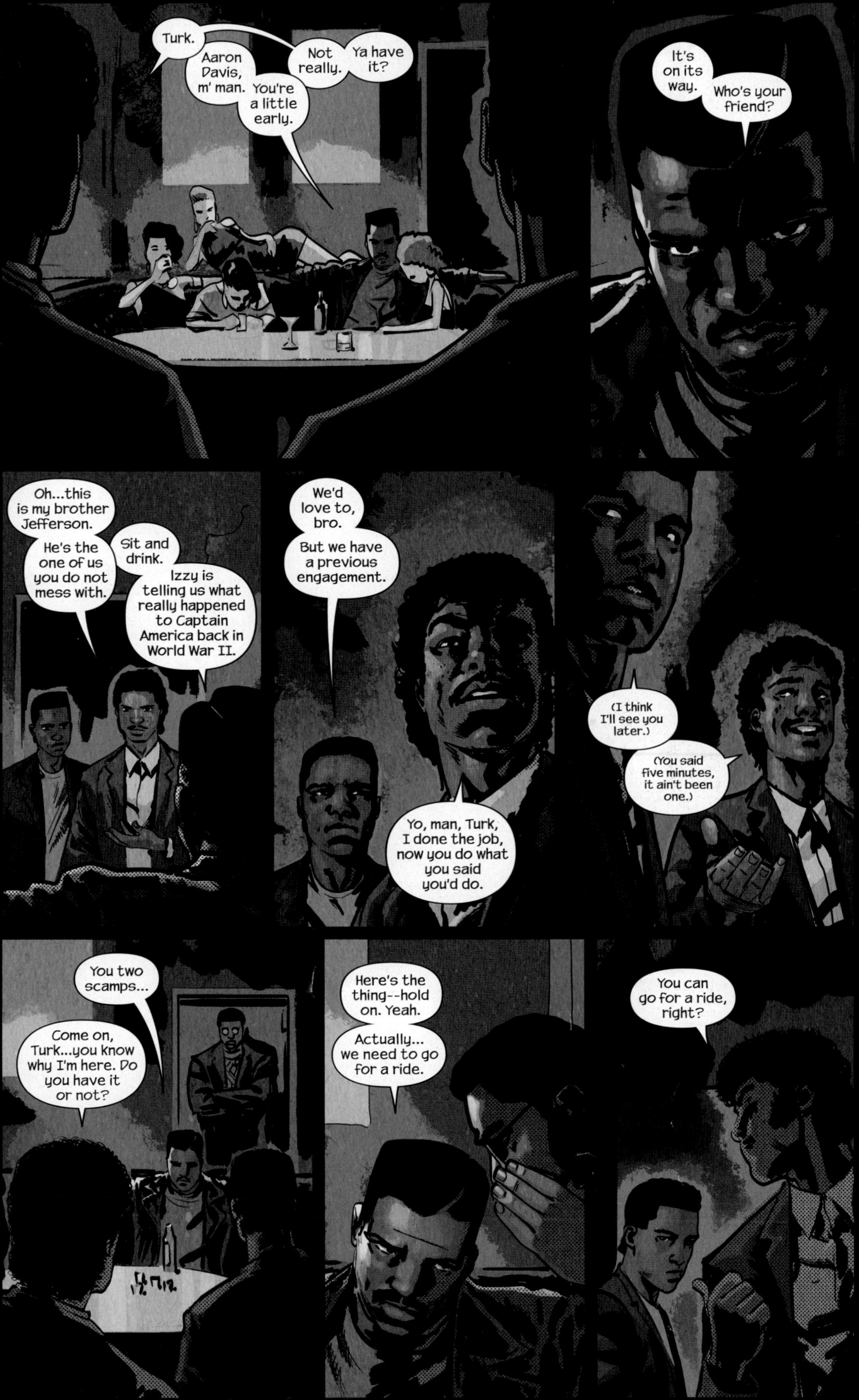
Turk.
Aaron Davis, m' man.
You're a little early.
Not really.
Ya have it?
It's on its way.
Who's your friend?
Oh...this is my brother Jefferson.
He's the one of us you do not mess with.
Sit and drink.
Izzy is telling us what really happened to Captain America back in World War II.
We'd love to, bro.
But we have a previous engagement.
Yo, man, Turk, I done the job, now you do what you said you'd do.
(I think I'll see you later.)
(You said five minutes, it ain't been one.)
You two scamps...
Come on, Turk...you know why I'm here. Do you have it or not?
Here's the thing--hold on. Yeah.
Actually... we need to go for a ride.
You can go for a ride, right?

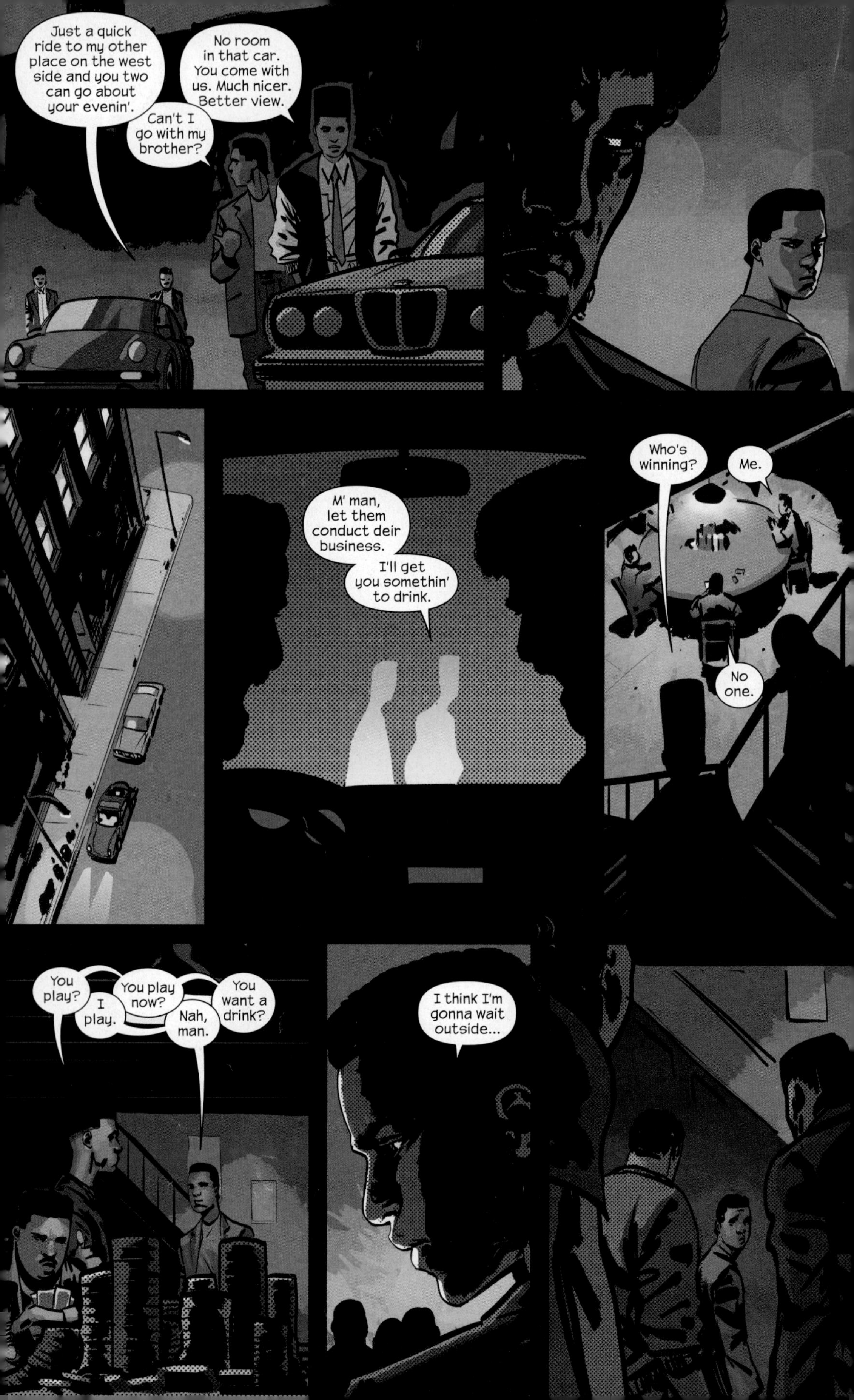

Just a quick ride to my other place on the west side and you two can go about your evenin'.
Can't I go with my brother?
No room in that car. You come with us. Much nicer. Better view.
M' man, let them conduct deir business.
I'll get you somethin' to drink.
Who's winning?
Me.
No one.
You play?
I play.
You play now?
Nah, man.
You want a drink?
I think I'm gonna wait outside...

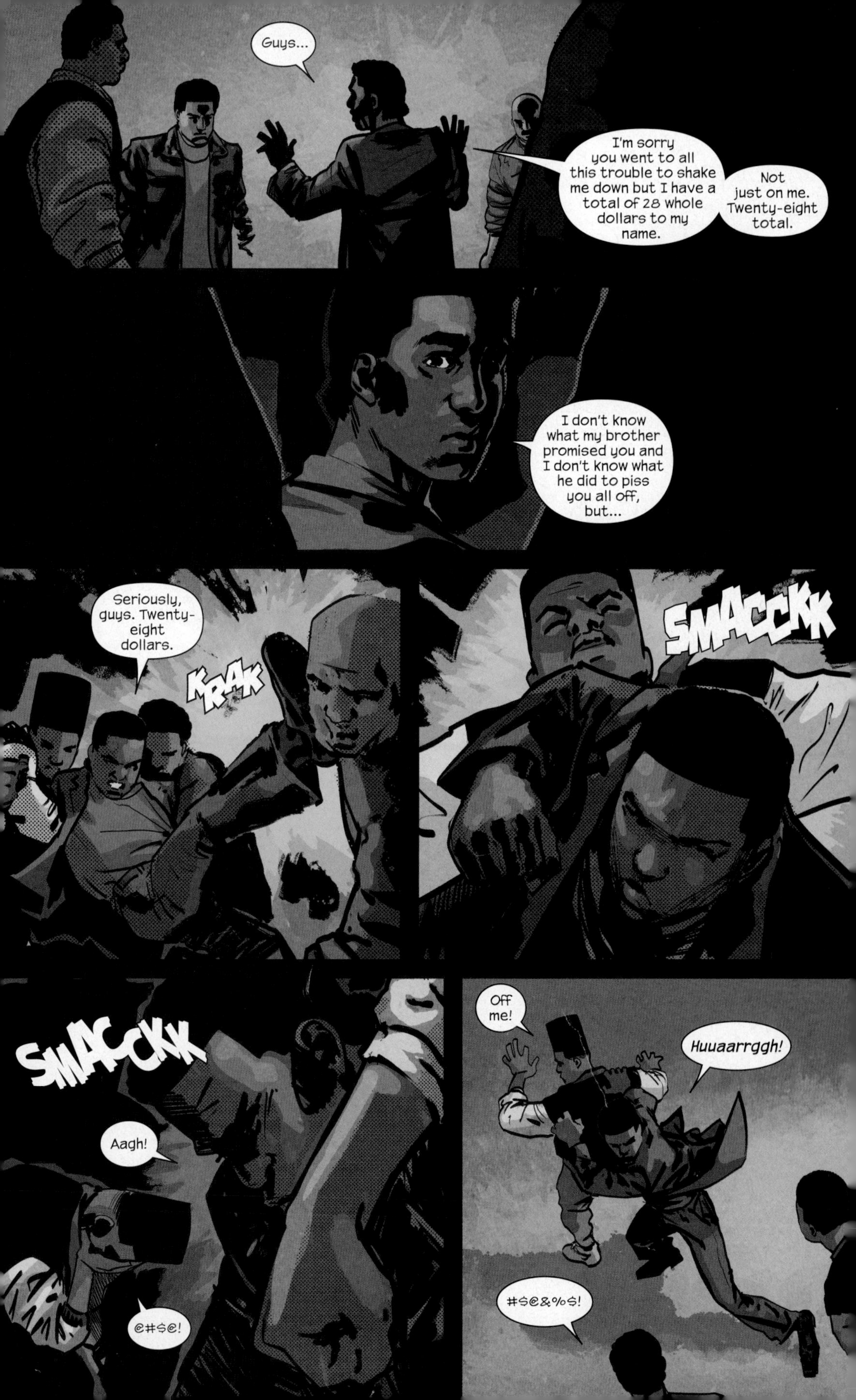
Guys...
I'm sorry you went to all this trouble to shake me down but I have a total of 28 whole dollars to my name.
Not just on me. Twenty-eight total.
I don't know what my brother promised you and I don't know what he did to piss you all off, but...
Seriously, guys. Twenty-eight dollars.
KRAK
SMACCKK
SMACCKK
Aagh!
@#$@!
Off me!
Huuaarrggh!
#$@&%$!

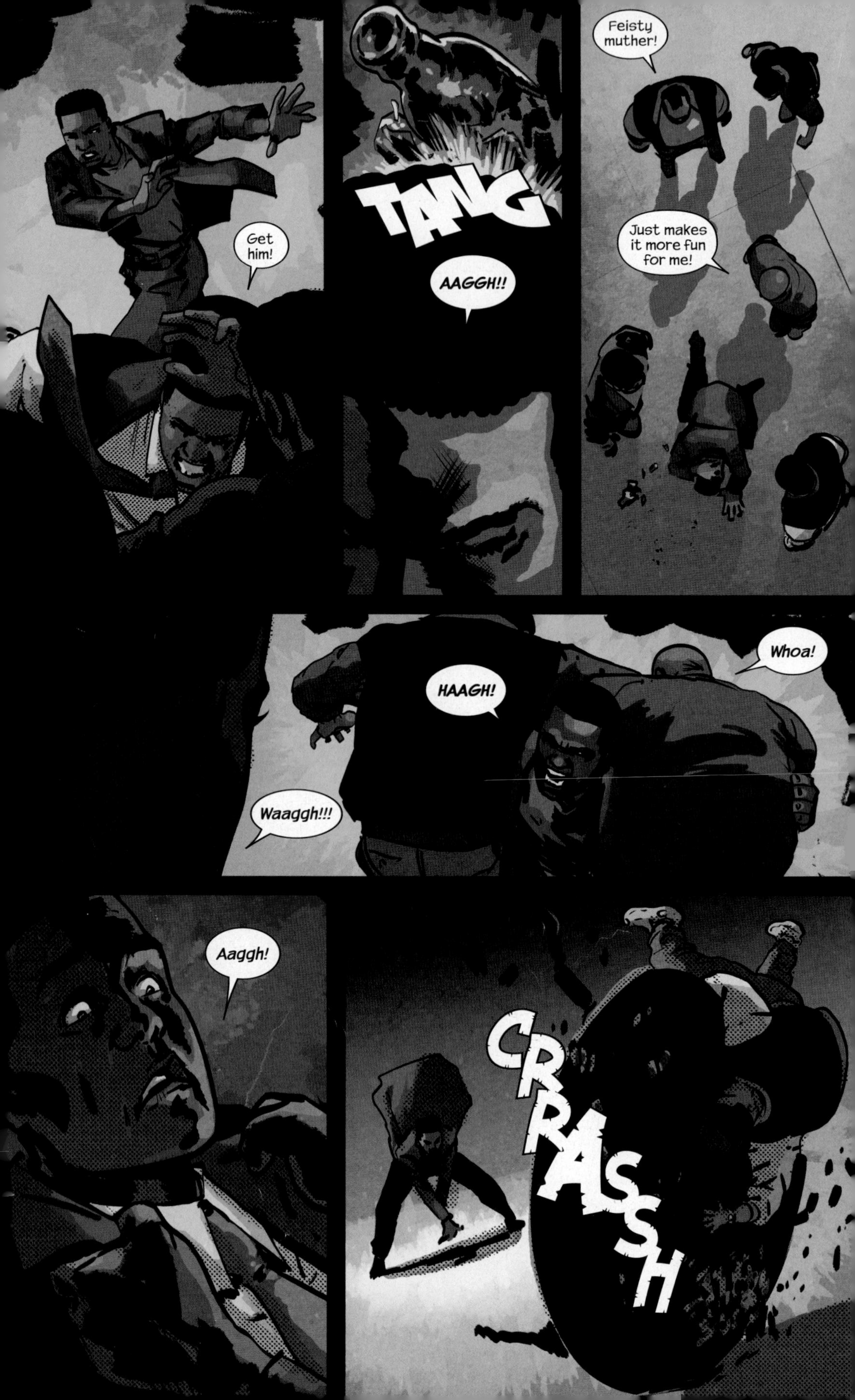
Get him!
TANG
AAGGH!!
Feisty muther!
Just makes it more fun for me!
HAAGH!
Whoa!
Waaggh!!!
Aaggh!
CRRASSH

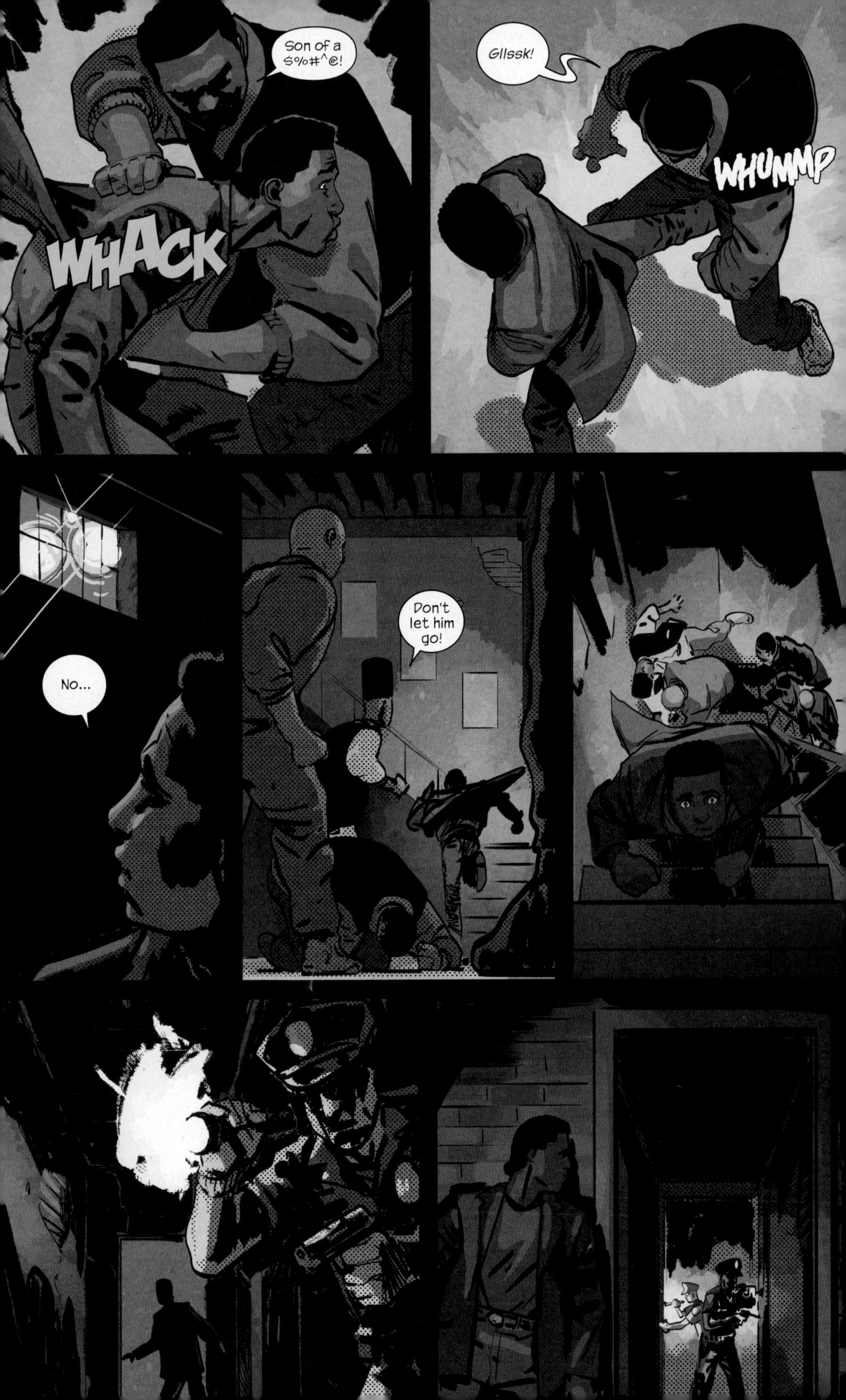
Son of a $%#^@!
WHACK
Gllssk!
WHUMMP
No...
Don't let him go!

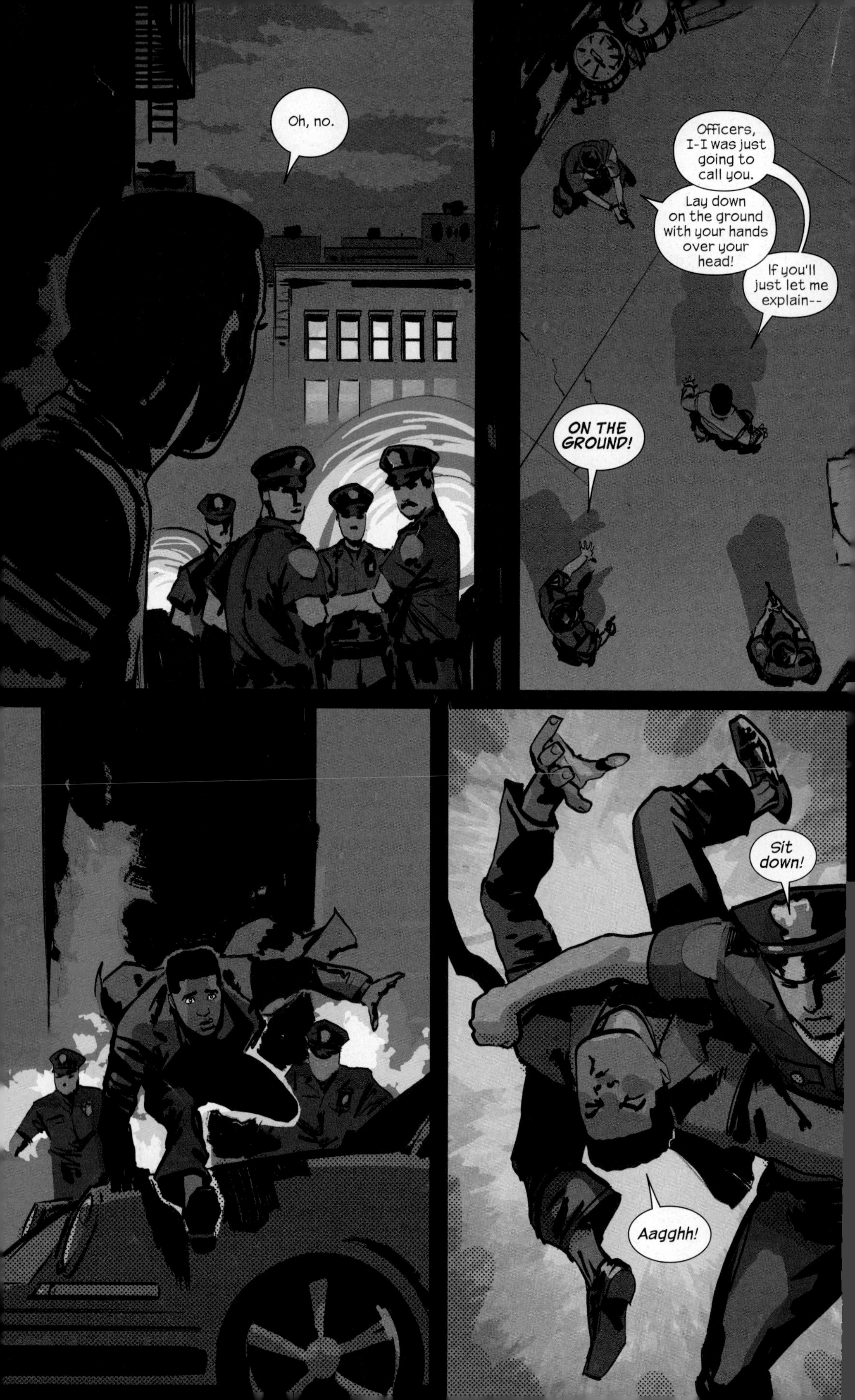
Oh, no.
Officers, I-I was just going to call you.
Lay down on the ground with your hands over your head!
If you'll just let me explain--
ON THE GROUND!
Sit down!
Aagghh!

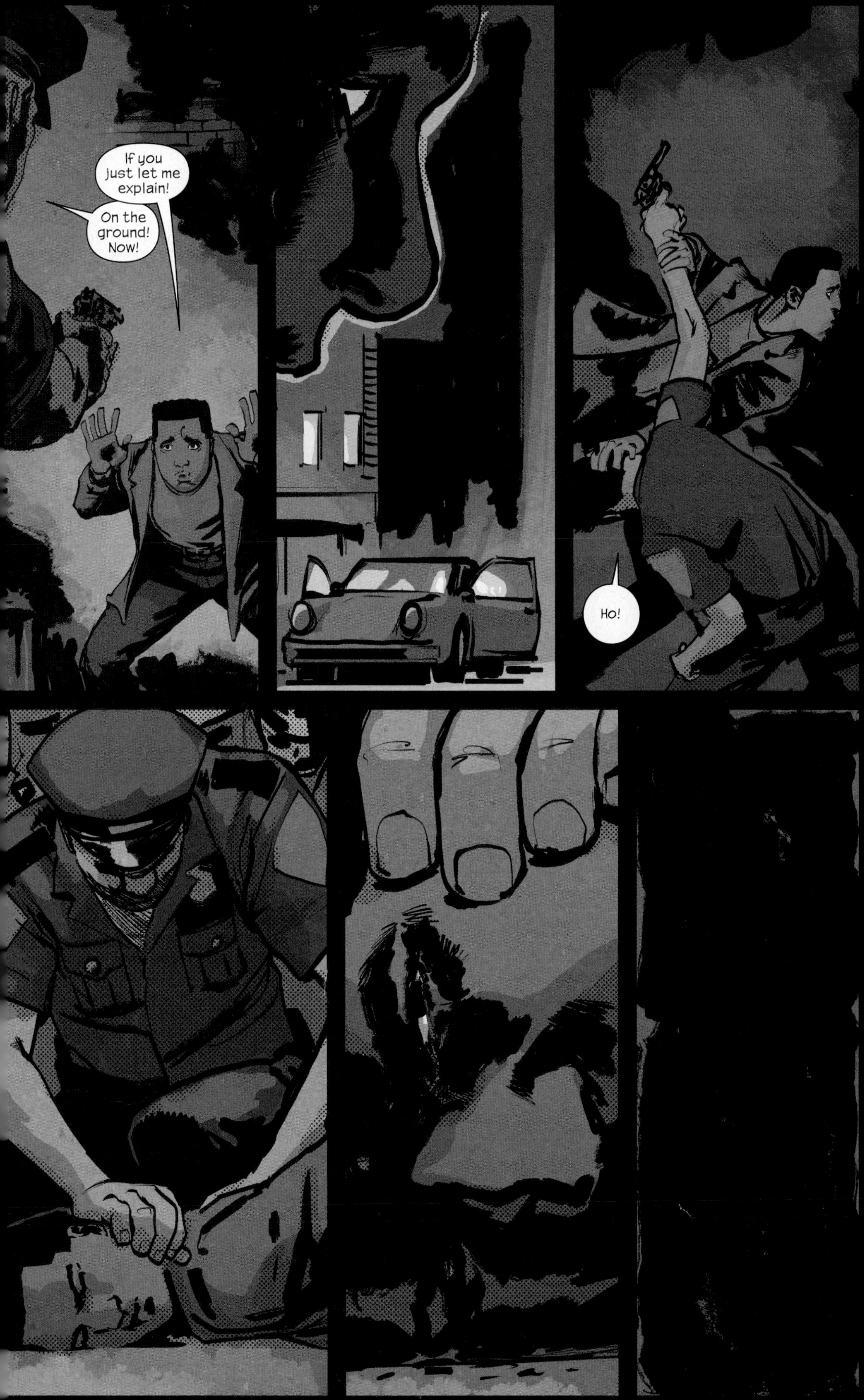
If you just let me explain!
On the ground! Now!
Ho!

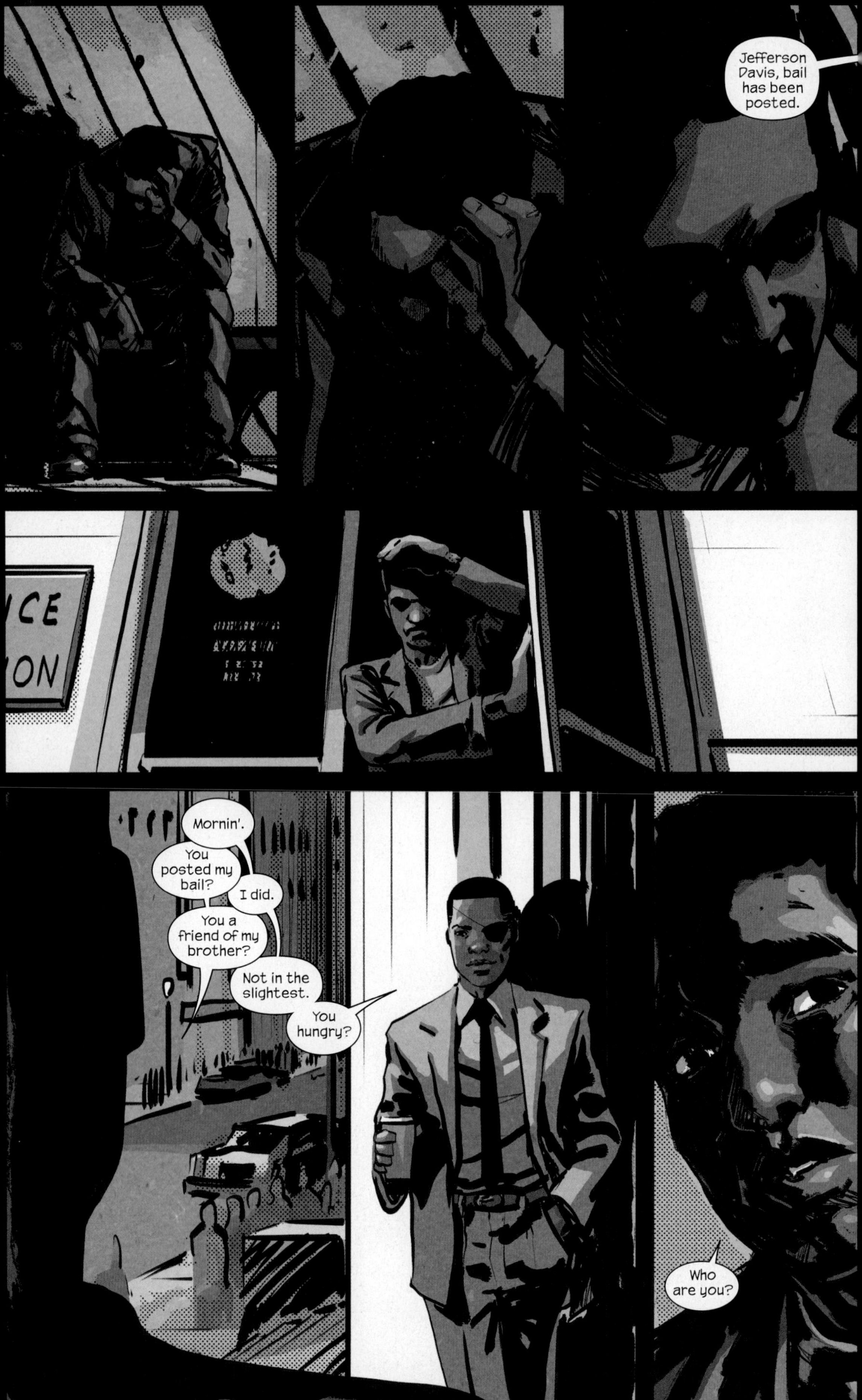
Jefferson Davis, bail has been posted.
Mornin'.
You posted my bail?
I did.
You a friend of my brother?
Not in the slightest.
You hungry?
Who are you?

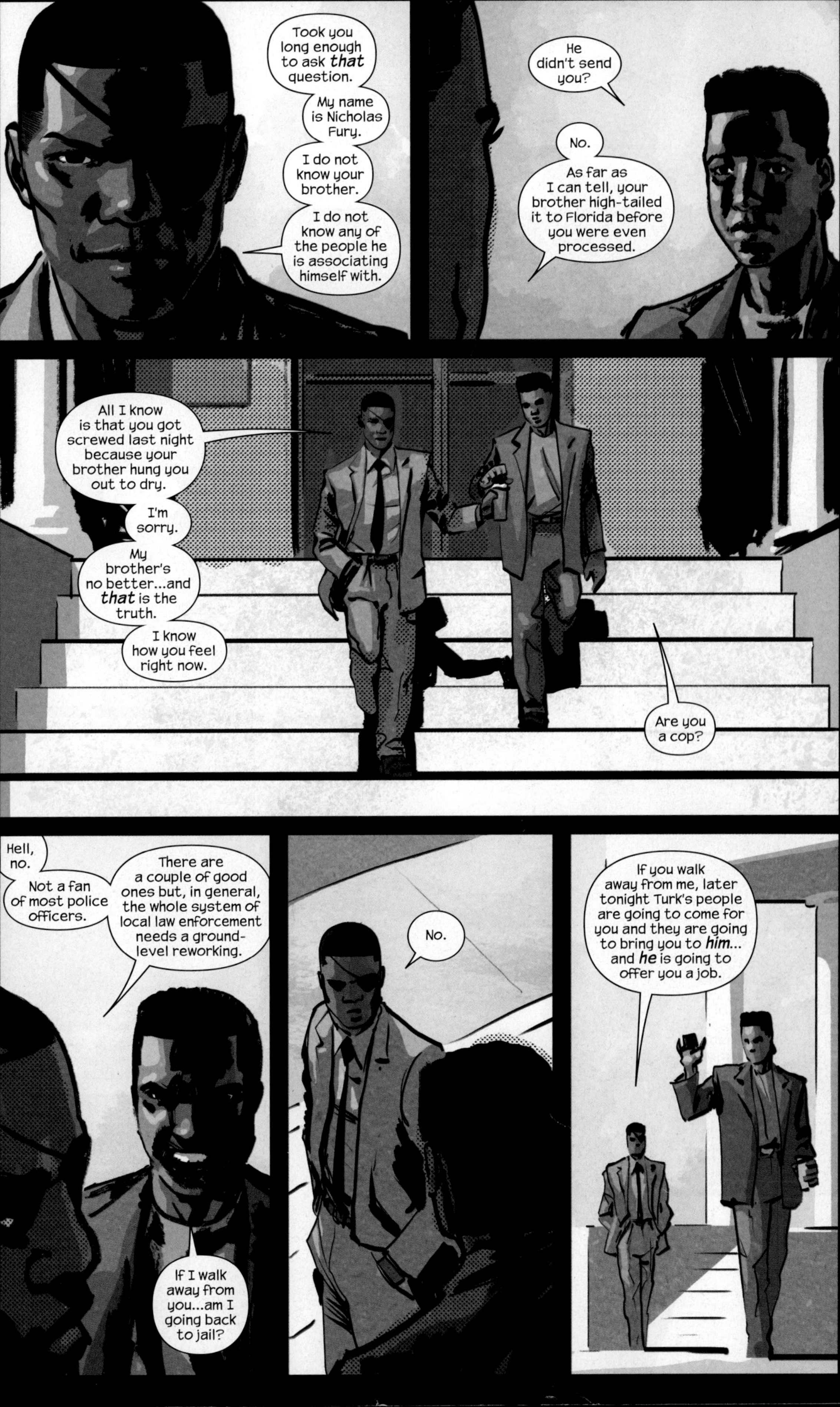
Took you long enough to ask *that* question.
My name is Nicholas Fury.
I do not know your brother.
I do not know any of the people he is associating himself with.
He didn't send you?
No.
As far as I can tell, your brother high-tailed it to Florida before you were even processed.
All I know is that you got screwed last night because your brother hung you out to dry.
I'm sorry.
My brother's no better...and *that* is the truth.
I know how you feel right now.
Are you a cop?
Hell, no.
Not a fan of most police officers.
There are a couple of good ones but, in general, the whole system of local law enforcement needs a ground-level reworking.
If I walk away from you...am I going back to jail?
No.
If you walk away from me, later tonight Turk's people are going to come for you and they are going to bring you to *him*... and *he* is going to offer you a job.

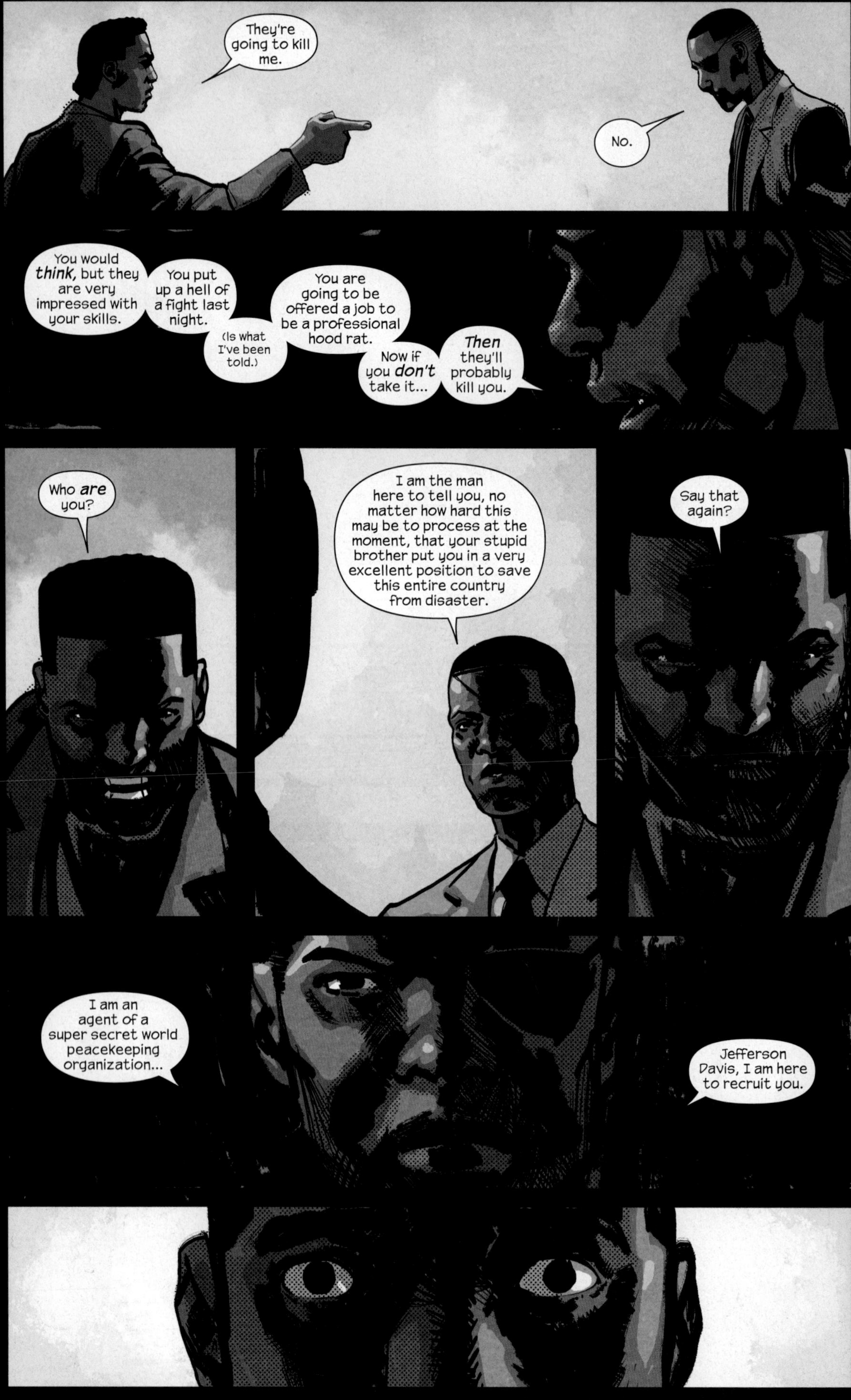
They're going to kill me.
No.
You would *think*, but they are very impressed with your skills.
You put up a hell of a fight last night.
(Is what I've been told.)
You are going to be offered a job to be a professional hood rat.
Now if you *don't* take it...
*Then* they'll probably kill you.
Who *are* you?
I am the man here to tell you, no matter how hard this may be to process at the moment, that your stupid brother put you in a very excellent position to save this entire country from disaster.
Say that again?
I am an agent of a super secret world peacekeeping organization...
Jefferson Davis, I am here to recruit you.

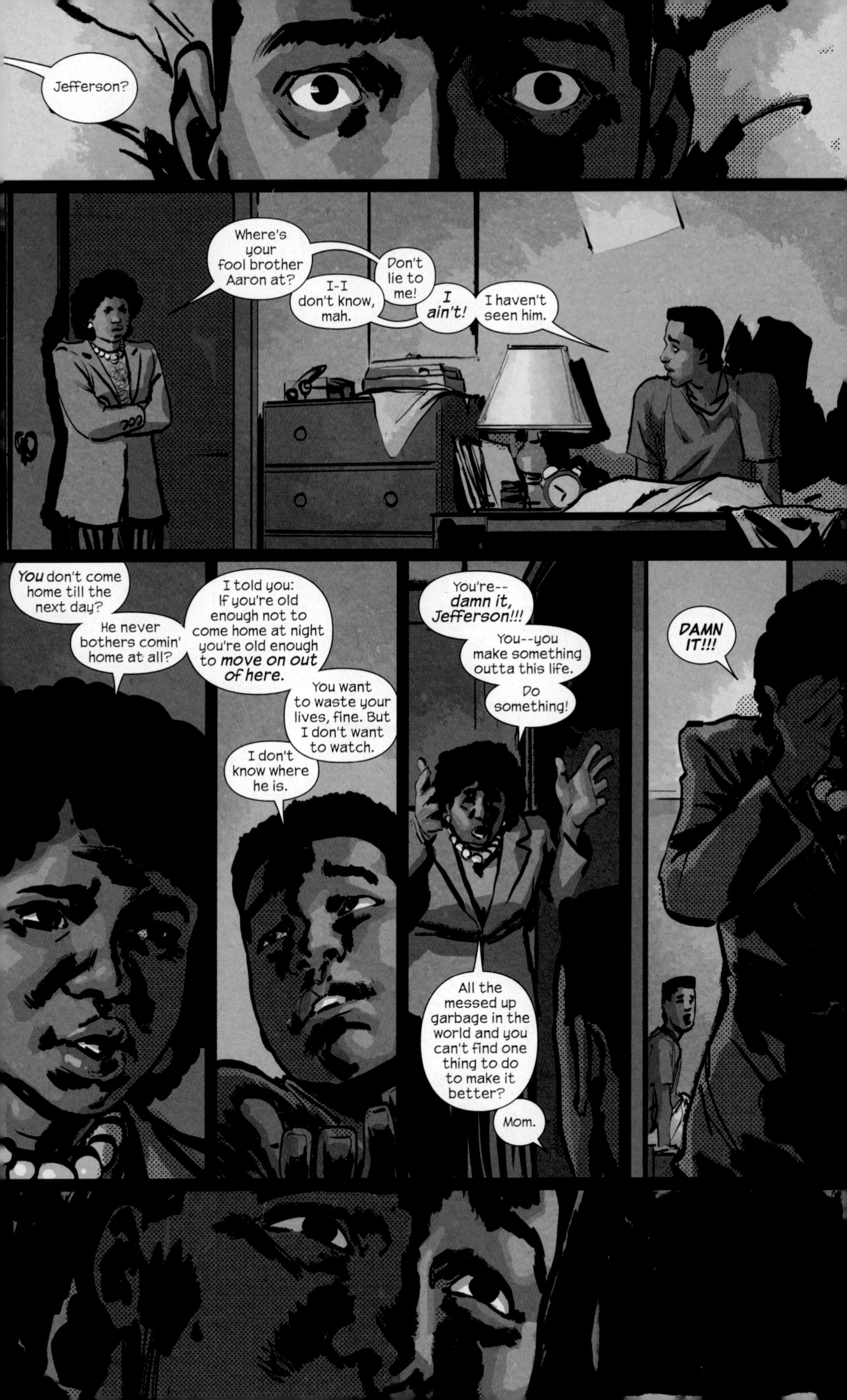
Jefferson?
Where's your fool brother Aaron at?
I-I don't know, mah.
Don't lie to me!
I ain't!
I haven't seen him.
You don't come home till the next day?
He never bothers comin' home at all?
I told you: If you're old enough not to come home at night you're old enough to move on out of here.
You want to waste your lives, fine. But I don't want to watch.
I don't know where he is.
You're-- damn it, Jefferson!!!
You--you make something outta this life.
Do something!
All the messed up garbage in the world and you can't find one thing to do to make it better?
Mom.
DAMN IT!!!

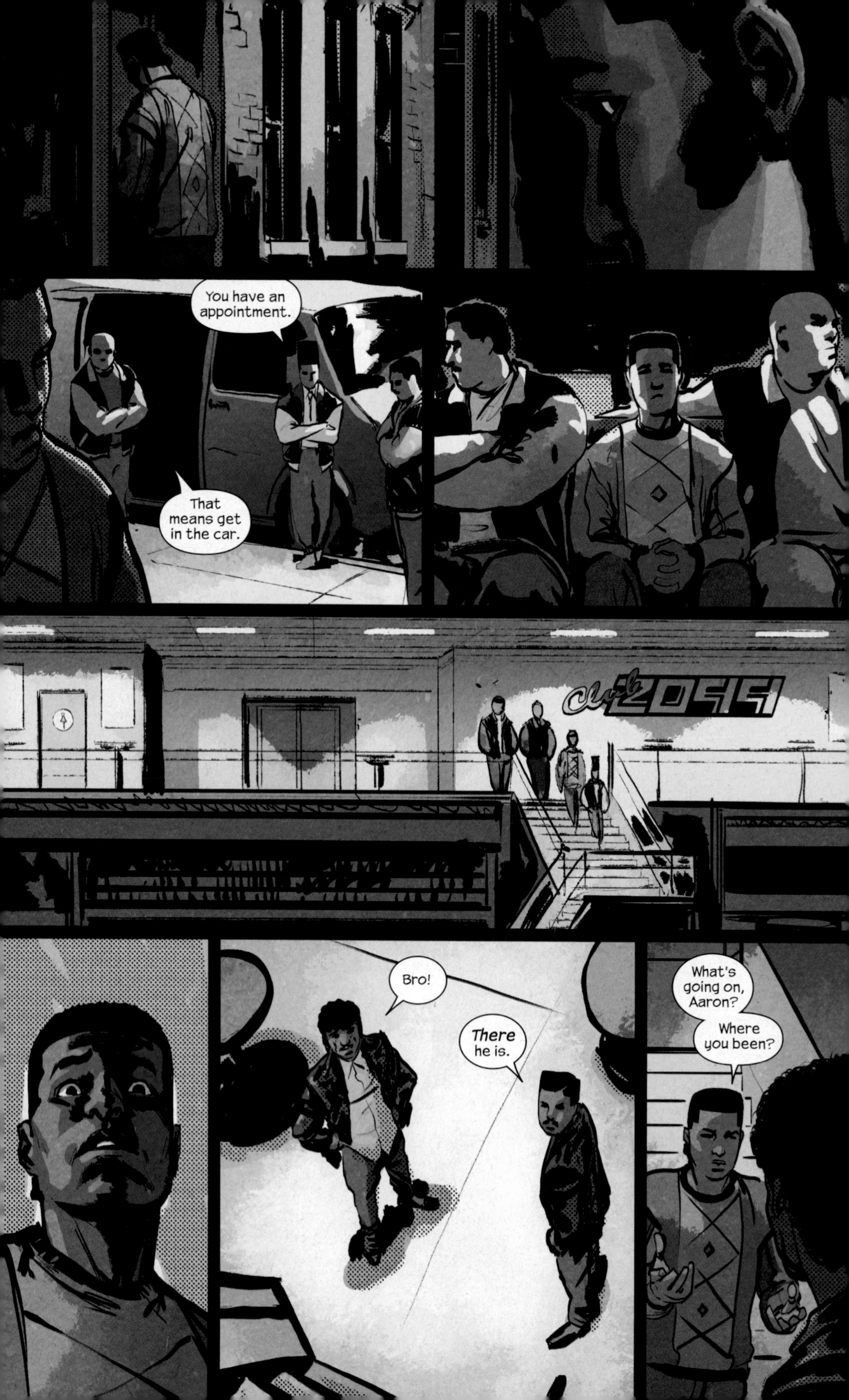
You have an appointment.
That means get in the car.
Club 2099
Bro!
There he is.
What's going on, Aaron?
Where you been?

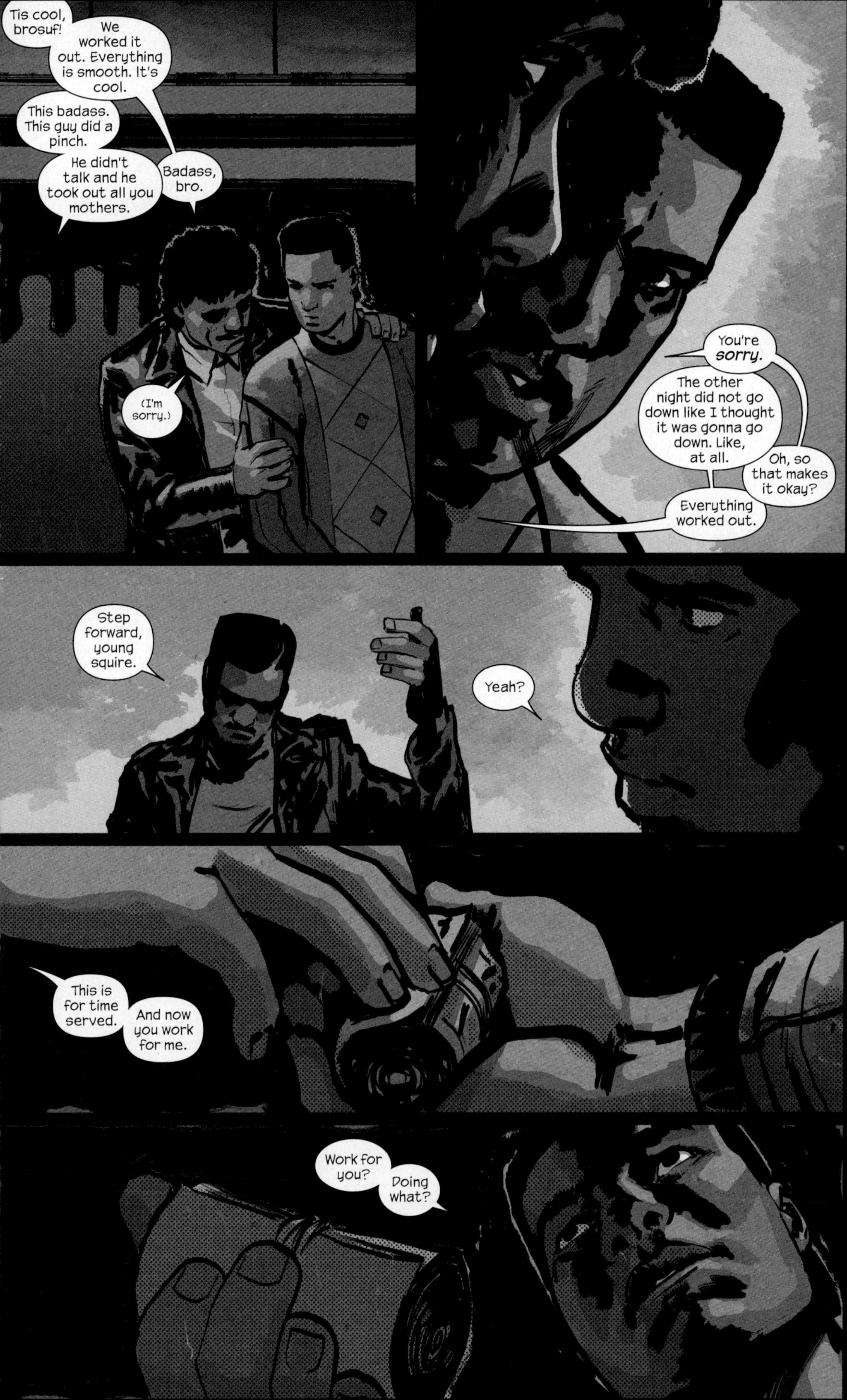
Tis cool, brosuf!
We worked it out. Everything is smooth. It's cool.
This badass. This guy did a pinch.
He didn't talk and he took out all you mothers.
Badass, bro.
(I'm sorry.)
You're *sorry.*
The other night did not go down like I thought it was gonna go down. Like, at all.
Oh, so that makes it okay?
Everything worked out.
Step forward, young squire.
Yeah?
This is for time served.
And now you work for me.
Work for you?
Doing what?

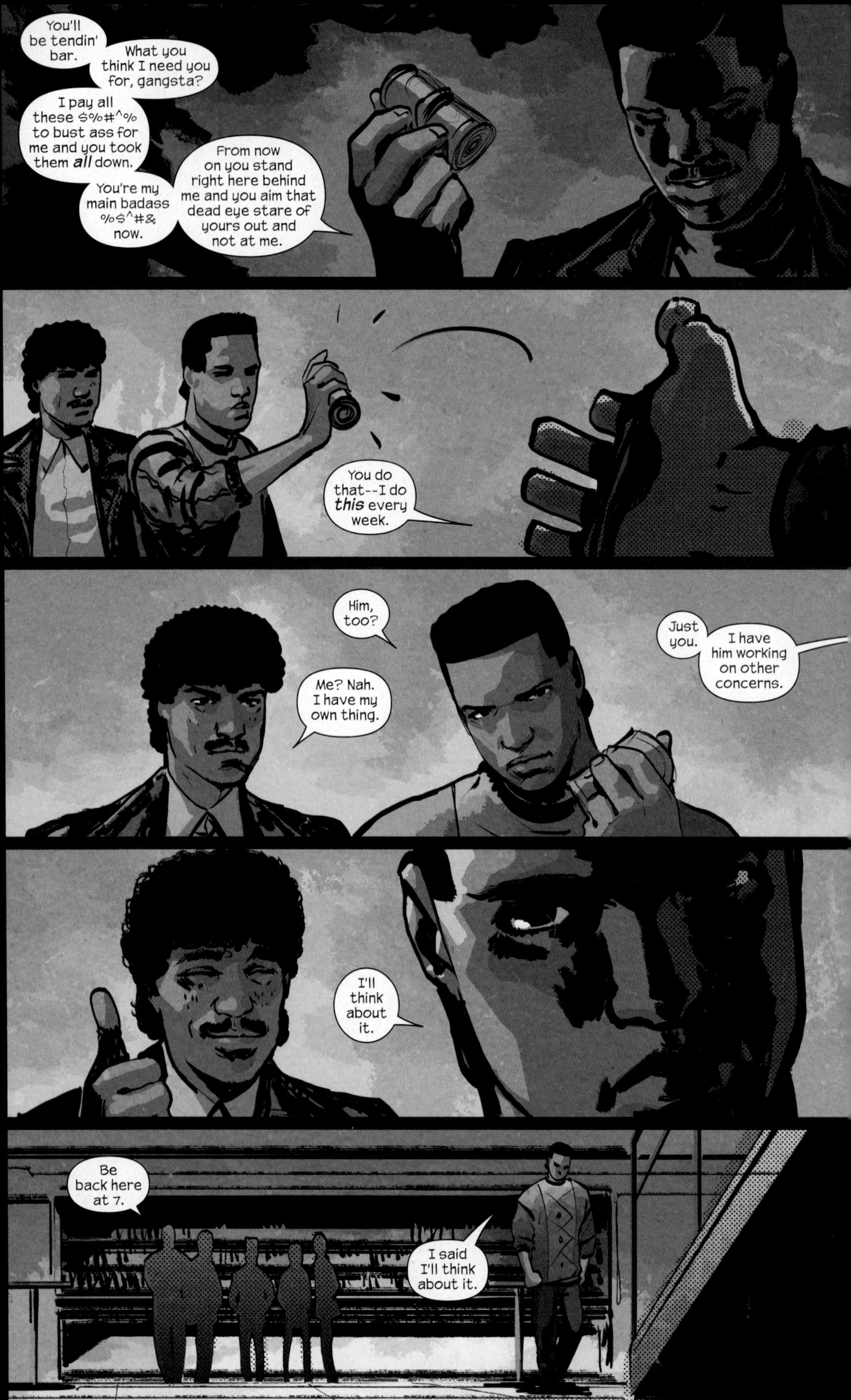

You'll be tendin' bar.
What you think I need you for, gangsta?
I pay all these $%#^% to bust ass for me and you took them *all* down.
You're my main badass %$^#& now.
From now on you stand right here behind me and you aim that dead eye stare of yours out and not at me.
You do that--I do *this* every week.
Him, too?
Me? Nah. I have my own thing.
Just you.
I have him working on other concerns.
I'll think about it.
Be back here at 7.
I said I'll think about it.

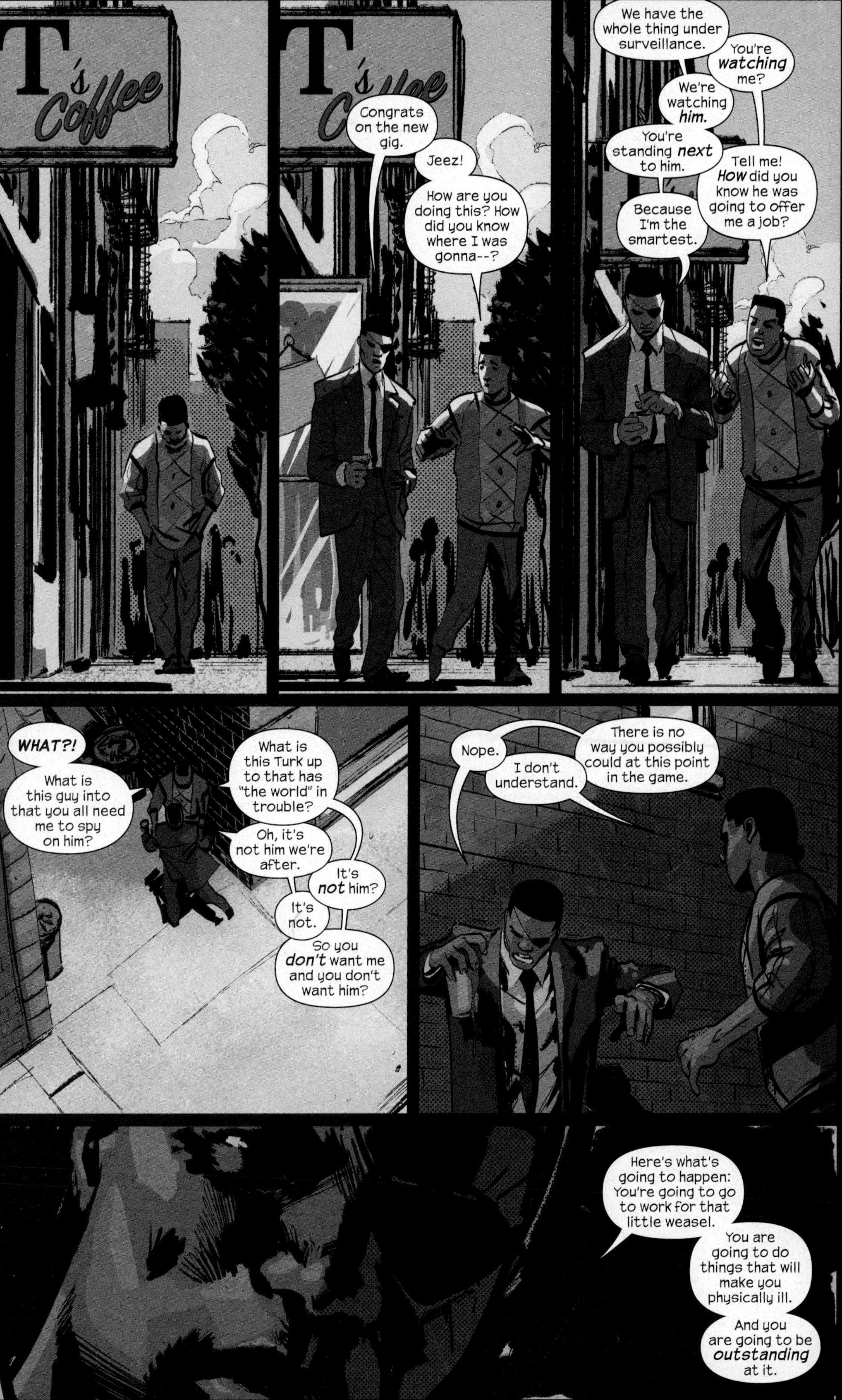
T's Coffee
Congrats on the new gig.
Jeez!
How are you doing this? How did you know where I was gonna--?
We have the whole thing under surveillance.
You're *watching* me?
We're watching *him.*
You're standing *next* to him.
Tell me! *HOW* did you know he was going to offer me a job?
Because I'm the smartest.
*WHAT?!*
What is this guy into that you all need me to spy on him?
What is this Turk up to that has "the world" in trouble?
Oh, it's not him we're after.
It's *not* him?
It's not.
So you *don't* want me and you don't want him?
Nope.
There is no way you possibly could at this point in the game.
I don't understand.
Here's what's going to happen: You're going to go to work for that little weasel.
You are going to do things that will make you physically ill.
And you are going to be *outstanding* at it.

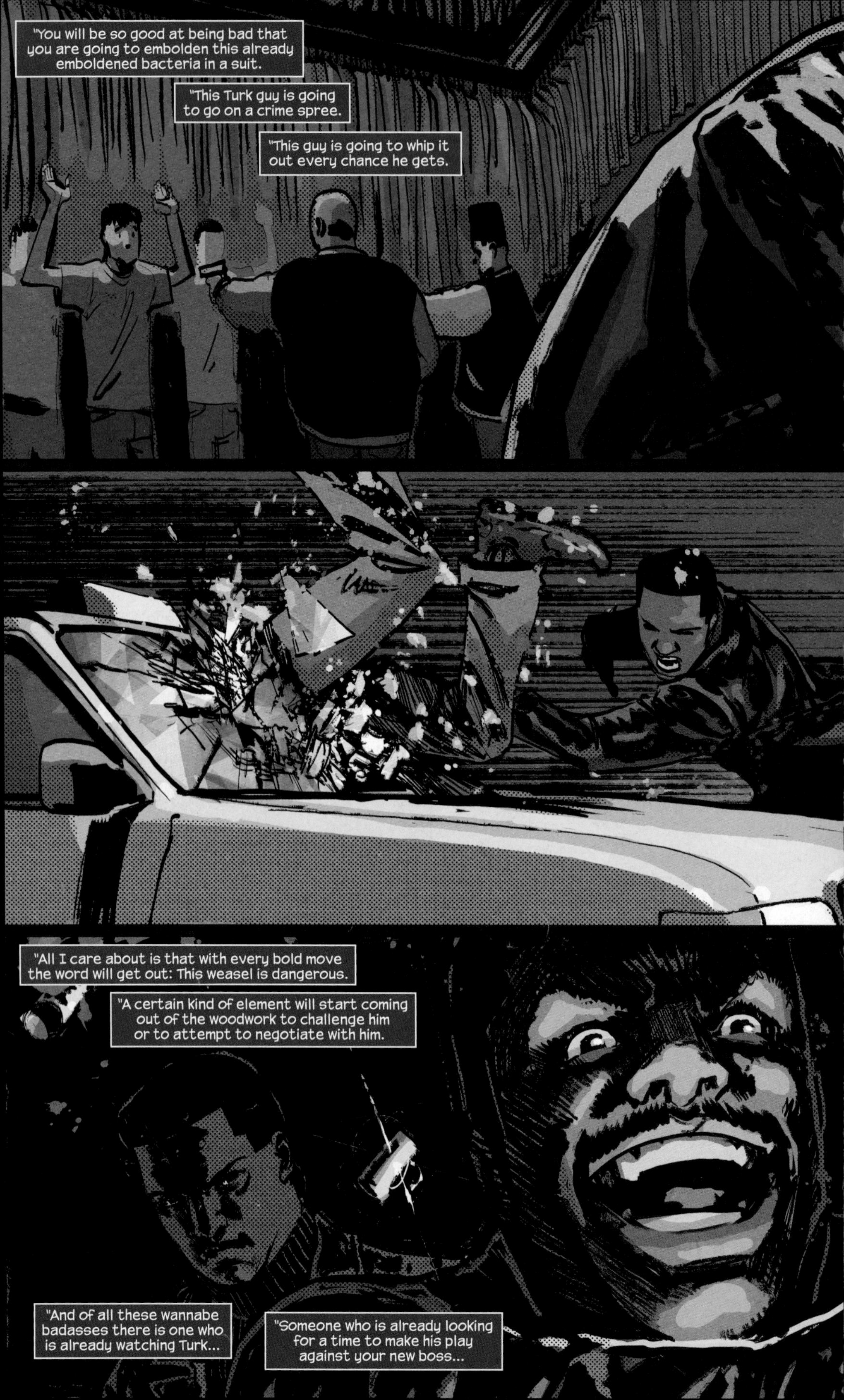
"You will be so good at being bad that you are going to embolden this already emboldened bacteria in a suit.
"This Turk guy is going to go on a crime spree.
"This guy is going to whip it out every chance he gets.
"All I care about is that with every bold move the word will get out: This weasel is dangerous.
"A certain kind of element will start coming out of the woodwork to challenge him or to attempt to negotiate with him.
"And of all these wannabe badasses there is one who is already watching Turk...
"Someone who is already looking for a time to make his play against your new boss...

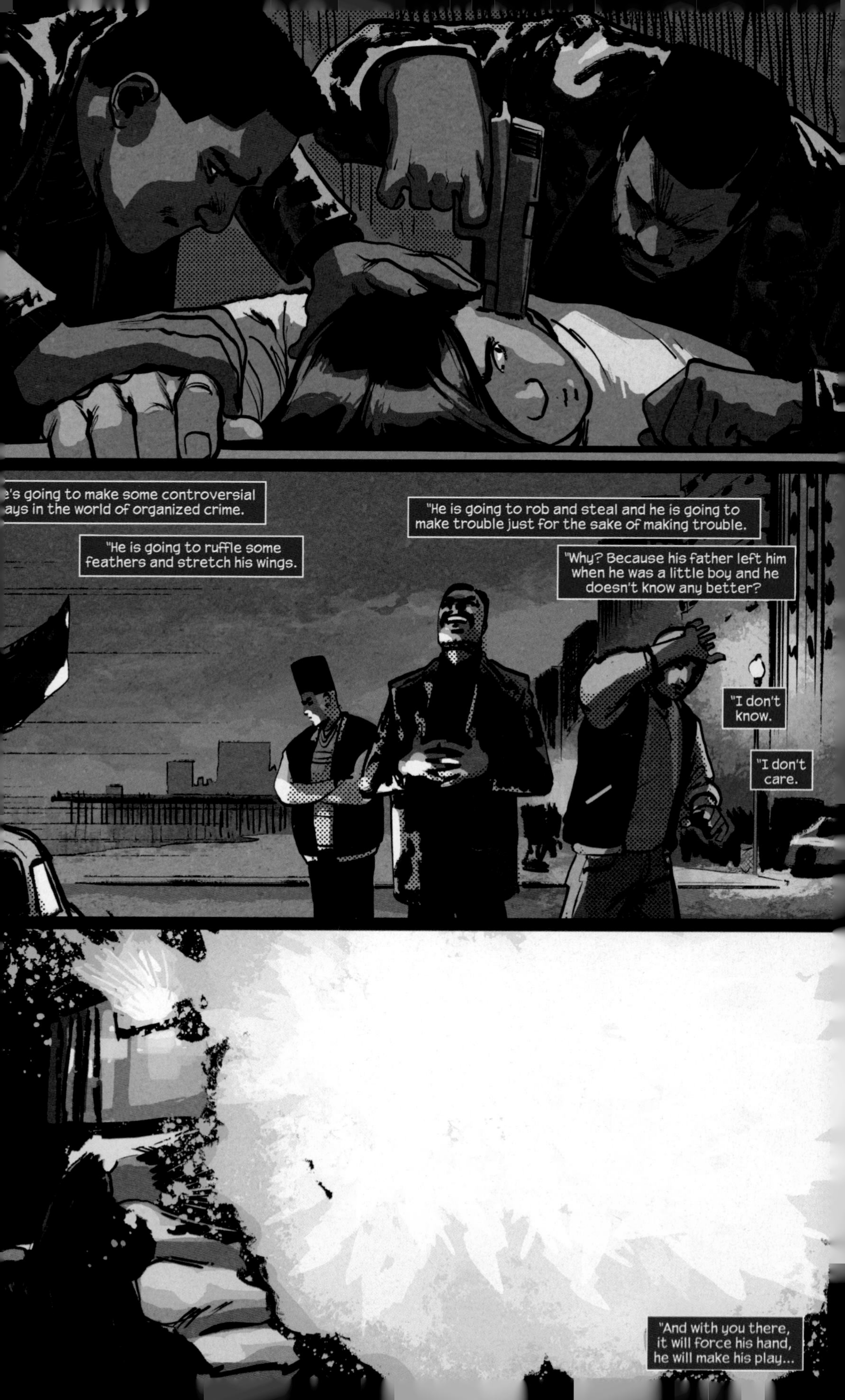
e's going to make some controversial
ays in the world of organized crime.
"He is going to ruffle some feathers and stretch his wings.
"He is going to rob and steal and he is going to make trouble just for the sake of making trouble.
"Why? Because his father left him when he was a little boy and he doesn't know any better?
"I don't know.
"I don't care.
"And with you there, it will force his hand, he will make his play...

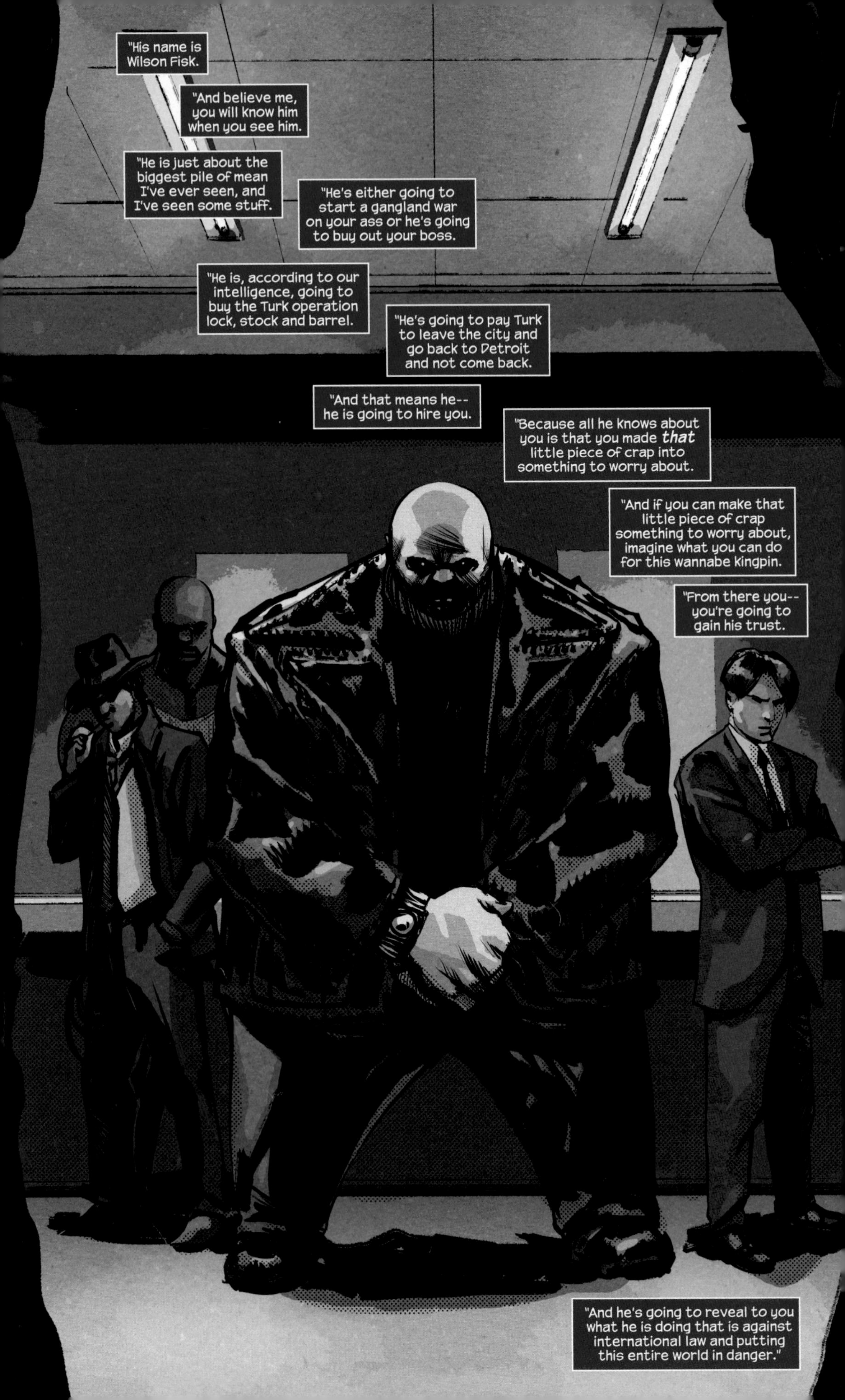
"His name is Wilson Fisk.
"And believe me, you will know him when you see him.
"He is just about the biggest pile of mean I've ever seen, and I've seen some stuff.
"He's either going to start a gangland war on your ass or he's going to buy out your boss.
"He is, according to our intelligence, going to buy the Turk operation lock, stock and barrel.
"He's going to pay Turk to leave the city and go back to Detroit and not come back.
"And that means he-- he is going to hire you.
"Because all he knows about you is that you made *that* little piece of crap into something to worry about.
"And if you can make that little piece of crap something to worry about, imagine what you can do for this wannabe Kingpin.
"From there you-- you're going to gain his trust.
"And he's going to reveal to you what he is doing that is against international law and putting this entire world in danger."

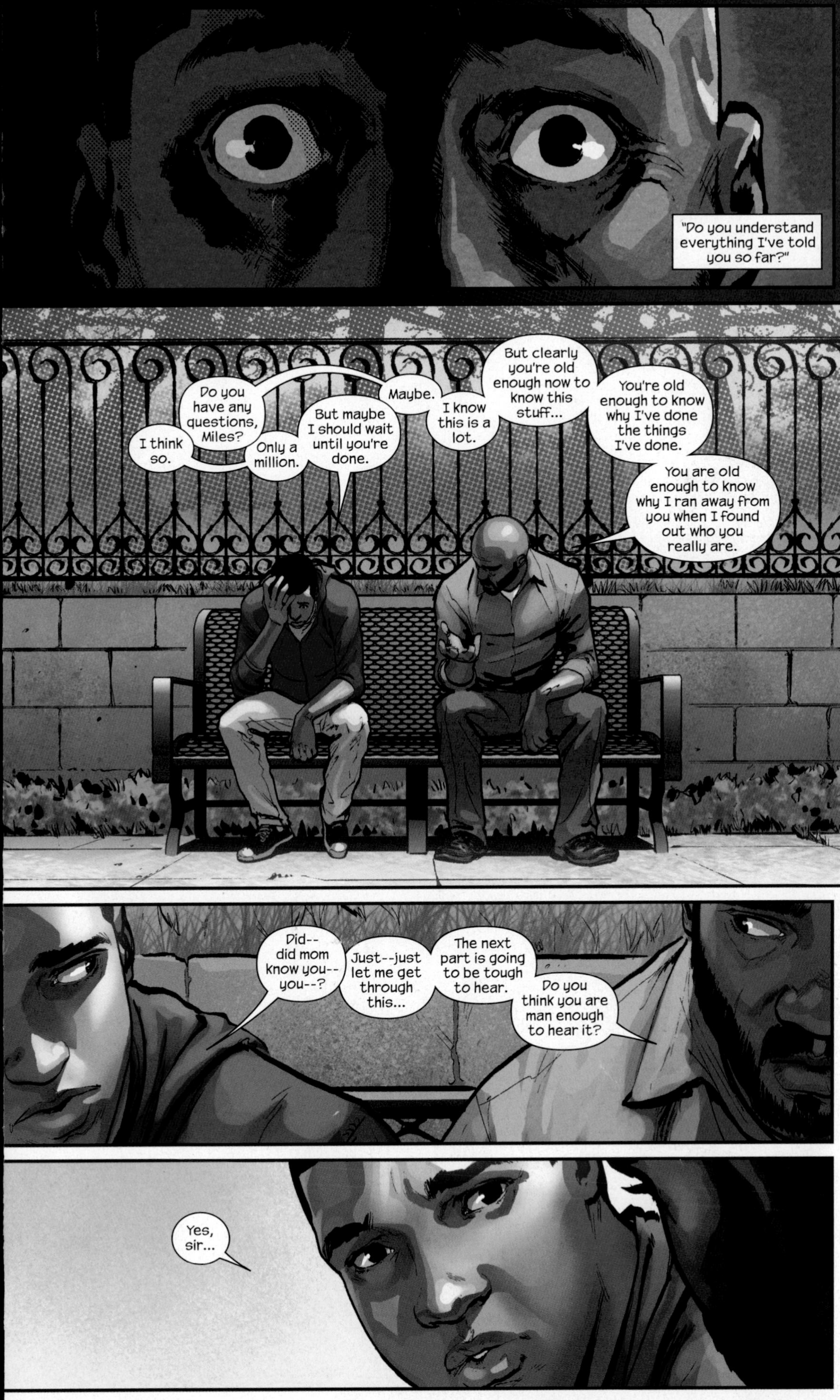
"Do you understand everything I've told you so far?"
I think so.
Do you have any questions, Miles?
Maybe.
Only a million.
But maybe I should wait until you're done.
I know this is a lot.
But clearly you're old enough now to know this stuff...
You're old enough to know why I've done the things I've done.
You are old enough to know why I ran away from you when I found out who you really are.
Did-- did mom know you-- you--?
Just--just let me get through this...
The next part is going to be tough to hear.
Do you think you are man enough to hear it?
Yes, sir...

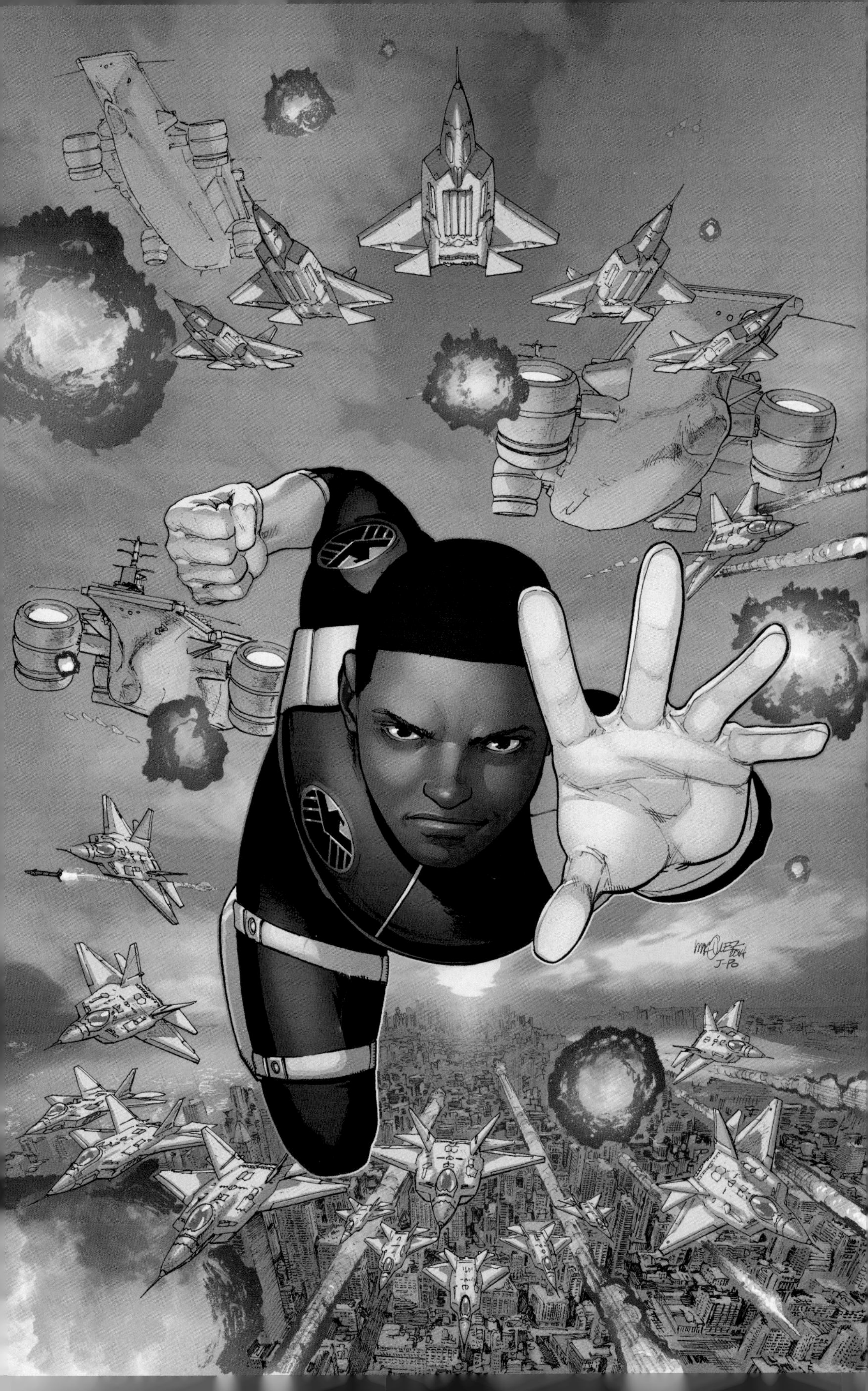

You were an undercover agent of S.H.I.E.L.D.?

Working inside the Kingpin's organization?

No one mentioned me to you?

No.

Good.

That means someone kept their word.

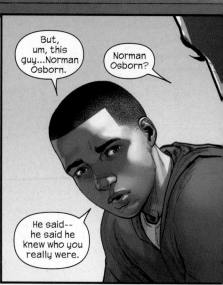

But, um, this guy...Norman Osborn.

Norman Osborn?

He said-- he said he knew who you really were.

That's not good.

Well, he's dead now, so...

I didn't do it.

He just, mid-fight, you know, keeled over.

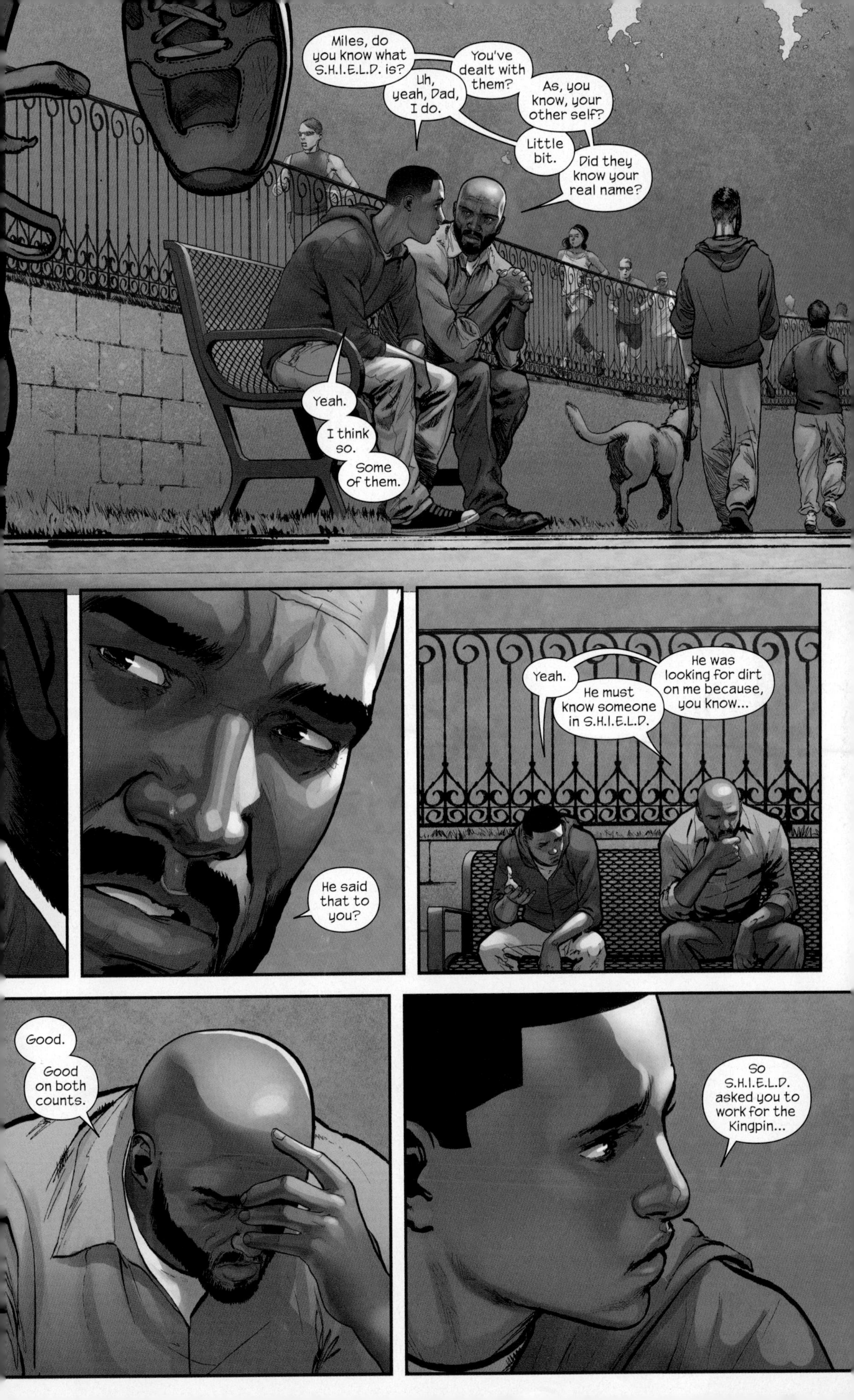
Miles, do you know what S.H.I.E.L.D. is?
Uh, yeah, Dad, I do.
You've dealt with them?
Little bit.
As, you know, your other self?
Did they know your real name?
Yeah.
I think so.
Some of them.
He said that to you?
Yeah.
He was looking for dirt on me because, you know...
He must know someone in S.H.I.E.L.D.
Good.
Good on both counts.
So S.H.I.E.L.D. asked you to work for the Kingpin...

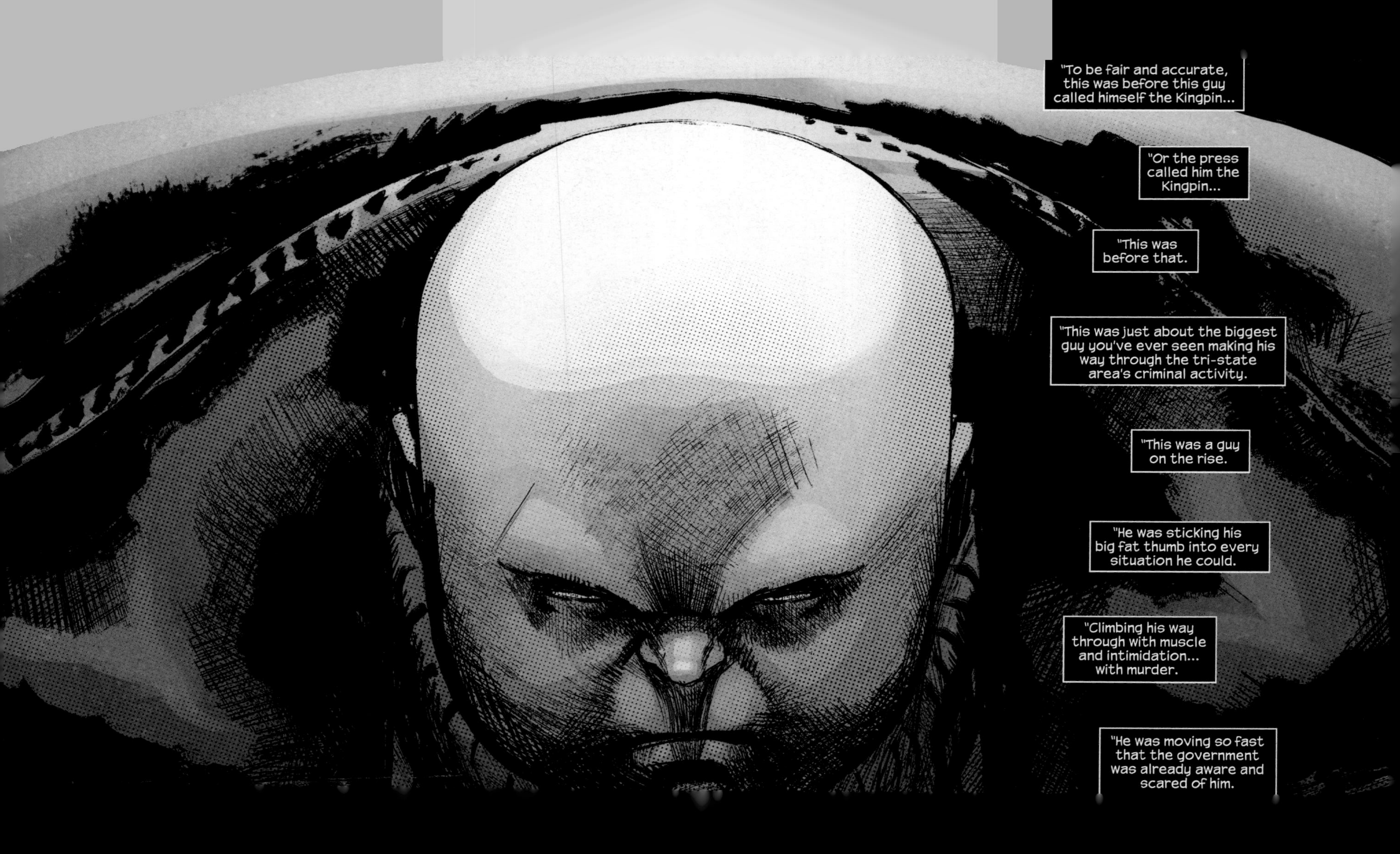
"To be fair and accurate, this was before this guy called himself the Kingpin...
"Or the press called him the Kingpin...
"This was before that.
"This was just about the biggest guy you've ever seen making his way through the tri-state area's criminal activity.
"This was a guy on the rise.
"He was sticking his big fat thumb into every situation he could.
"Climbing his way through with muscle and intimidation... with murder.
"He was moving so fast that the government was already aware and scared of him.

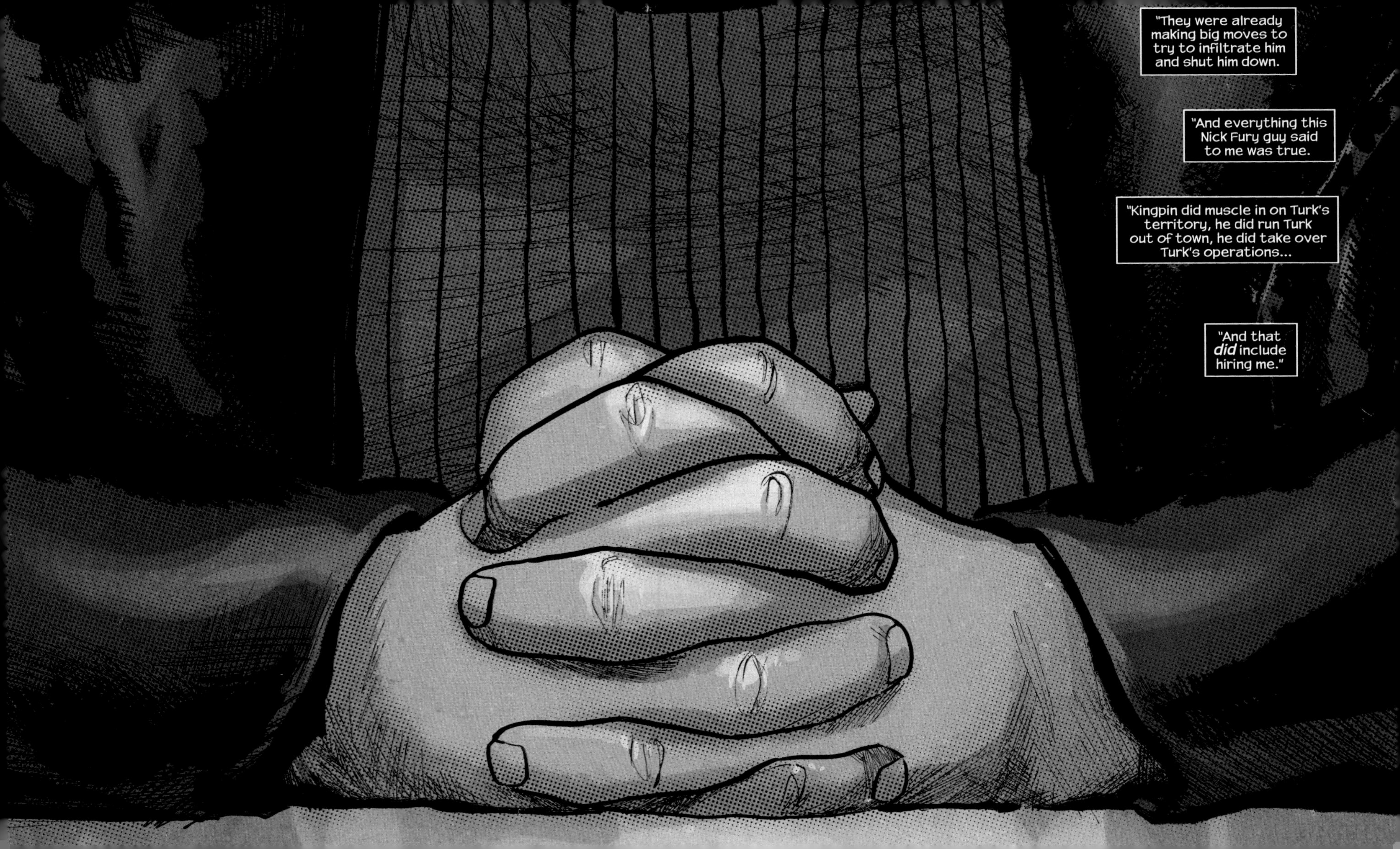
"They were already making big moves to try to infiltrate him and shut him down.
"And everything this Nick Fury guy said to me was true.
"Kingpin did muscle in on Turk's territory, he did run Turk out of town, he did take over Turk's operations...
"And that *did* include hiring me."

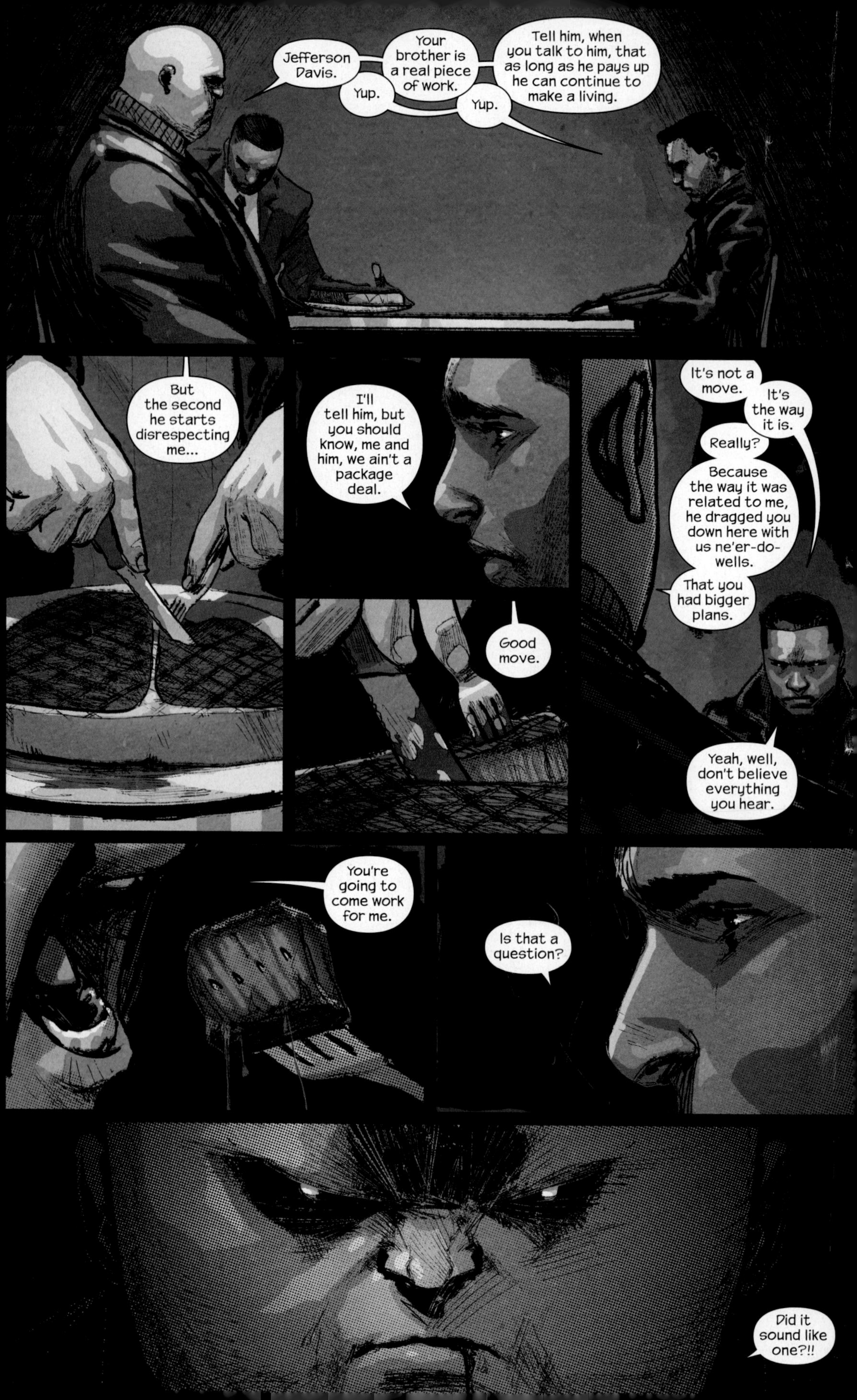
Jefferson Davis.
Your brother is a real piece of work.
Yup.
Tell him, when you talk to him, that as long as he pays up he can continue to make a living.
Yup.
But the second he starts disrespecting me...
I'll tell him, but you should know, me and him, we ain't a package deal.
Good move.
It's not a move.
It's the way it is.
Really?
Because the way it was related to me, he dragged you down here with us ne'er-do-wells.
That you had bigger plans.
Yeah, well, don't believe everything you hear.
You're going to come work for me.
Is that a question?
Did it sound like one?!!

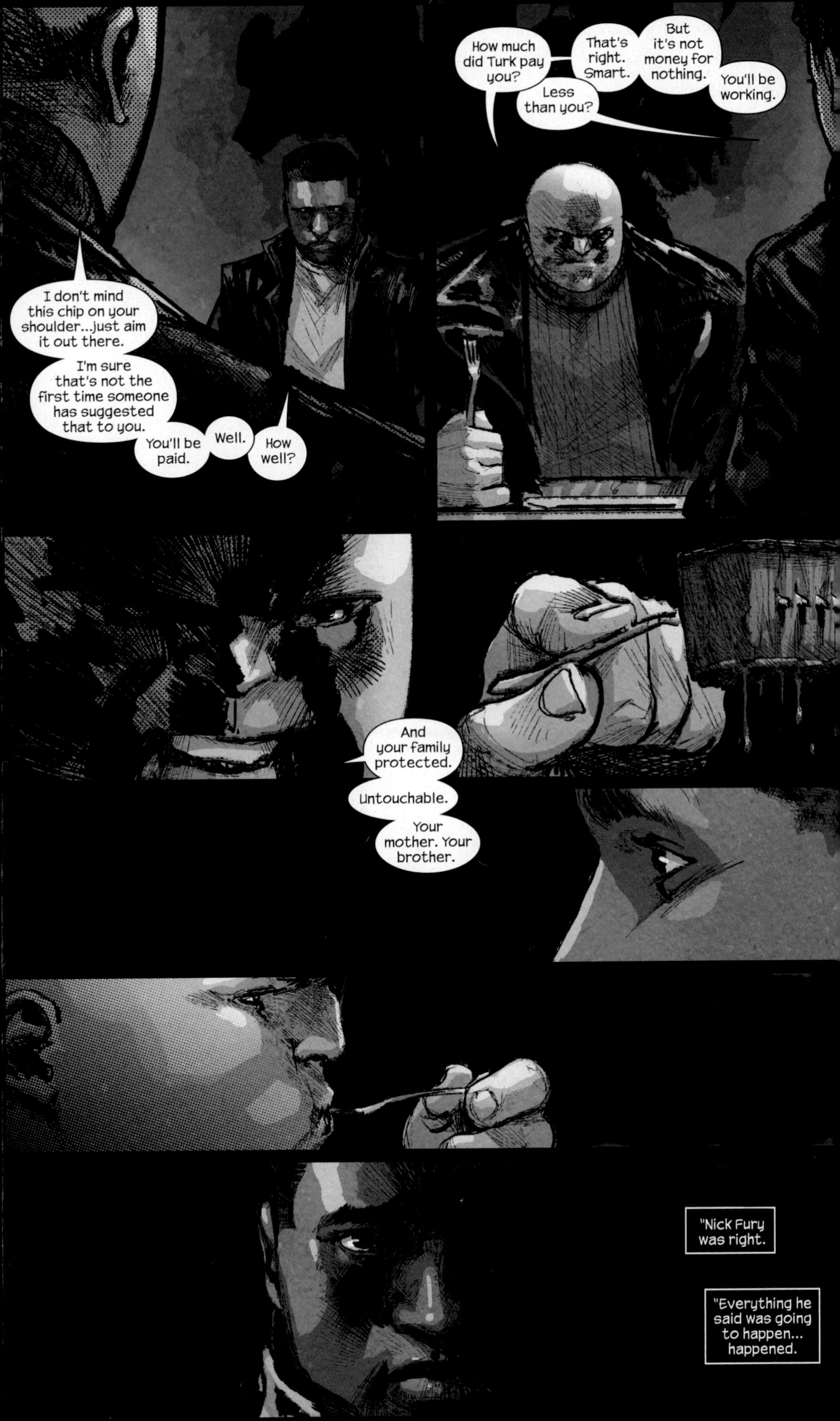
I don't mind this chip on your shoulder...just aim it out there.
I'm sure that's not the first time someone has suggested that to you.
You'll be paid.
Well.
How well?
How much did Turk pay you?
That's right. Smart.
But it's not money for nothing.
You'll be working.
Less than you?
And your family protected.
Untouchable.
Your mother. Your brother.
"Nick Fury was right.
"Everything he said was going to happen... happened.

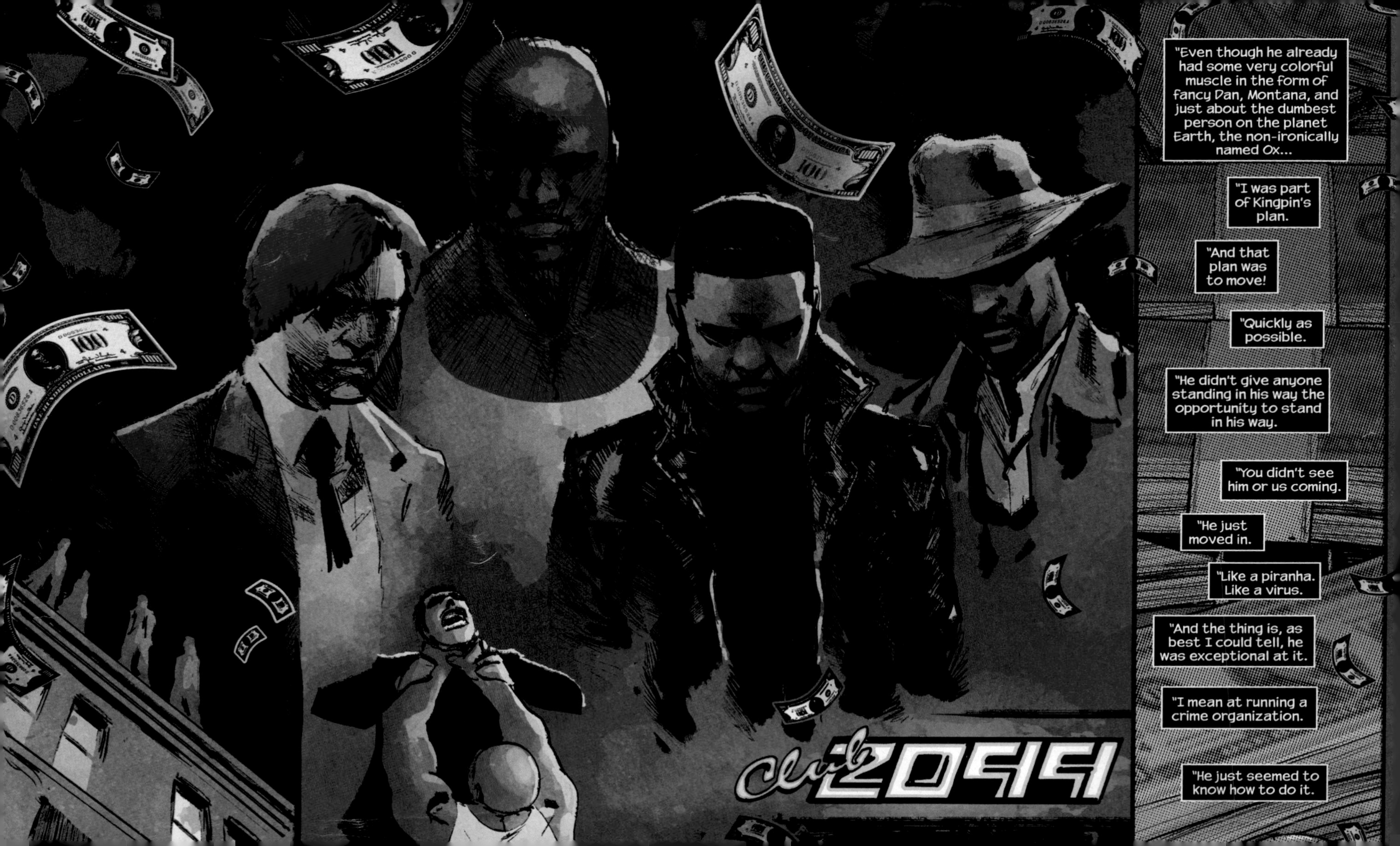
"Even though he already had some very colorful muscle in the form of fancy Dan, Montana, and just about the dumbest person on the planet Earth, the non-ironically named Ox...
"I was part of Kingpin's plan.
"And that plan was to move!
"Quickly as possible.
"He didn't give anyone standing in his way the opportunity to stand in his way.
"You didn't see him or us coming.
"He just moved in.
"Like a piranha. Like a virus.
"And the thing is, as best I could tell, he was exceptional at it.
"I mean at running a crime organization.
"He just seemed to know how to do it.
club 2099

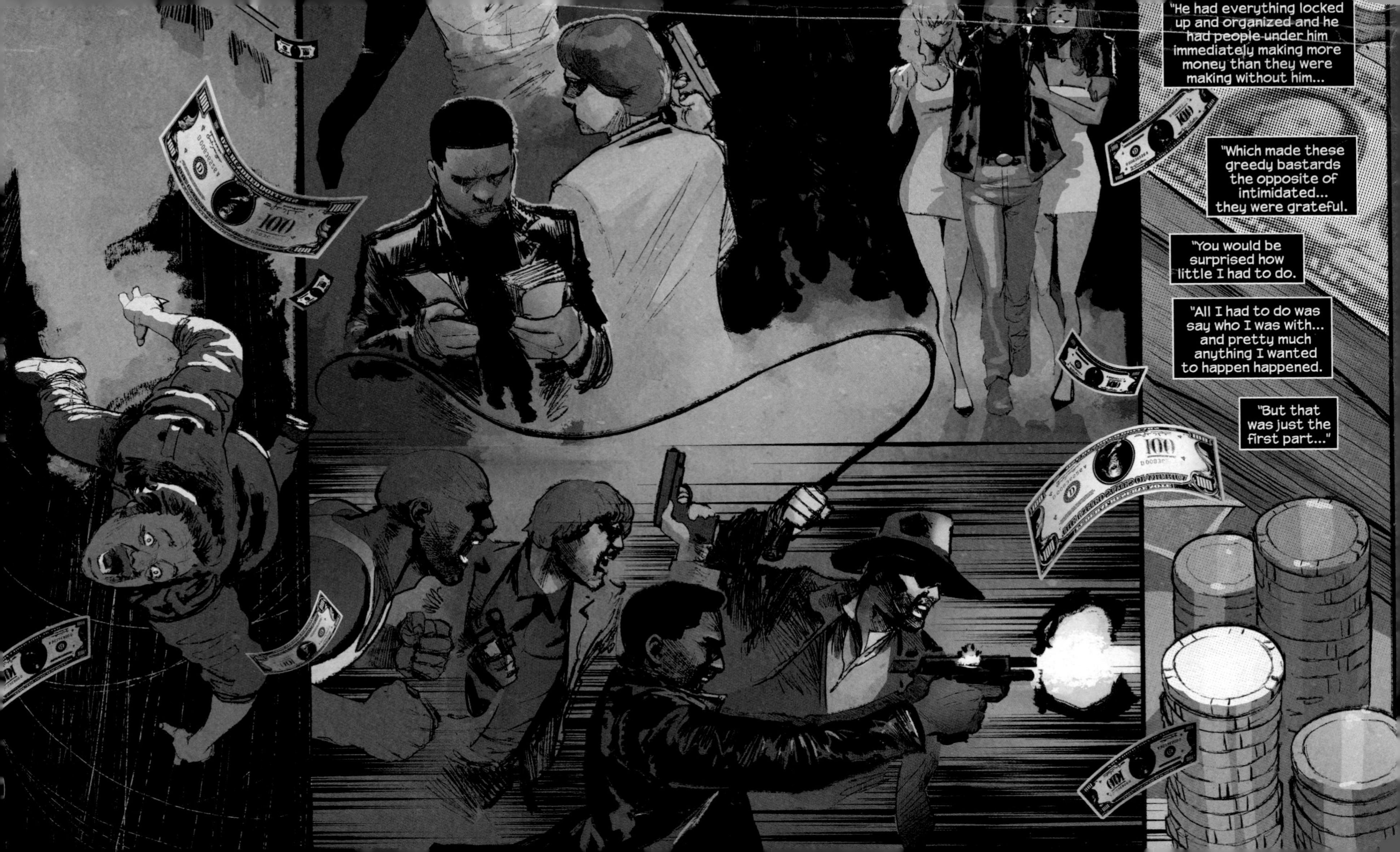
"He had everything locked up and organized and he had people under him immediately making more money than they were making without him...
"Which made these greedy bastards the opposite of intimidated... they were grateful.
"You would be surprised how little I had to do.
"All I had to do was say who I was with... and pretty much anything I wanted to happen happened.
"But that was just the first part..."

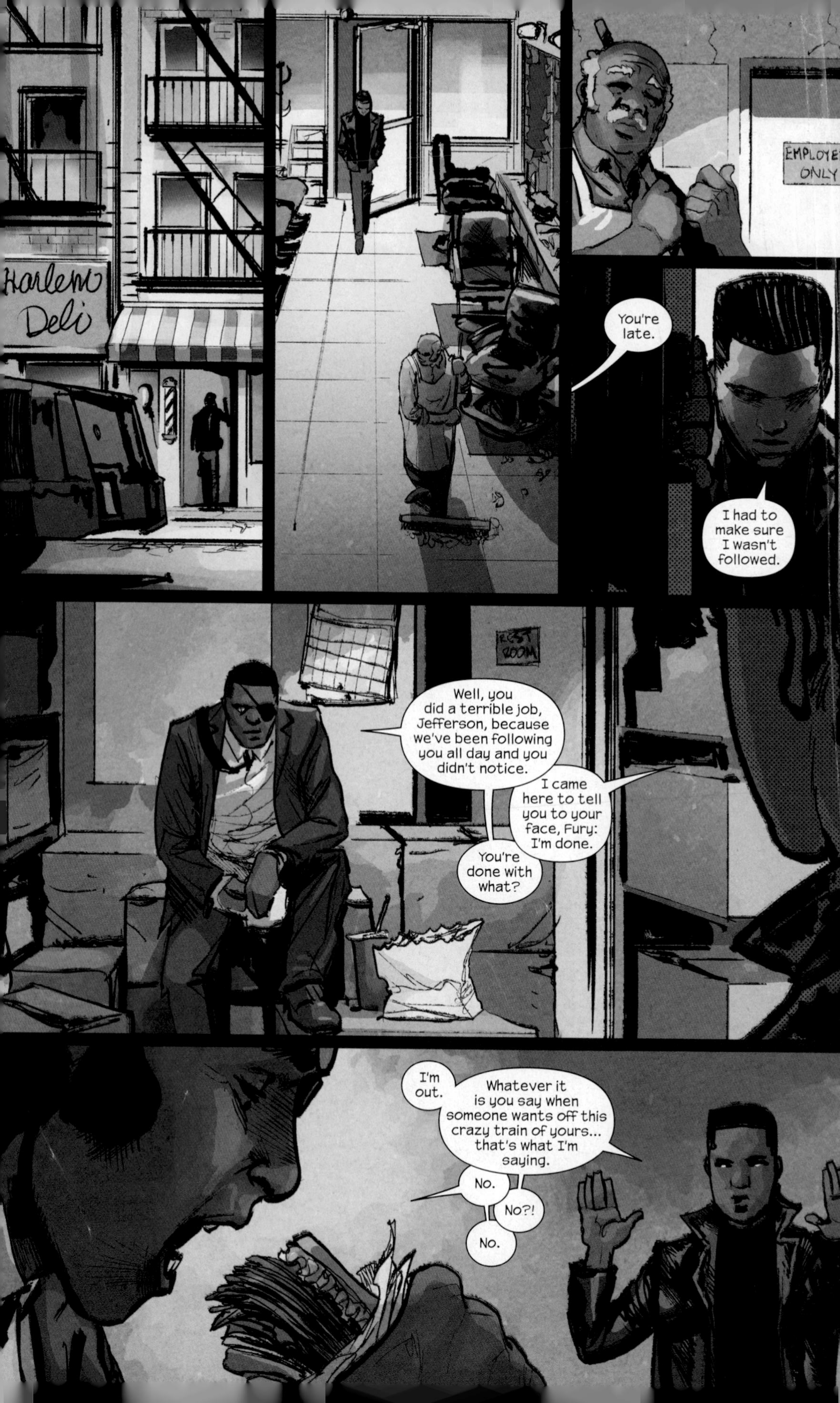
Harlem Deli
EMPLOYEES ONLY
You're late.
I had to make sure I wasn't followed.
REST ROOM
Well, you did a terrible job, Jefferson, because we've been following you all day and you didn't notice.
I came here to tell you to your face, Fury: I'm done.
You're done with what?
I'm out.
Whatever it is you say when someone wants off this crazy train of yours... that's what I'm saying.
No.
No?!
No.

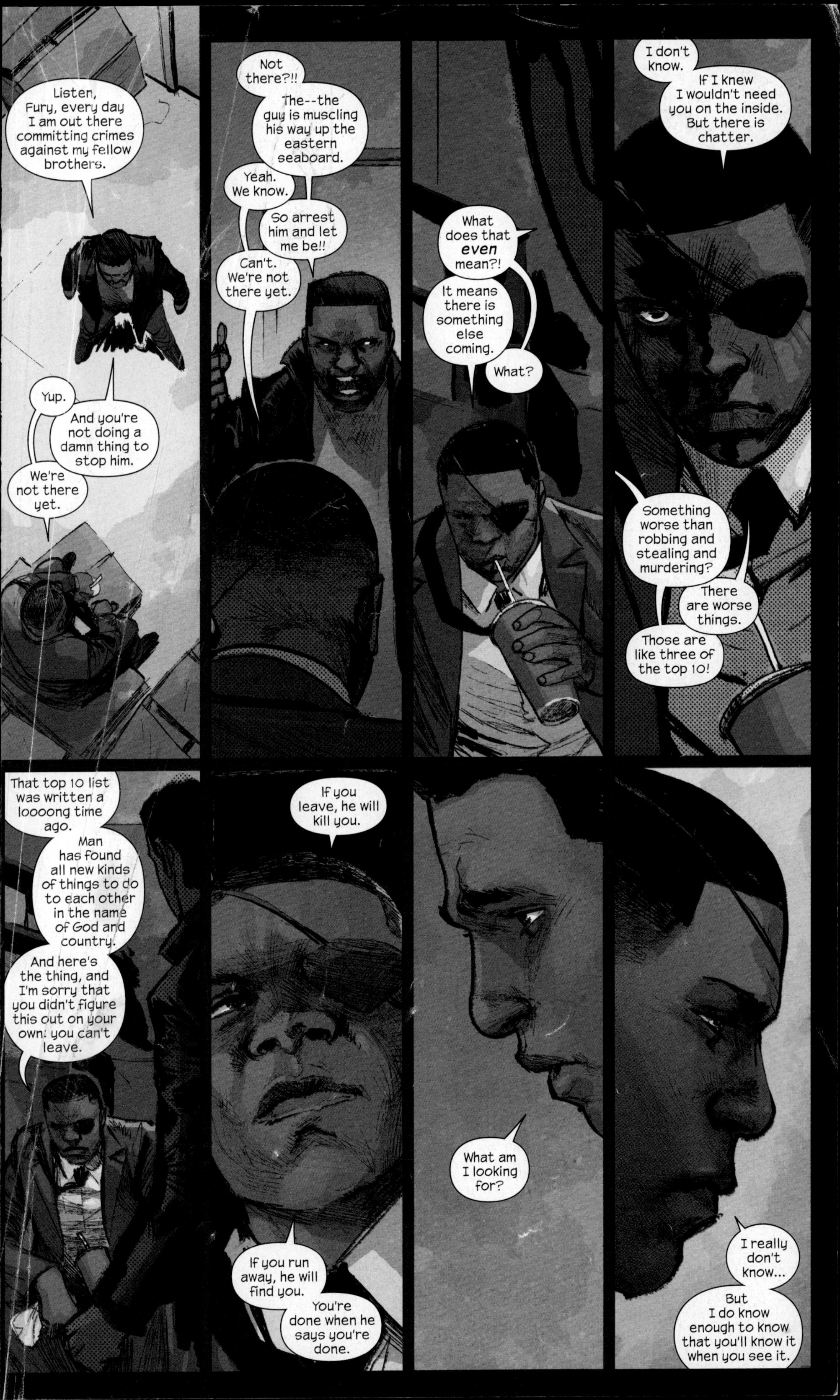
Listen, Fury, every day I am out there committing crimes against my fellow brothers.
Yup.
And you're not doing a damn thing to stop him.
We're not there yet.
Not there?!!
The--the guy is muscling his way up the eastern seaboard.
Yeah. We know.
So arrest him and let me be!!
Can't. We're not there yet.
What does that even mean?!
It means there is something else coming.
What?
I don't know.
If I knew I wouldn't need you on the inside. But there is chatter.
Something worse than robbing and stealing and murdering?
There are worse things.
Those are like three of the top 10!
That top 10 list was written a loooong time ago.
Man has found all new kinds of things to do to each other in the name of God and country.
And here's the thing, and I'm sorry that you didn't figure this out on your own: you can't leave.
If you leave, he will kill you.
If you run away, he will find you.
You're done when he says you're done.
What am I looking for?
I really don't know...
But I do know enough to know that you'll know it when you see it.

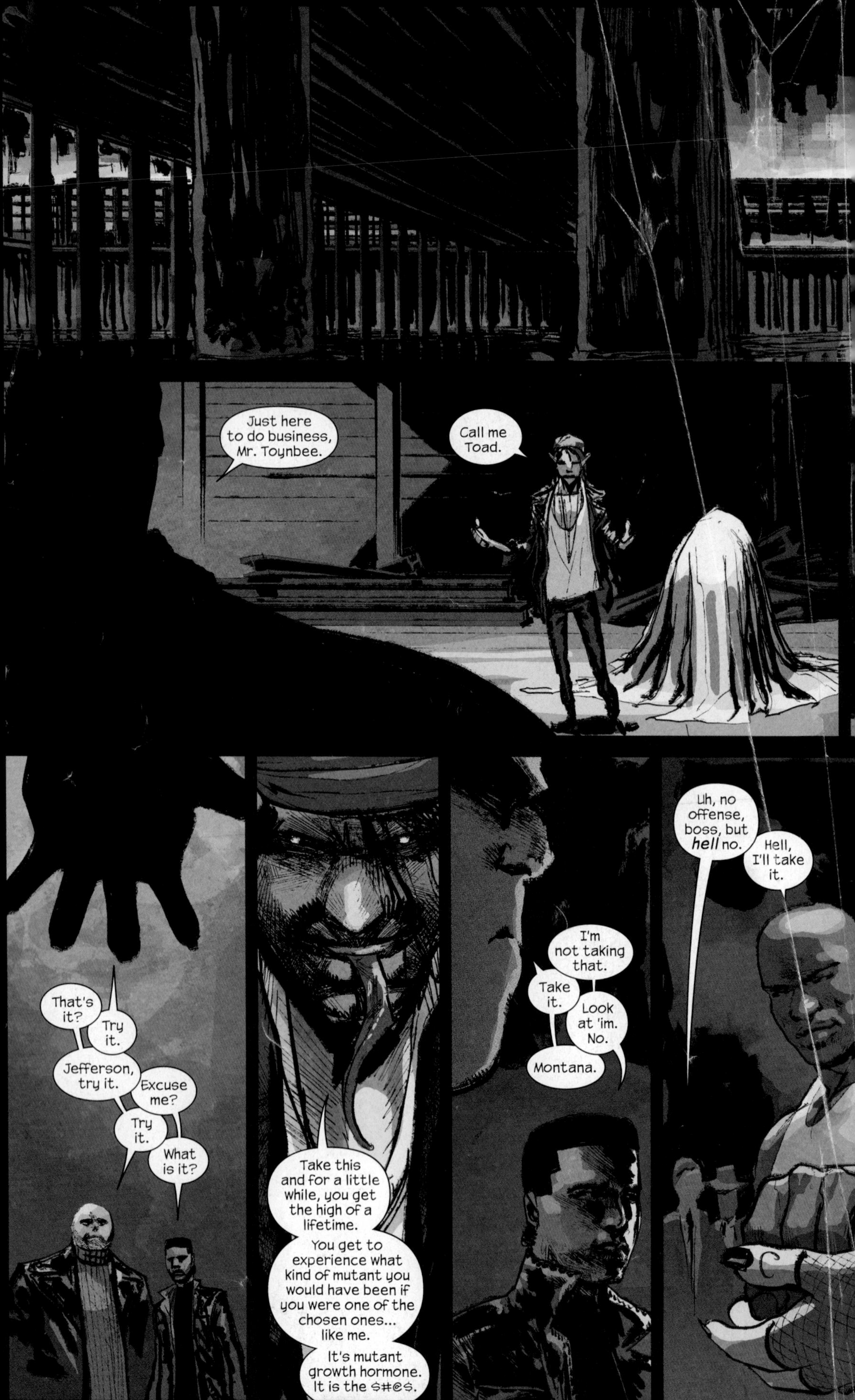
Just here to do business, Mr. Toynbee.
Call me Toad.
That's it?
Try it.
Jefferson, try it.
Excuse me?
Try it.
What is it?
Take this and for a little while, you get the high of a lifetime.
You get to experience what kind of mutant you would have been if you were one of the chosen ones... like me.
It's mutant growth hormone. It is the $#@$.
I'm not taking that.
Take it.
Look at 'im. No.
Montana.
Uh, no offense, boss, but hell no.
Hell, I'll take it.

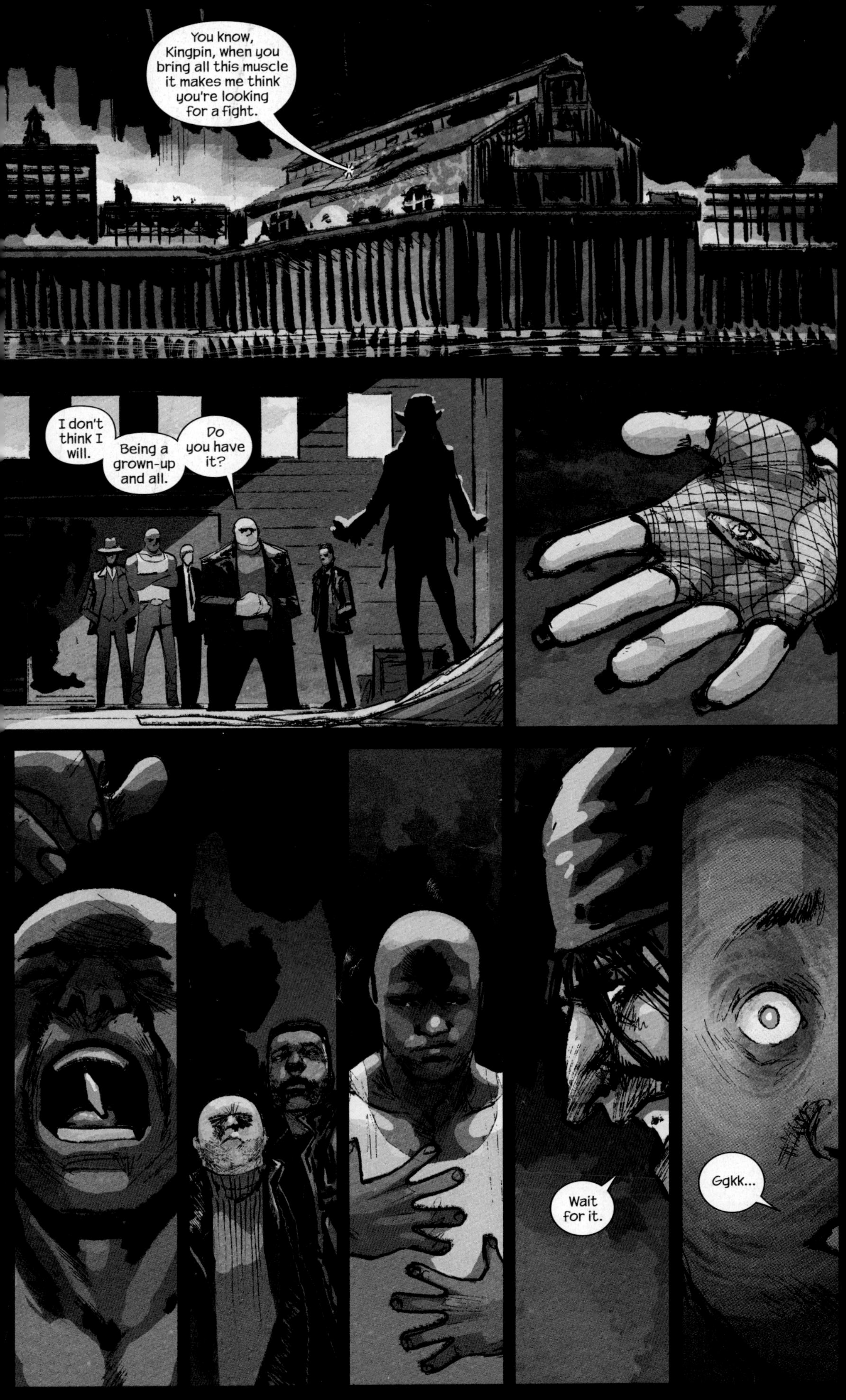
You know, Kingpin, when you bring all this muscle it makes me think you're looking for a fight.
I don't think I will.
Being a grown-up and all.
Do you have it?
Wait for it.
Ggkk...

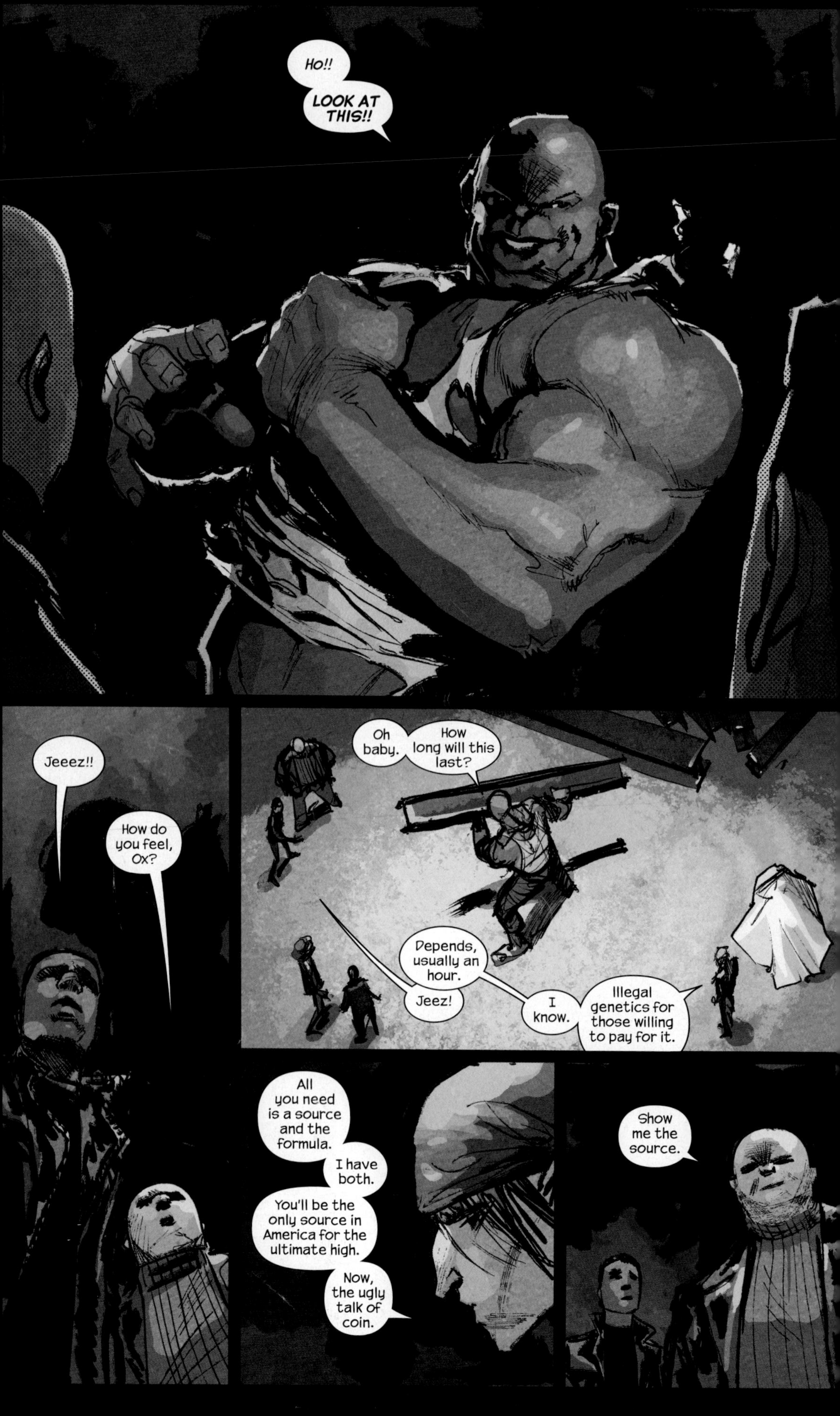
Ho!!
LOOK AT THIS!!
Jeeez!!
How do you feel, Ox?
Oh baby.
How long will this last?
Depends, usually an hour.
Jeez!
I know.
Illegal genetics for those willing to pay for it.
All you need is a source and the formula.
I have both.
You'll be the only source in America for the ultimate high.
Now, the ugly talk of coin.
Show me the source.

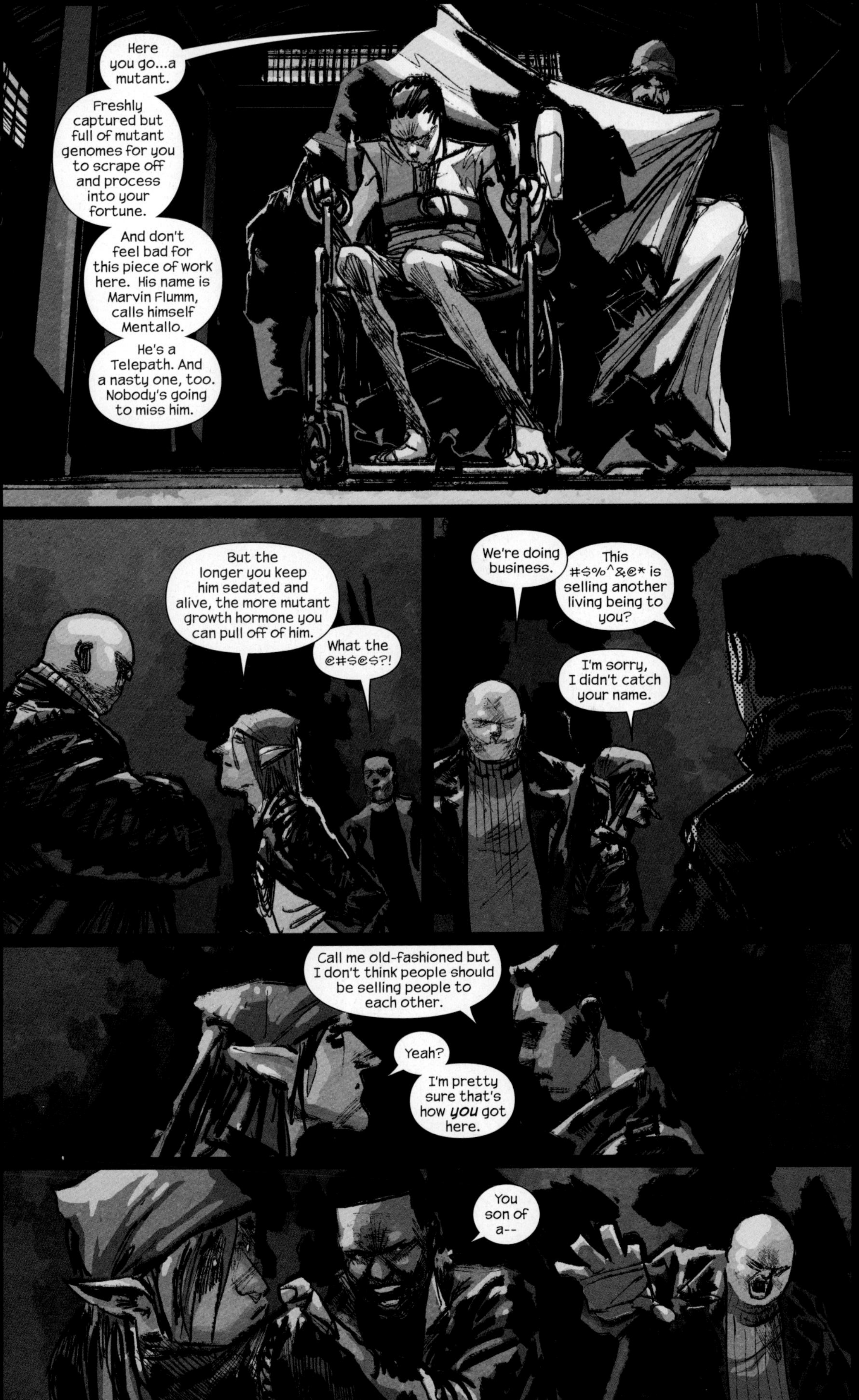
Here you go...a mutant.
Freshly captured but full of mutant genomes for you to scrape off and process into your fortune.
And don't feel bad for this piece of work here. His name is Marvin Flumm, calls himself Mentallo.
He's a Telepath. And a nasty one, too. Nobody's going to miss him.
But the longer you keep him sedated and alive, the more mutant growth hormone you can pull off of him.
What the @#$@$?!
We're doing business.
This #$%^&@* is selling another living being to you?
I'm sorry, I didn't catch your name.
Call me old-fashioned but I don't think people should be selling people to each other.
Yeah?
I'm pretty sure that's how *you* got here.
You son of a--

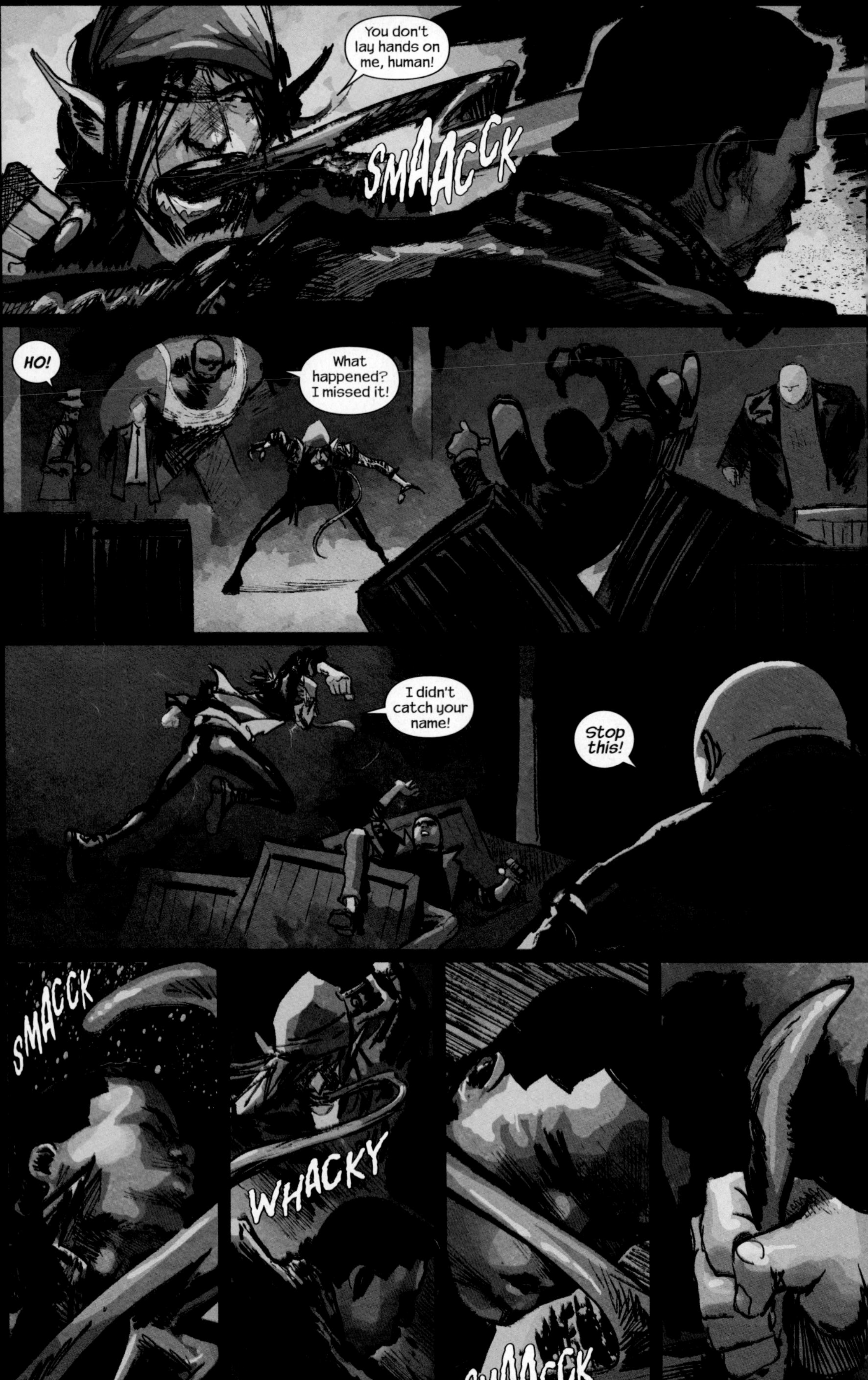
You don't lay hands on me, human!
SMAACCK
HO!
What happened? I missed it!
I didn't catch your name!
Stop this!
SMACCK
WHACKY
SMAACCK

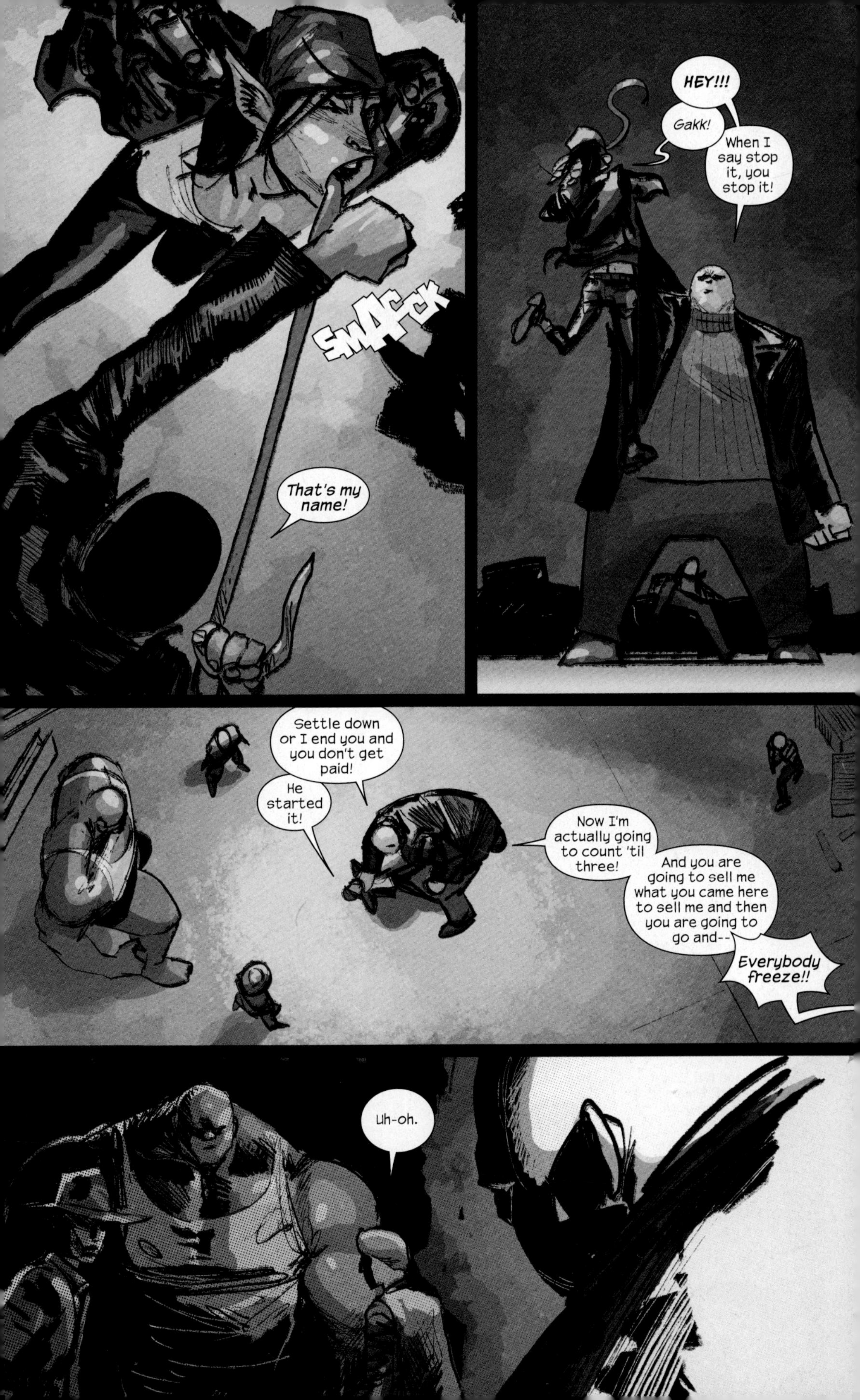
SMACK
That's my name!
HEY!!!
Gakk!
When I say stop it, you stop it!
Settle down or I end you and you don't get paid!
He started it!
Now I'm actually going to count 'til three!
And you are going to sell me what you came here to sell me and then you are going to go and--
Everybody freeze!!
Uh-oh.

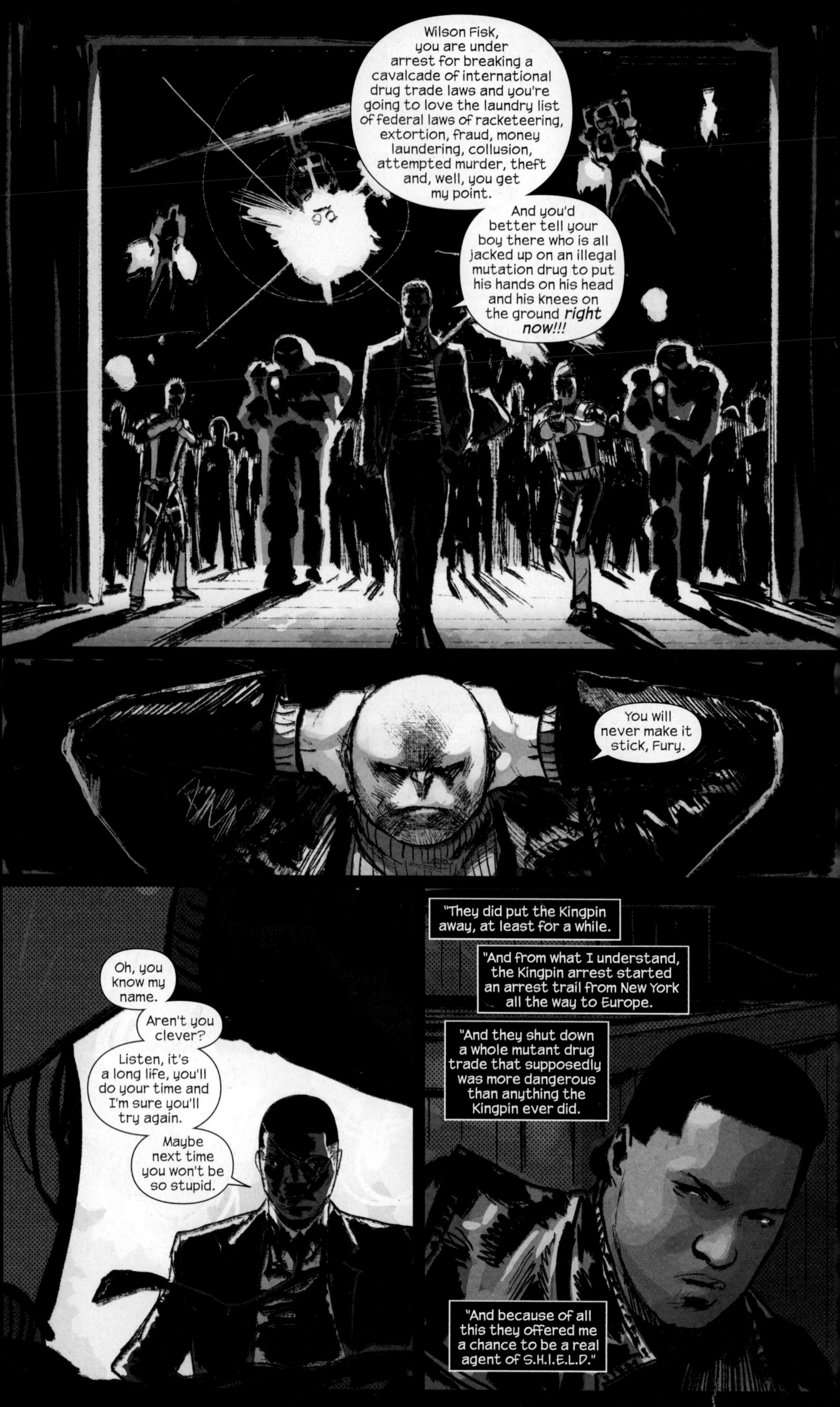
Wilson Fisk, you are under arrest for breaking a cavalcade of international drug trade laws and you're going to love the laundry list of federal laws of racketeering, extortion, fraud, money laundering, collusion, attempted murder, theft and, well, you get my point.
And you'd better tell your boy there who is all jacked up on an illegal mutation drug to put his hands on his head and his knees on the ground *right now!!!*
You will never make it stick, Fury.
Oh, you know my name.
Aren't you clever?
Listen, it's a long life, you'll do your time and I'm sure you'll try again.
Maybe next time you won't be so stupid.
"They did put the Kingpin away, at least for a while.
"And from what I understand, the Kingpin arrest started an arrest trail from New York all the way to Europe.
"And they shut down a whole mutant drug trade that supposedly was more dangerous than anything the Kingpin ever did.
"And because of all this they offered me a chance to be a real agent of S.H.I.E.L.D."

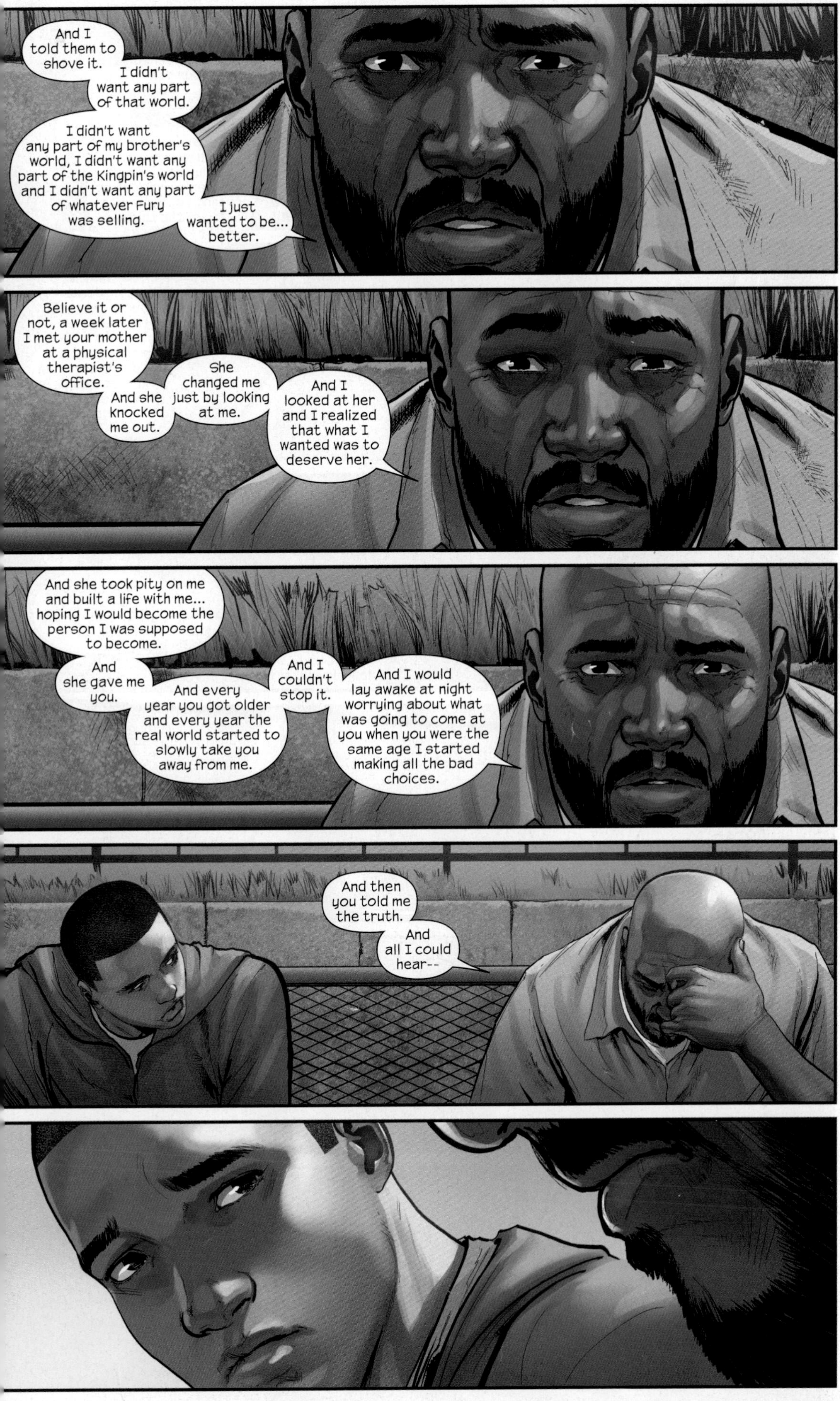
And I told them to shove it.
I didn't want any part of that world.
I didn't want any part of my brother's world, I didn't want any part of the Kingpin's world and I didn't want any part of whatever Fury was selling.
I just wanted to be... better.
Believe it or not, a week later I met your mother at a physical therapist's office.
And she knocked me out.
She changed me just by looking at me.
And I looked at her and I realized that what I wanted was to deserve her.
And she took pity on me and built a life with me... hoping I would become the person I was supposed to become.
And she gave me you.
And every year you got older and every year the real world started to slowly take you away from me.
And I couldn't stop it.
And I would lay awake at night worrying about what was going to come at you when you were the same age I started making all the bad choices.
And then you told me the truth.
And all I could hear--

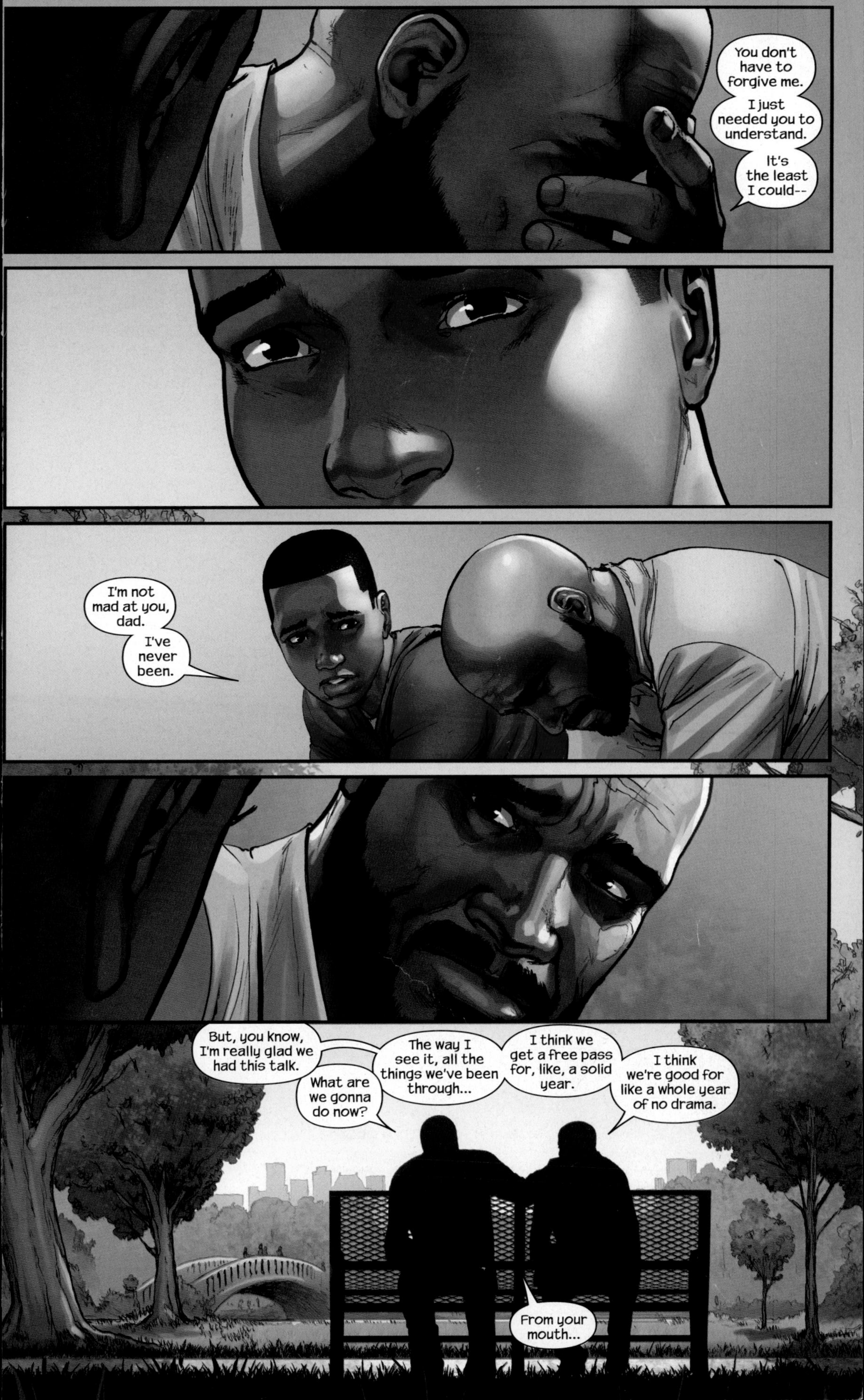
You don't have to forgive me.
I just needed you to understand.
It's the least I could--
I'm not mad at you, dad.
I've never been.
But, you know, I'm really glad we had this talk.
What are we gonna do now?
The way I see it, all the things we've been through...
I think we get a free pass for, like, a solid year.
I think we're good for like a whole year of no drama.
From your mouth...

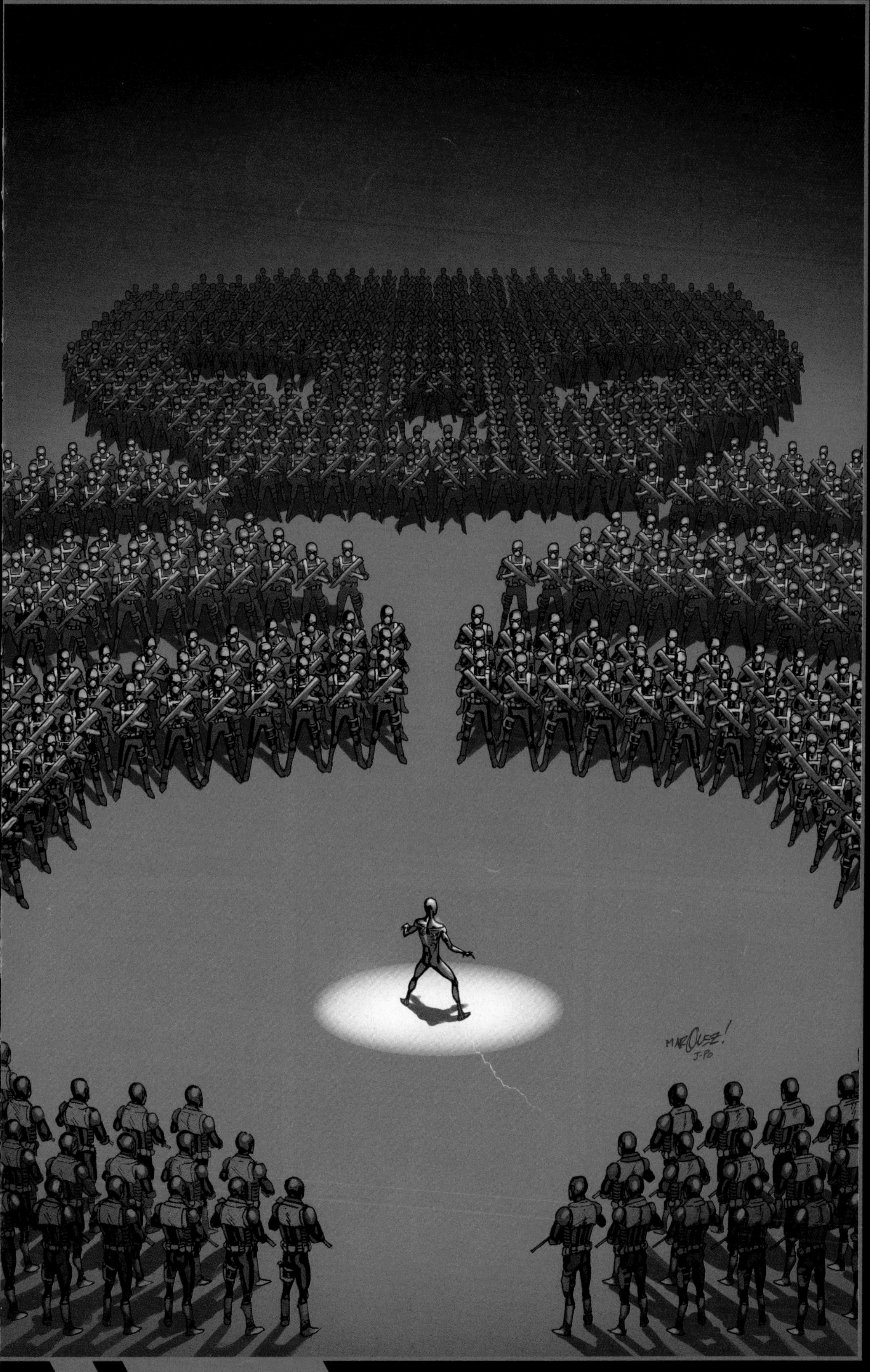
MARQUEZ!
J-Po

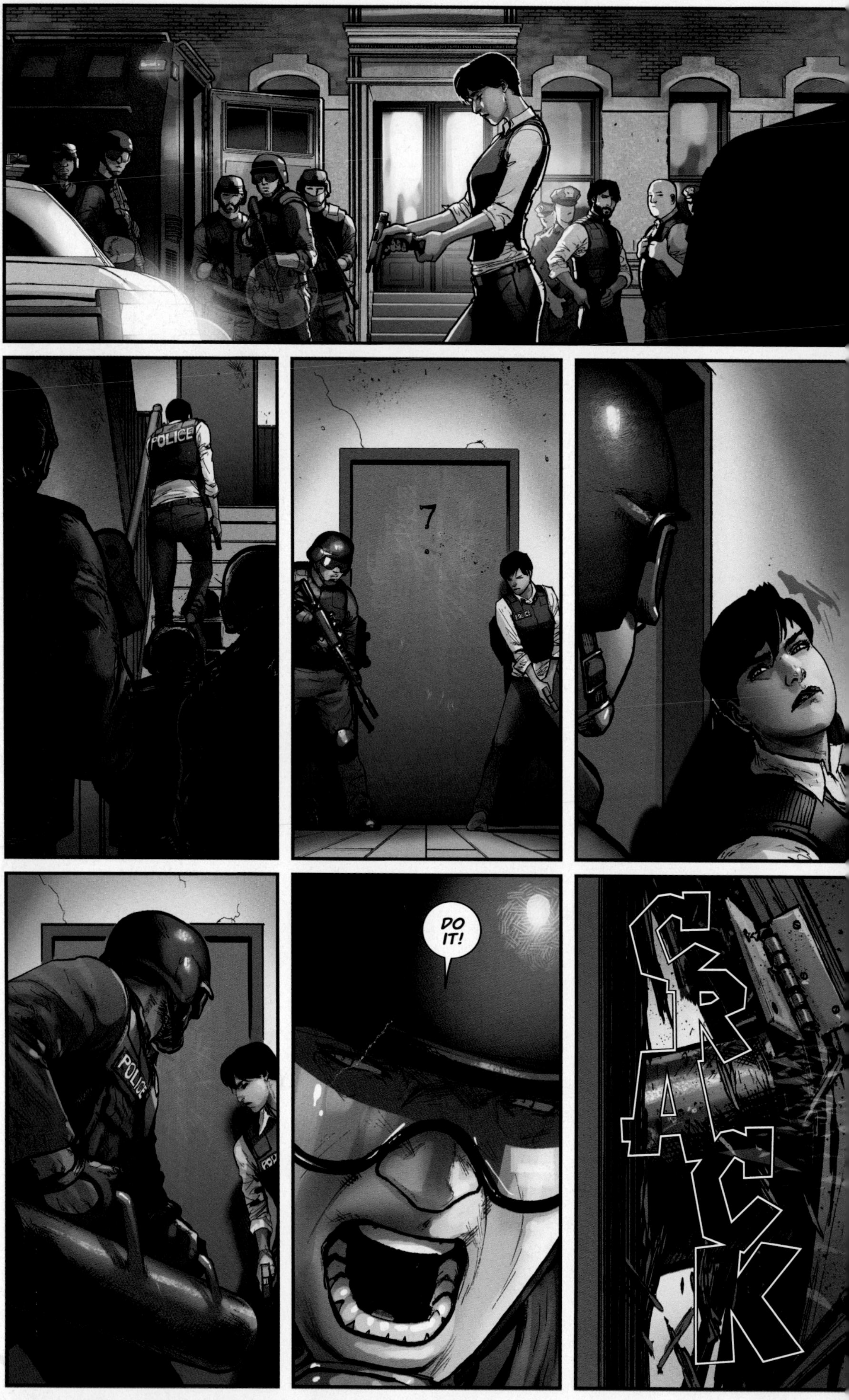
POLICE
7
DO IT!
POLICE
CRACK

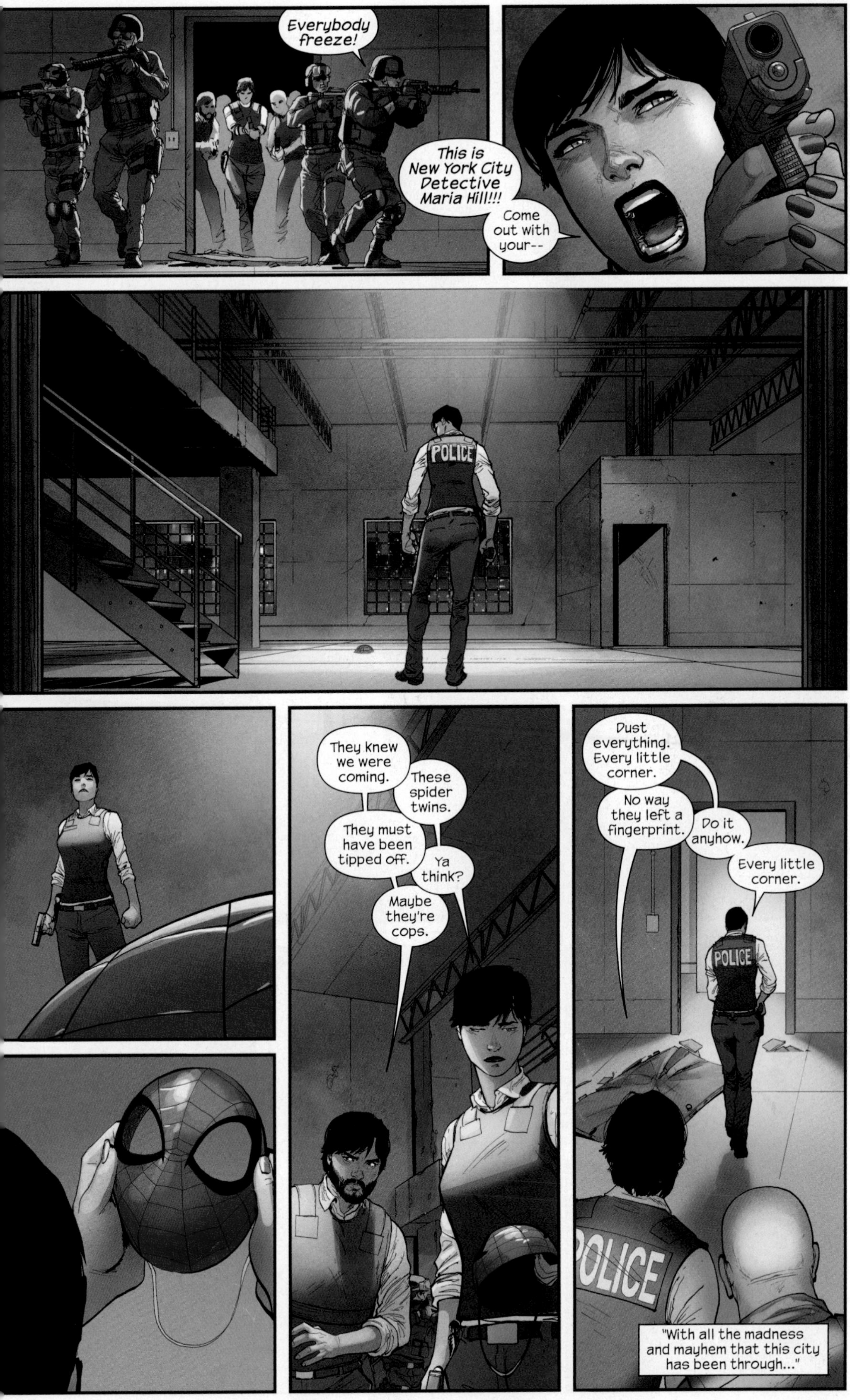
Everybody freeze!
This is New York City Detective Maria Hill!!!
Come out with your--
POLICE
They knew we were coming.
These spider twins.
They must have been tipped off.
Ya think?
Maybe they're cops.
Dust everything. Every little corner.
No way they left a fingerprint.
Do it anyhow.
Every little corner.
POLICE
POLICE
"With all the madness and mayhem that this city has been through..."

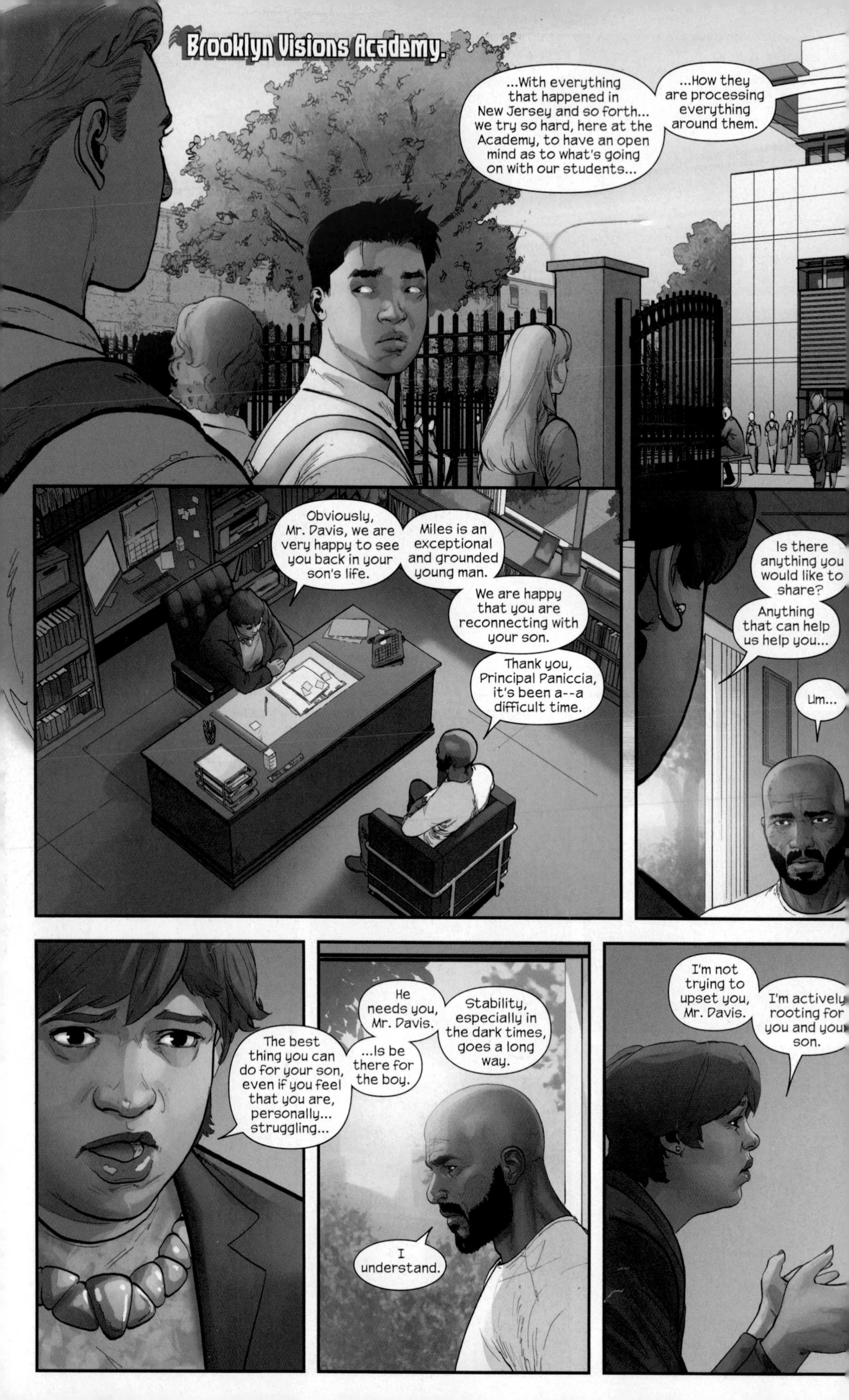

Brooklyn Visions Academy.
...With everything that happened in New Jersey and so forth... we try so hard, here at the Academy, to have an open mind as to what's going on with our students...
...How they are processing everything around them.
Obviously, Mr. Davis, we are very happy to see you back in your son's life.
Miles is an exceptional and grounded young man.
We are happy that you are reconnecting with your son.
Thank you, Principal Paniccia, it's been a--a difficult time.
Is there anything you would like to share?
Anything that can help us help you...
Um...
The best thing you can do for your son, even if you feel that you are, personally... struggling...
He needs you, Mr. Davis.
...Is be there for the boy.
Stability, especially in the dark times, goes a long way.
I understand.
I'm not trying to upset you, Mr. Davis.
I'm actively rooting for you and your son.

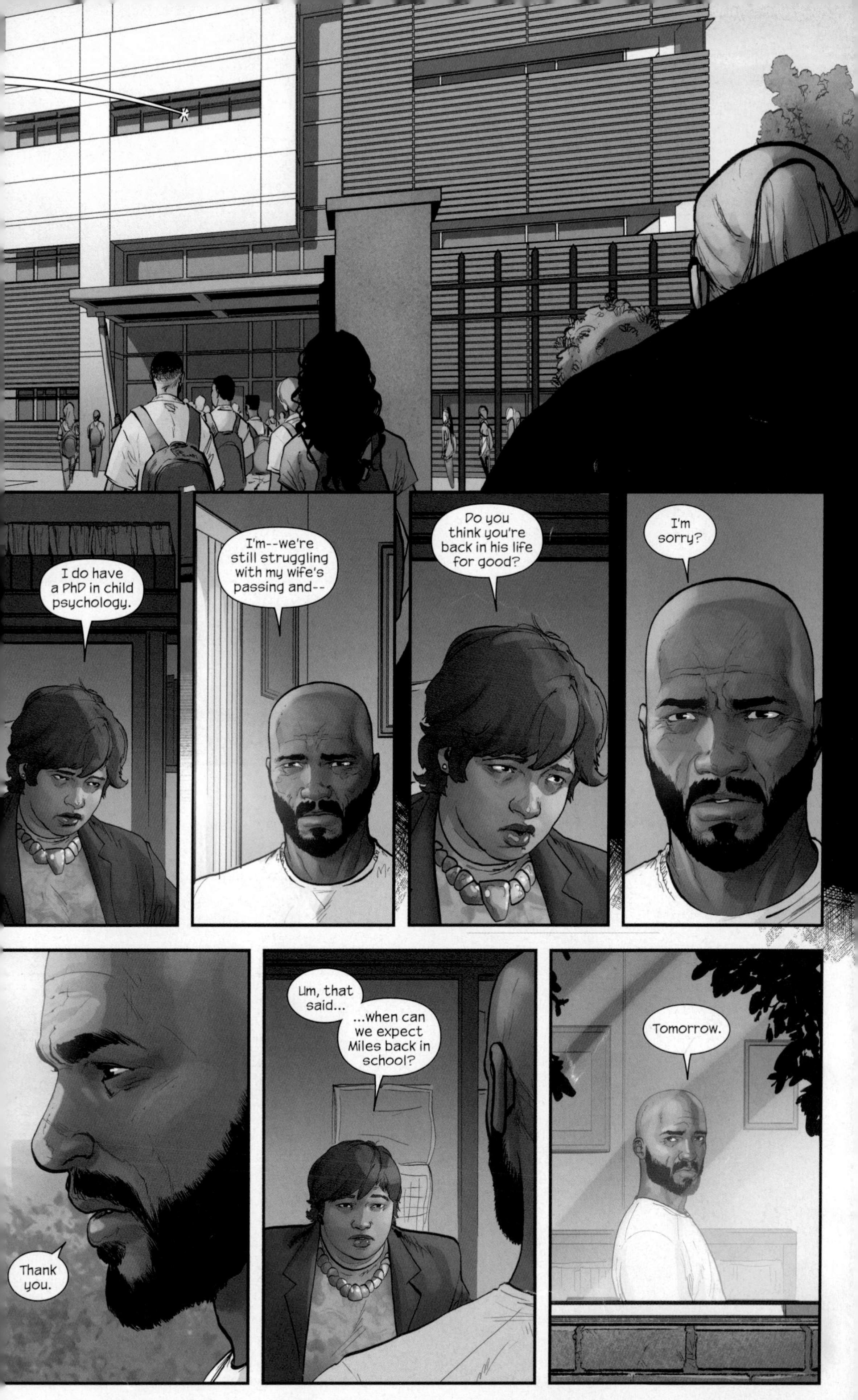

I do have a PhD in child psychology.
I'm--we're still struggling with my wife's passing and--
Do you think you're back in his life for good?
I'm sorry?
Thank you.
Um, that said...
...when can we expect Miles back in school?
Tomorrow.

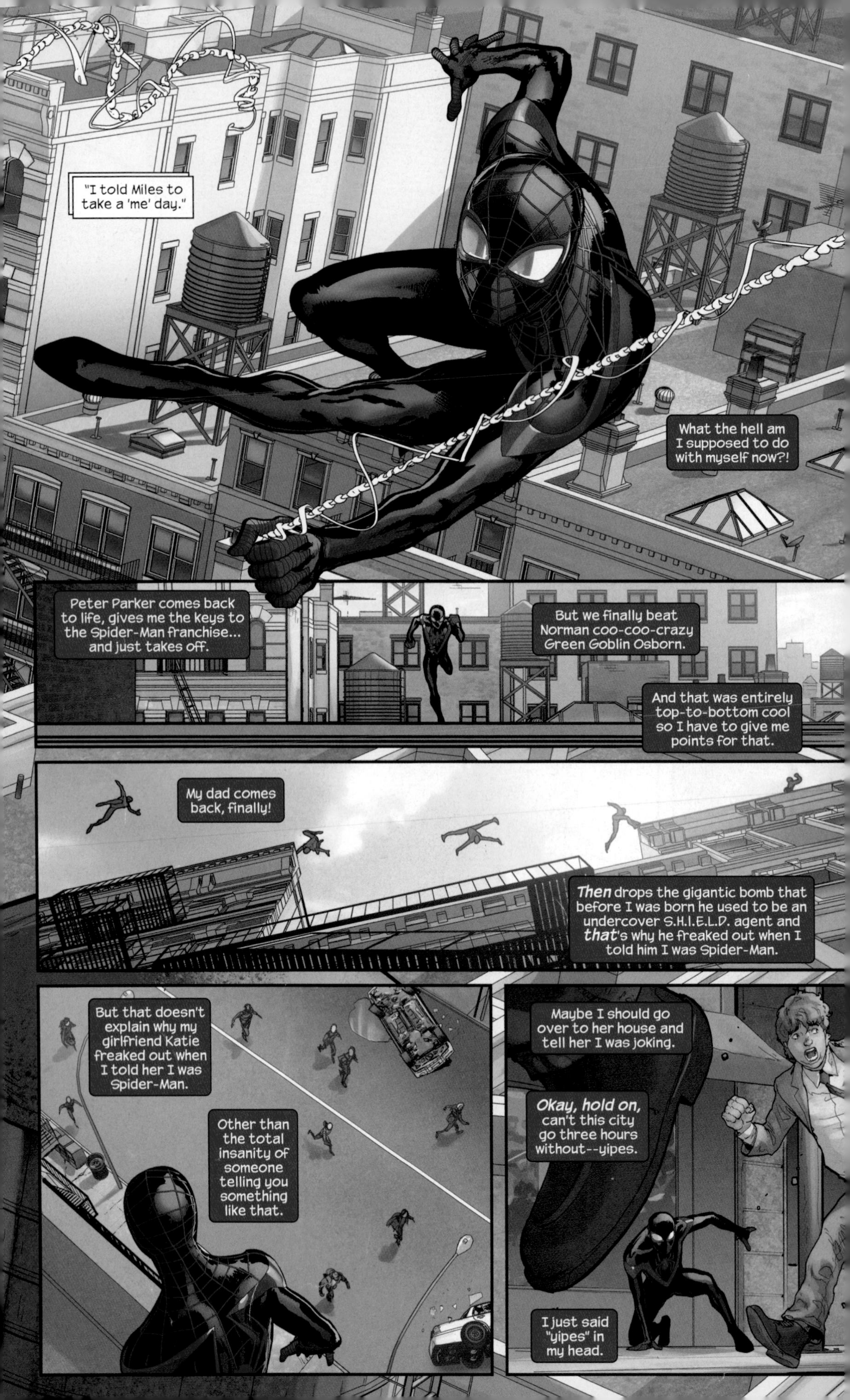
"I told Miles to take a 'me' day."
What the hell am I supposed to do with myself now?!
Peter Parker comes back to life, gives me the keys to the Spider-Man franchise... and just takes off.
But we finally beat Norman coo-coo-crazy Green Goblin Osborn.
And that was entirely top-to-bottom cool so I have to give me points for that.
My dad comes back, finally!
Then drops the gigantic bomb that before I was born he used to be an undercover S.H.I.E.L.D. agent and that's why he freaked out when I told him I was Spider-Man.
But that doesn't explain why my girlfriend Katie freaked out when I told her I was Spider-Man.
Other than the total insanity of someone telling you something like that.
Maybe I should go over to her house and tell her I was joking.
Okay, hold on, can't this city go three hours without--yipes.
I just said "yipes" in my head.

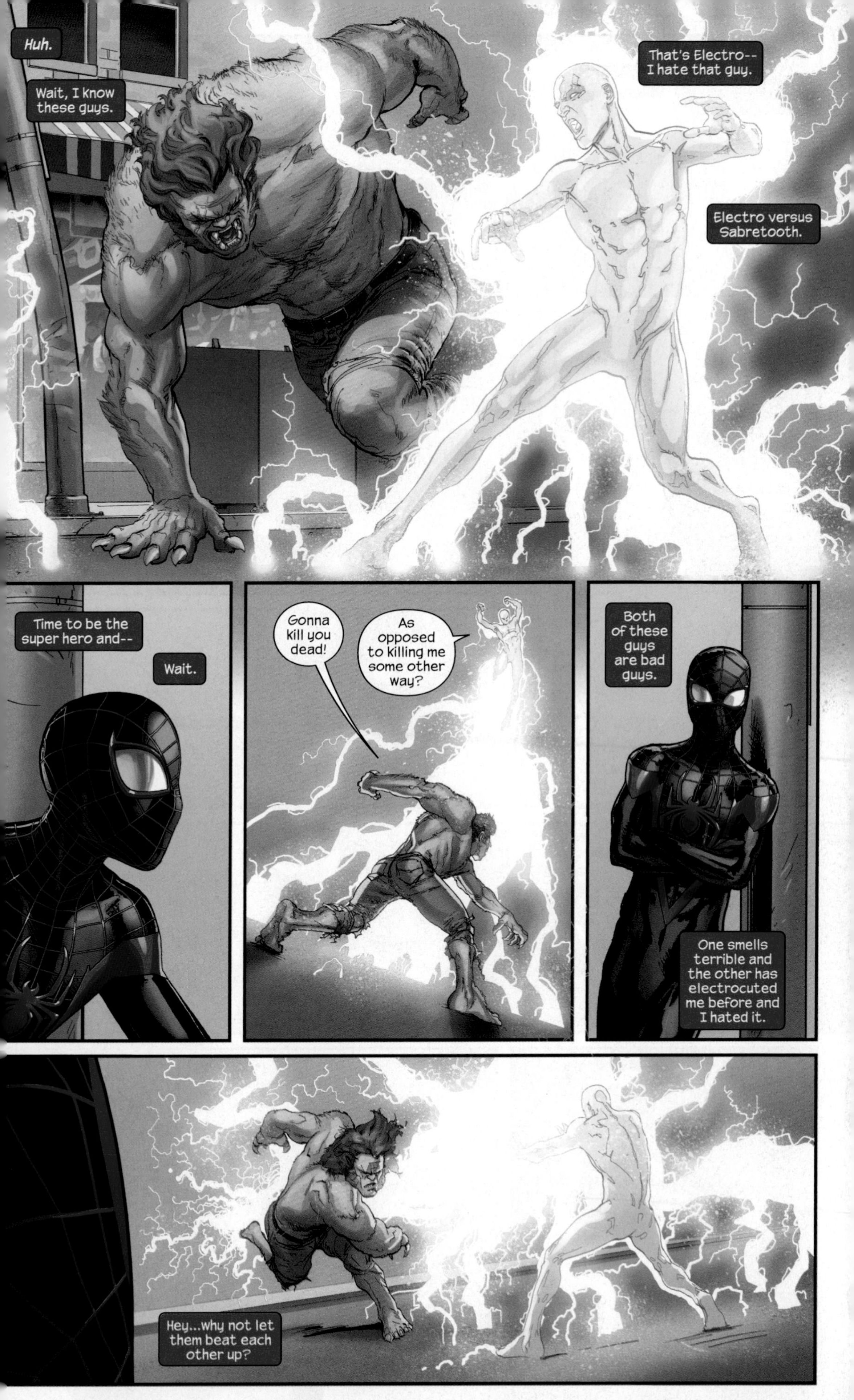
Huh.
Wait, I know these guys.
That's Electro-- I hate that guy.
Electro versus Sabretooth.
Time to be the super hero and--
Wait.
Gonna kill you dead!
As opposed to killing me some other way?
Both of these guys are bad guys.
One smells terrible and the other has electrocuted me before and I hated it.
Hey...why not let them beat each other up?

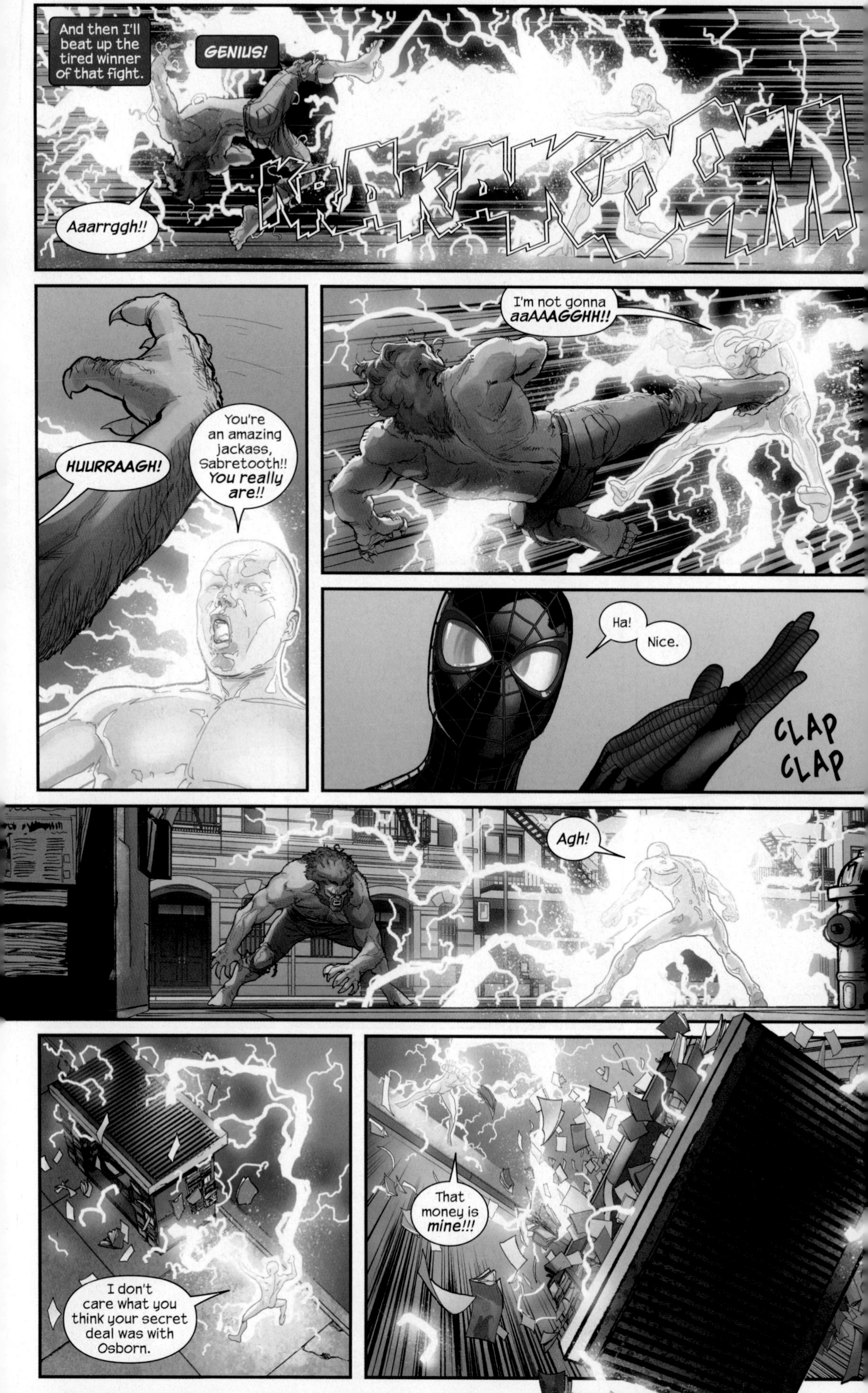
And then I'll beat up the tired winner of that fight.
GENIUS!
Aaarrggh!!
KRAKAKOOOM
HUURRAAGH!
You're an amazing jackass, Sabretooth!! You really are!!
I'm not gonna aaAAAGGHH!!
Ha!
Nice.
CLAP CLAP
Agh!
I don't care what you think your secret deal was with Osborn.
That money is mine!!!

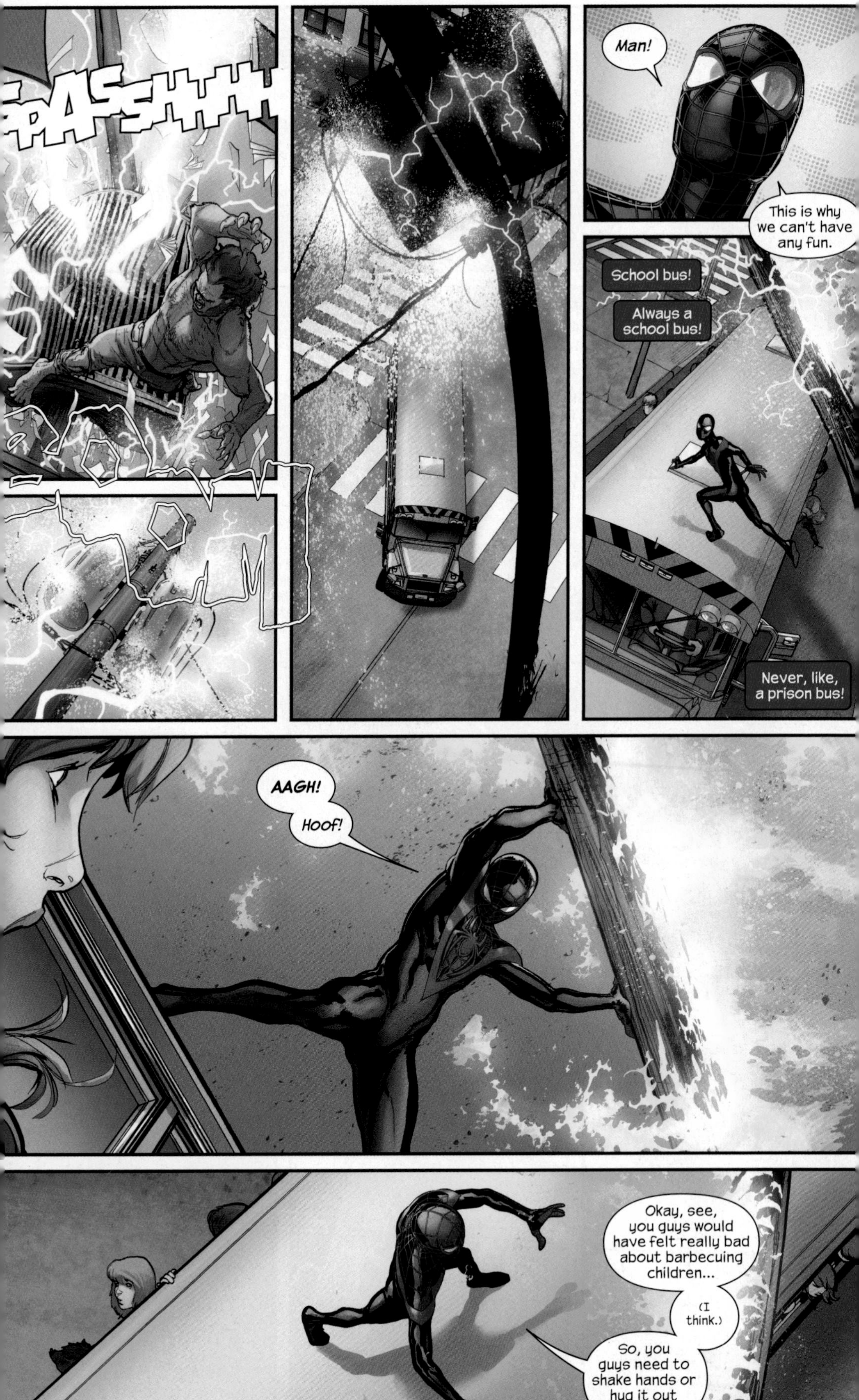
FPASHHH
Man!
This is why we can't have any fun.
School bus!
Always a school bus!
Never, like, a prison bus!
AAGH!
HOOF!
Okay, see, you guys would have felt really bad about barbecuing children...
(I think.)
So, you guys need to shake hands or hug it out and--

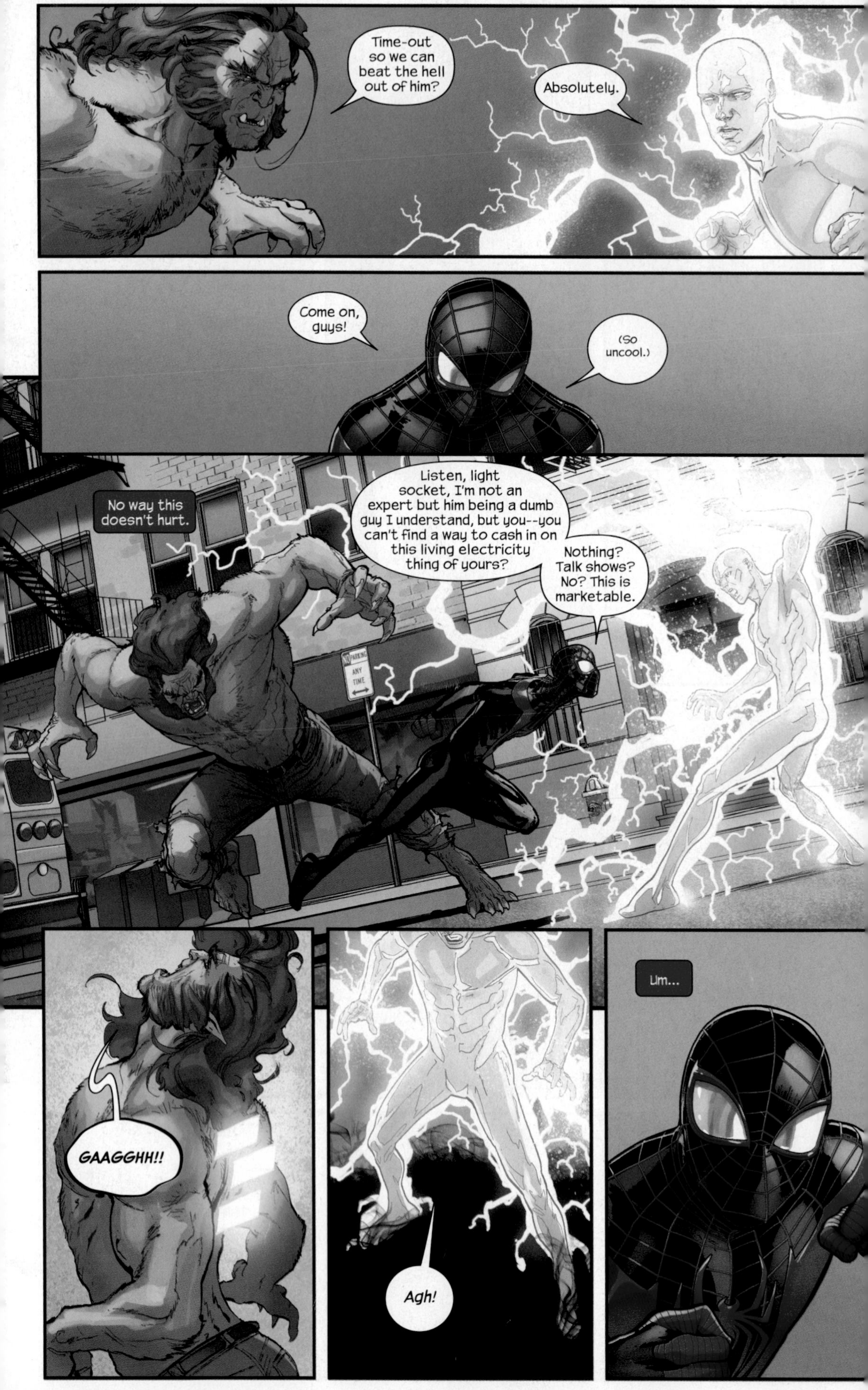
Time-out so we can beat the hell out of him?
Absolutely.
Come on, guys!
(So uncool.)
No way this doesn't hurt.
Listen, light socket, I'm not an expert but him being a dumb guy I understand, but you--you can't find a way to cash in on this living electricity thing of yours?
Nothing? Talk shows? No? This is marketable.
NO PARKING ANY TIME
GAAGGHH!!
Agh!
Um...

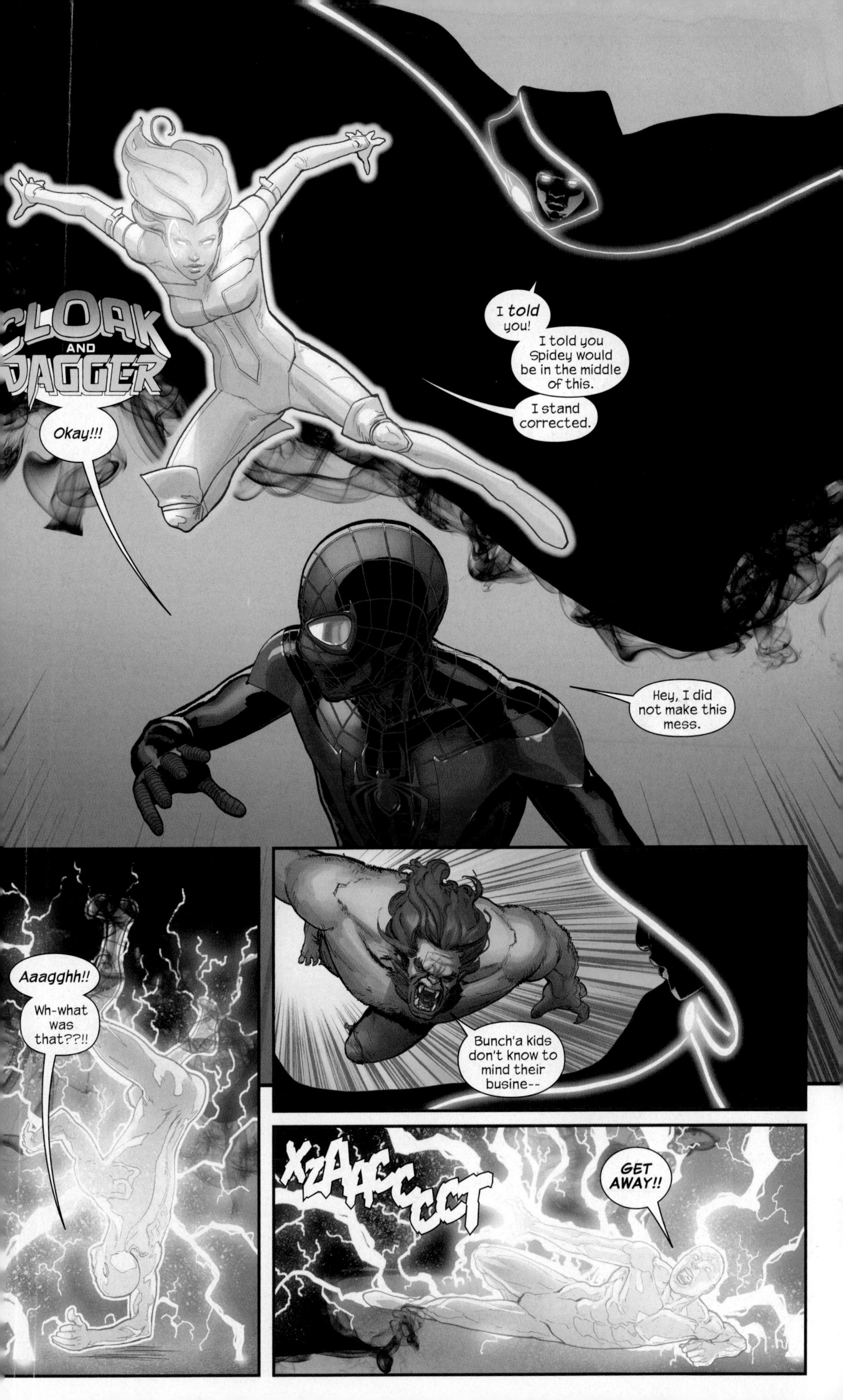
CLOAK AND DAGGER
Okay!!!
I told you!
I told you Spidey would be in the middle of this.
I stand corrected.
Hey, I did not make this mess.
Aaagghh!!
Wh-what was that??!!
Bunch'a kids don't know to mind their busine--
XZAACCCCT
GET AWAY!!

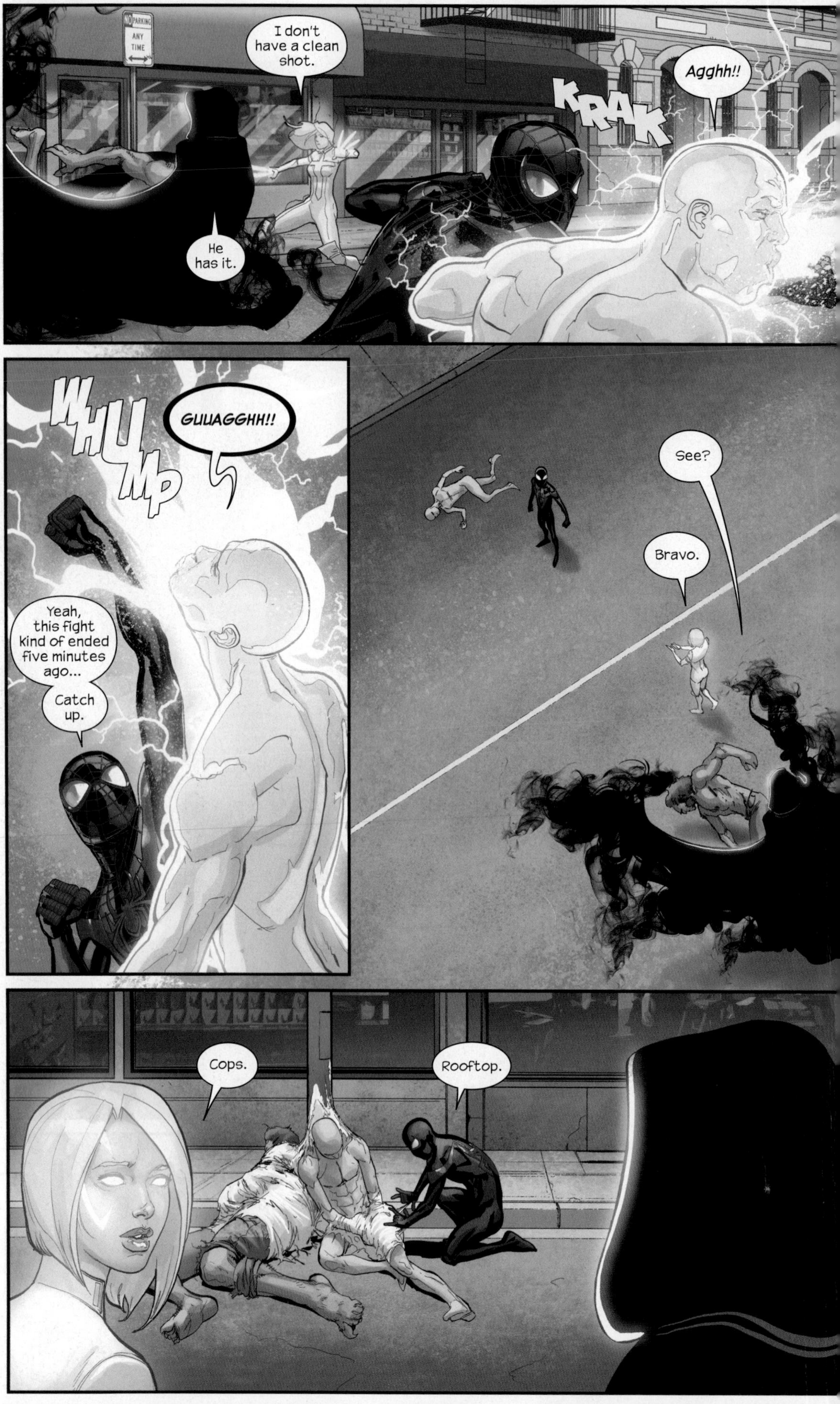
NO PARKING ANY TIME
I don't have a clean shot.
He has it.
KRAK
Agghh!!
WHUMP
GUUAGGHH!!
Yeah, this fight kind of ended five minutes ago...
Catch up.
See?
Bravo.
Cops.
Rooftop.

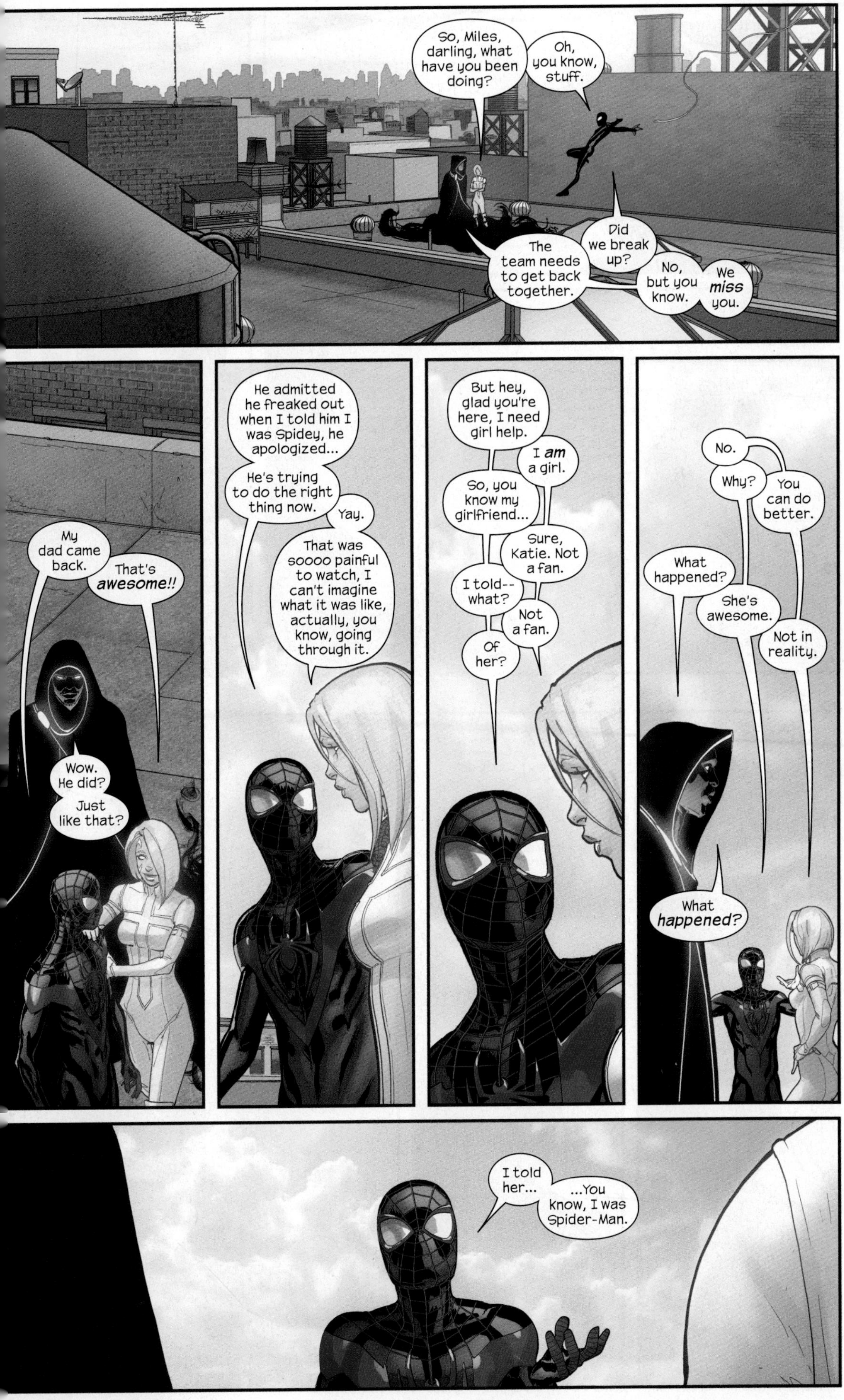

So, Miles, darling, what have you been doing?
Oh, you know, stuff.
Did we break up?
The team needs to get back together.
No, but you know.
We *miss* you.
My dad came back.
That's ***awesome!!***
Wow. He did?
Just like that?
He admitted he freaked out when I told him I was Spidey, he apologized...
He's trying to do the right thing now.
Yay.
That was soooo painful to watch, I can't imagine what it was like, actually, you know, going through it.
But hey, glad you're here, I need girl help.
I *am* a girl.
So, you know my girlfriend...
Sure, Katie. Not a fan.
I told-- what?
Not a fan.
Of her?
No.
Why?
You can do better.
What happened?
She's awesome.
Not in reality.
What ***happened?***
I told her...
...You know, I was Spider-Man.

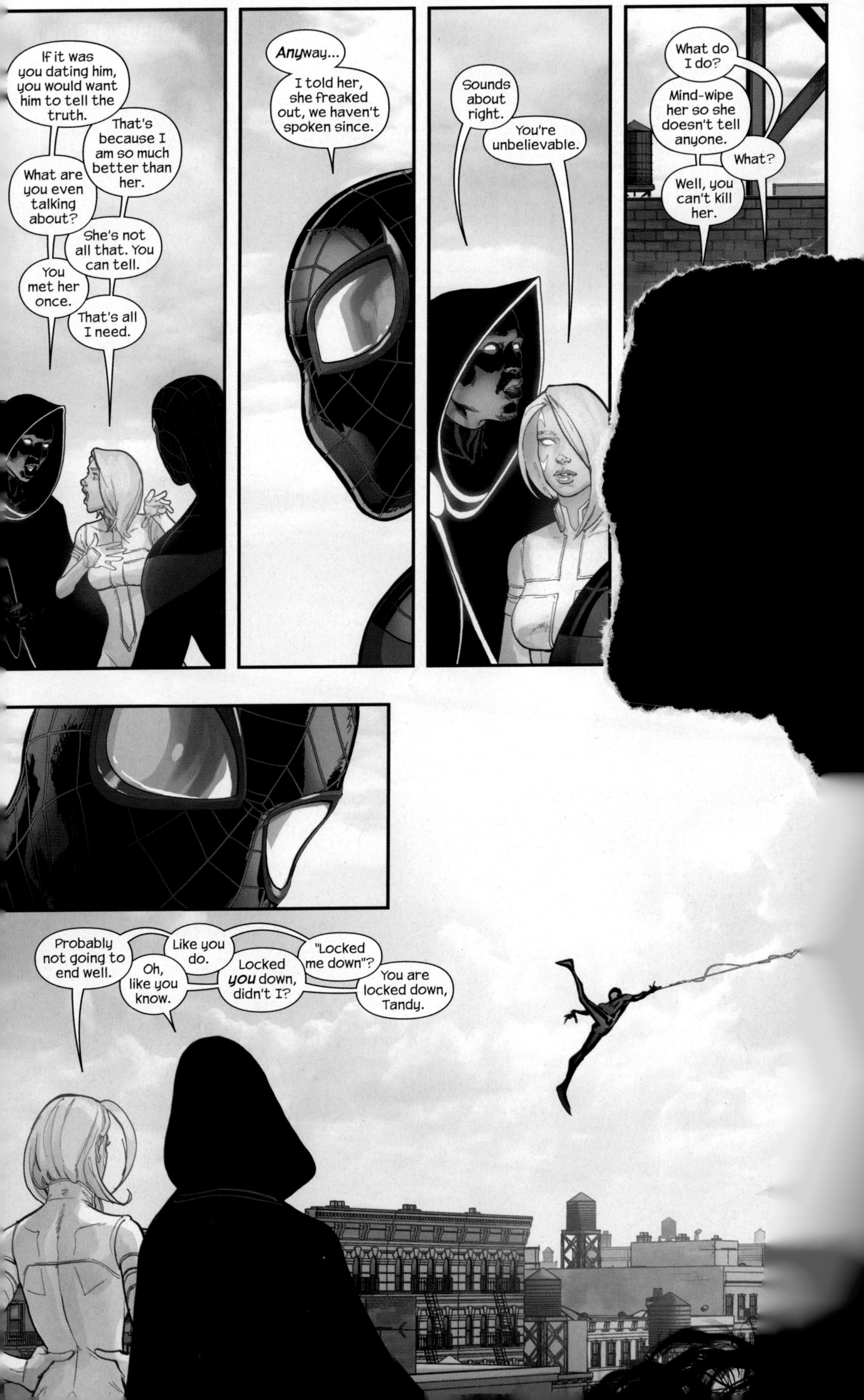
If it was you dating him, you would want him to tell the truth.
That's because I am so much better than her.
What are you even talking about?
She's not all that. You can tell.
You met her once.
That's all I need.
*Any*way...
I told her, she freaked out, we haven't spoken since.
Sounds about right.
You're unbelievable.
What do I do?
Mind-wipe her so she doesn't tell anyone.
What?
Well, you can't kill her.
Probably not going to end well.
Like you do.
Oh, like you know.
Locked *you* down, didn't I?
"Locked me down"?
You are locked down, Tandy.

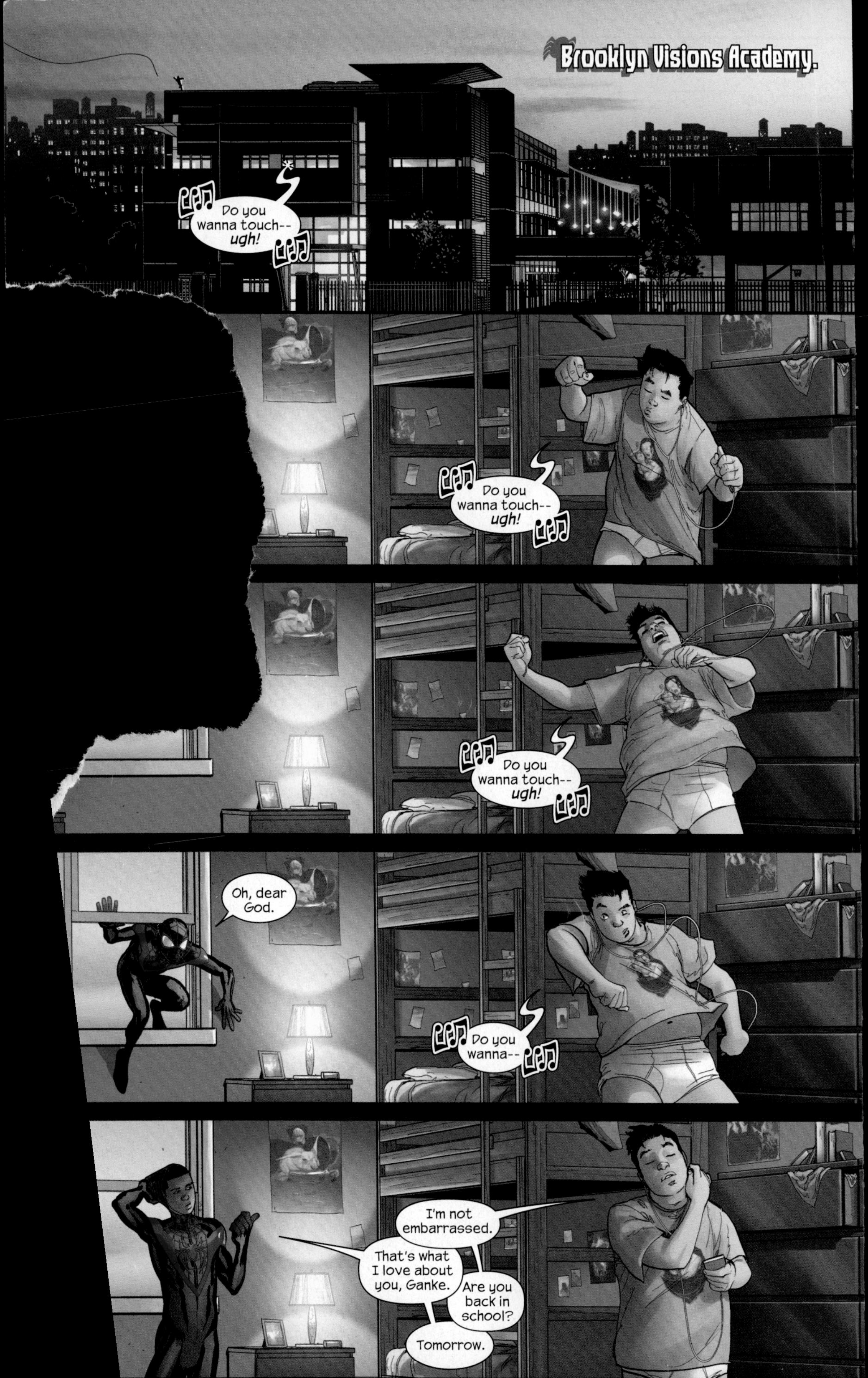
Brooklyn Visions Academy.
Do you wanna touch-- ugh!
Do you wanna touch-- ugh!
Do you wanna touch-- ugh!
Oh, dear God.
Do you wanna--
I'm not embarrassed.
That's what I love about you, Ganke.
Are you back in school?
Tomorrow.

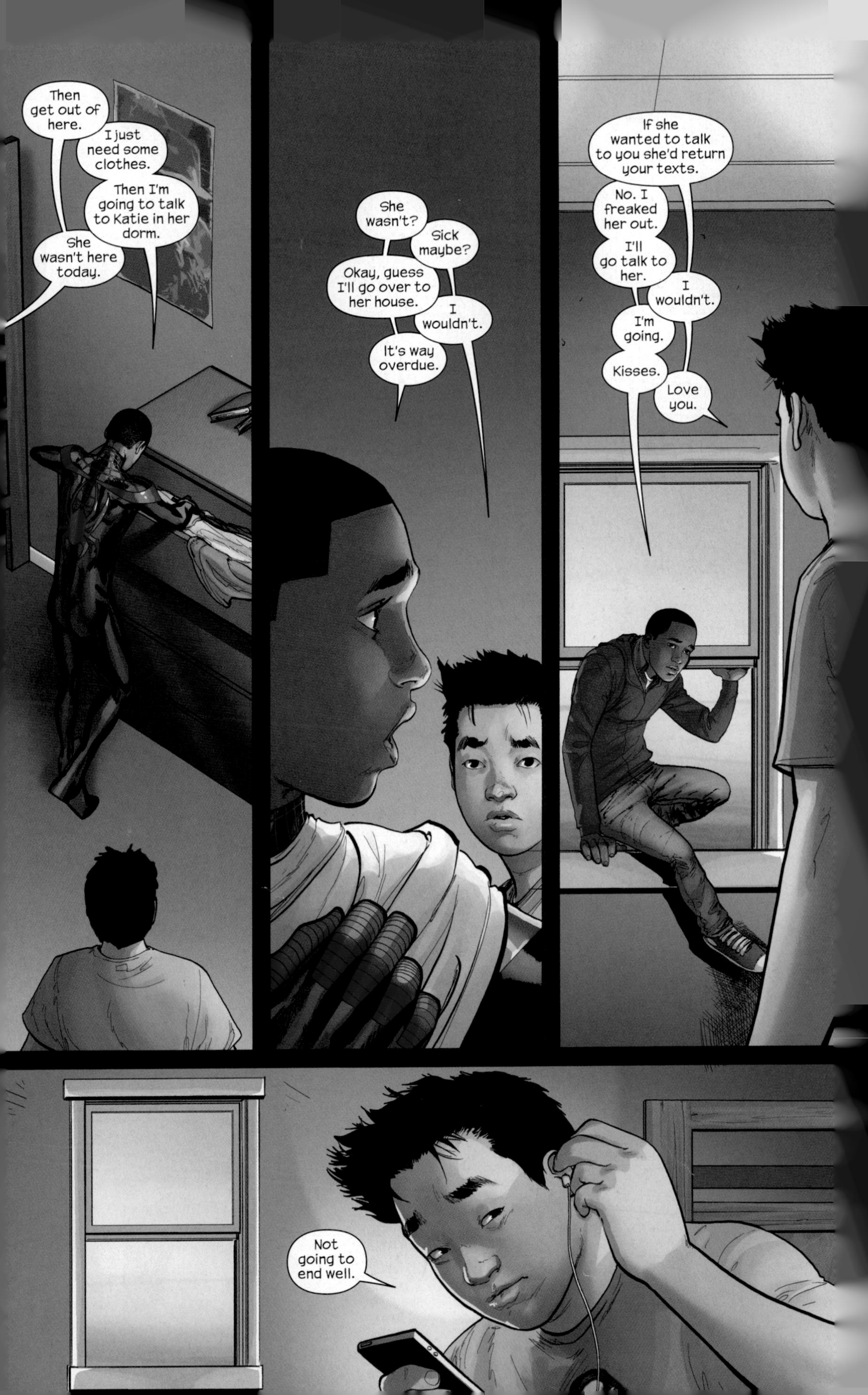
Then get out of here.
I just need some clothes.
Then I'm going to talk to Katie in her dorm.
She wasn't here today.
She wasn't?
Sick maybe?
Okay, guess I'll go over to her house.
I wouldn't.
It's way overdue.
If she wanted to talk to you she'd return your texts.
No. I freaked her out.
I'll go talk to her.
I wouldn't.
I'm going.
Kisses.
Love you.
Not going to end well.

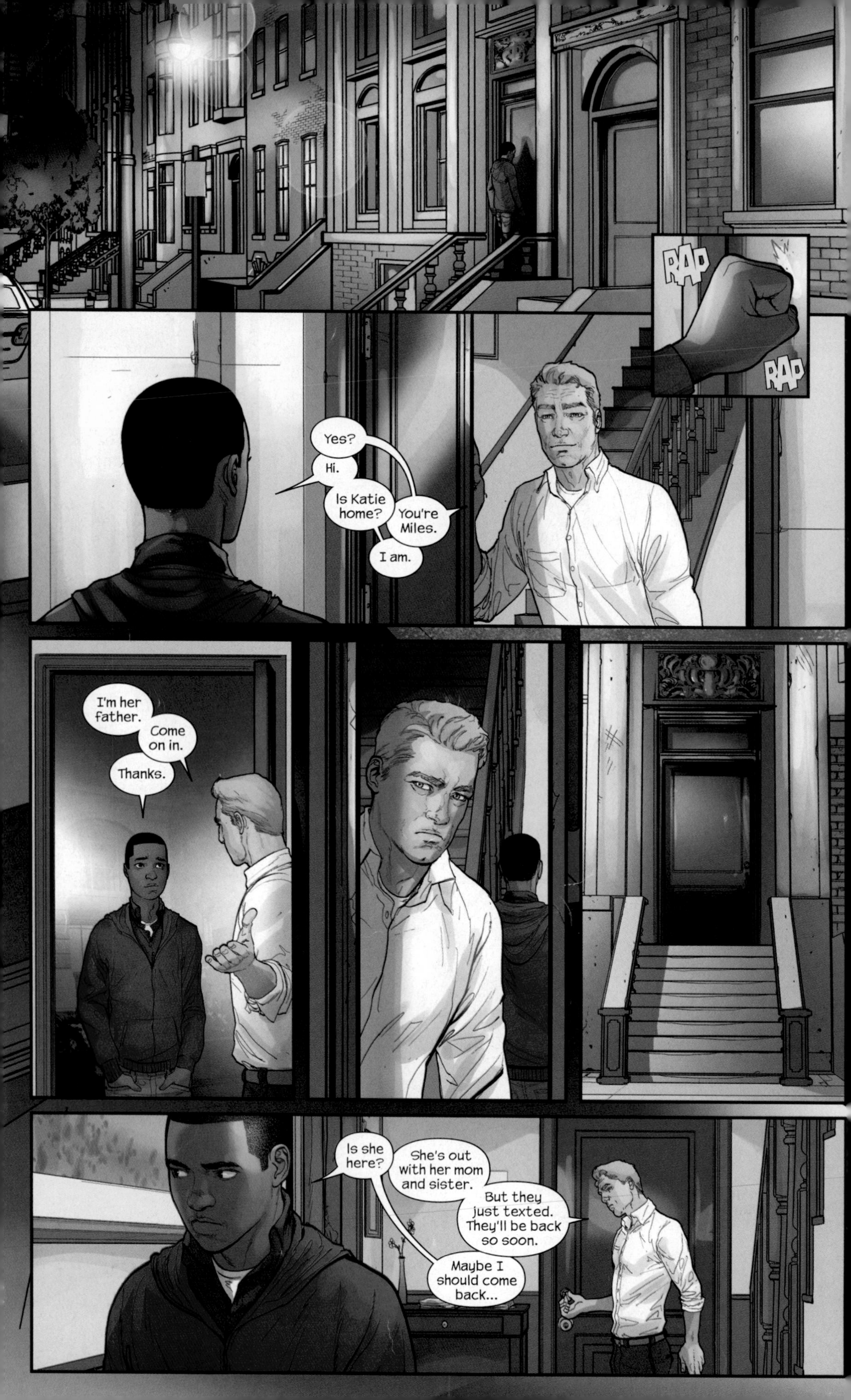
RAP
RAP
Yes?
Hi.
Is Katie home?
You're Miles.
I am.
I'm her father.
Come on in.
Thanks.
Is she here?
She's out with her mom and sister.
But they just texted. They'll be back so soon.
Maybe I should come back...

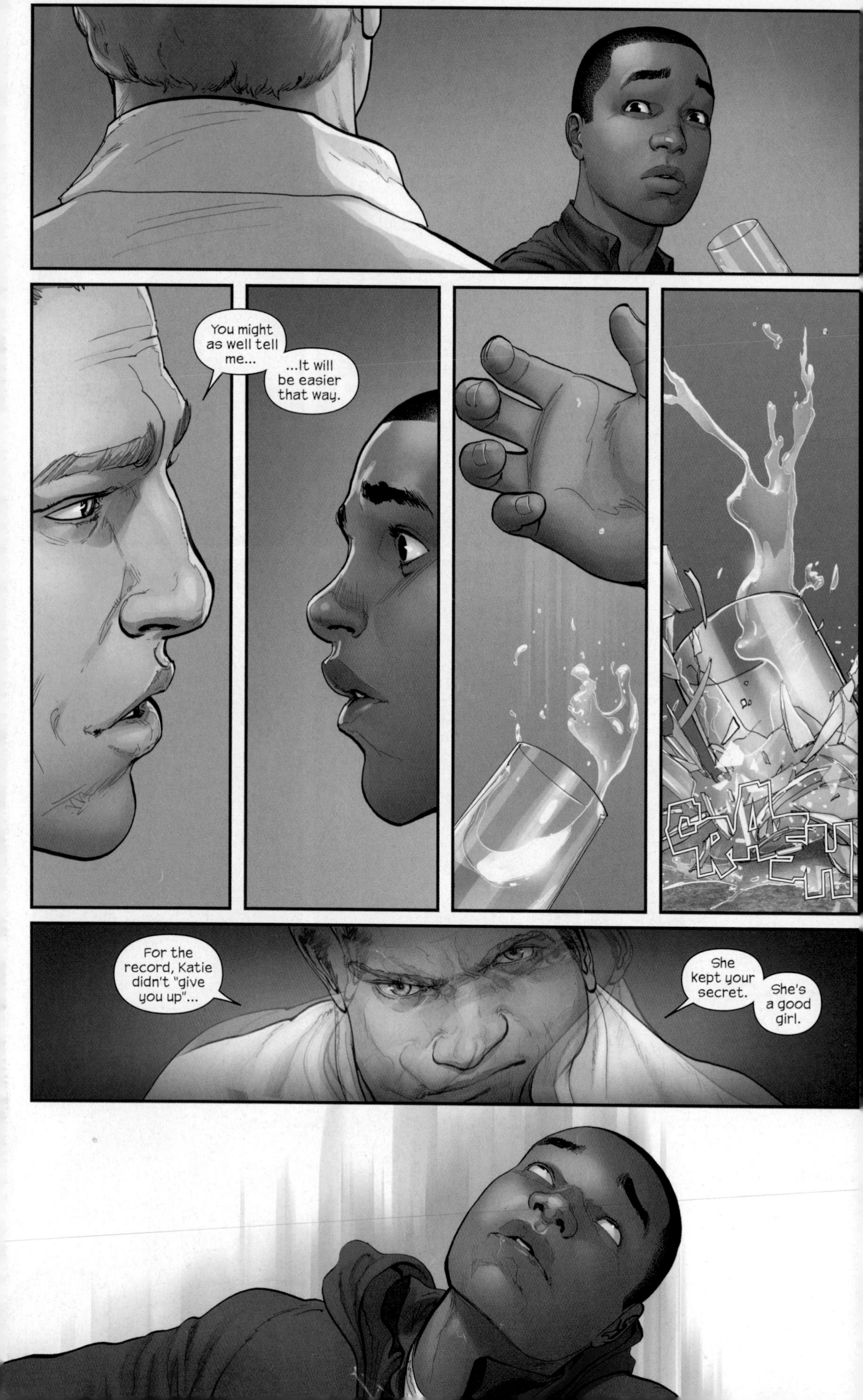
You might as well tell me...
...It will be easier that way.
CHSH
For the record, Katie didn't "give you up"...
She kept your secret.
She's a good girl.

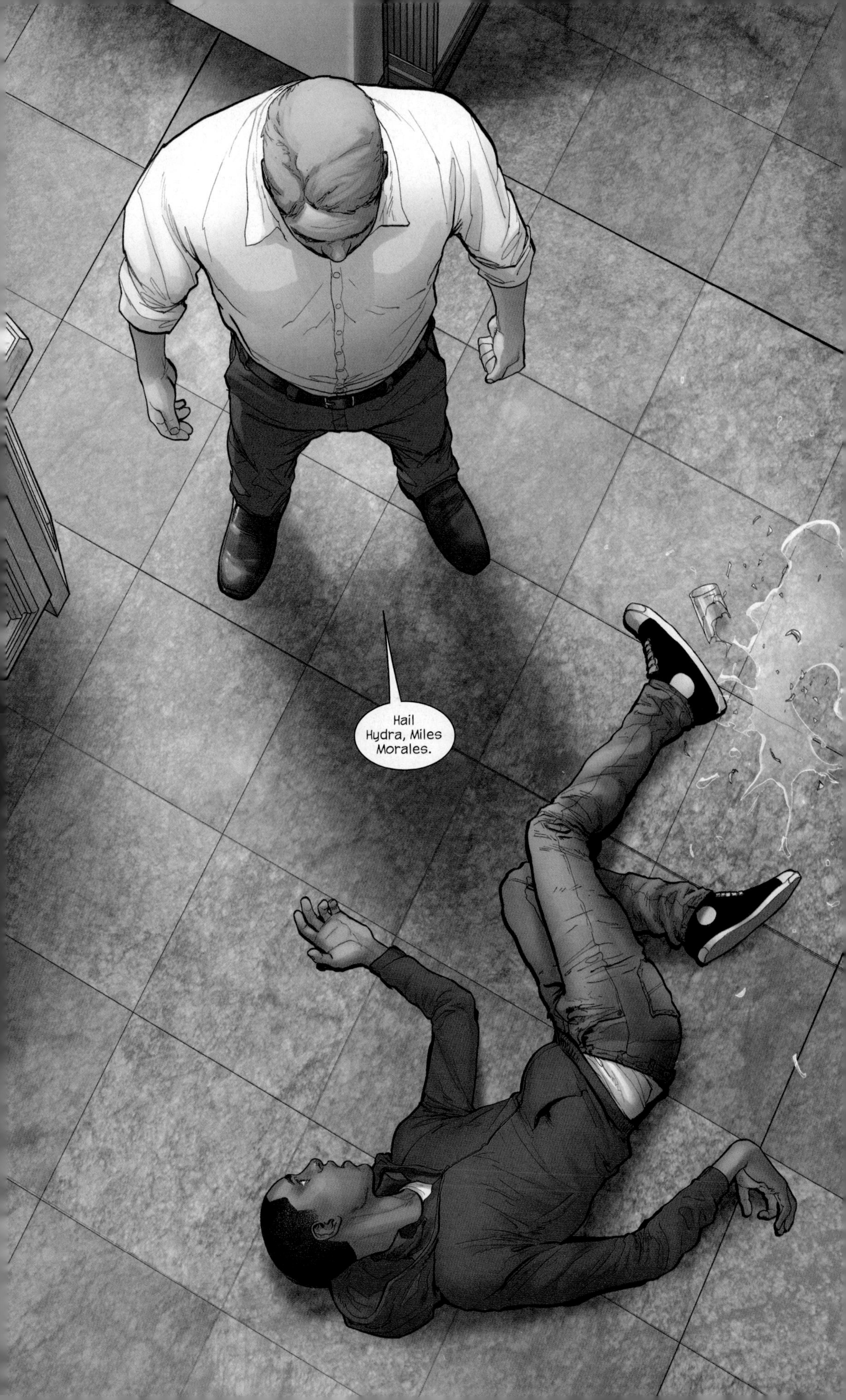
Hail Hydra, Miles Morales.

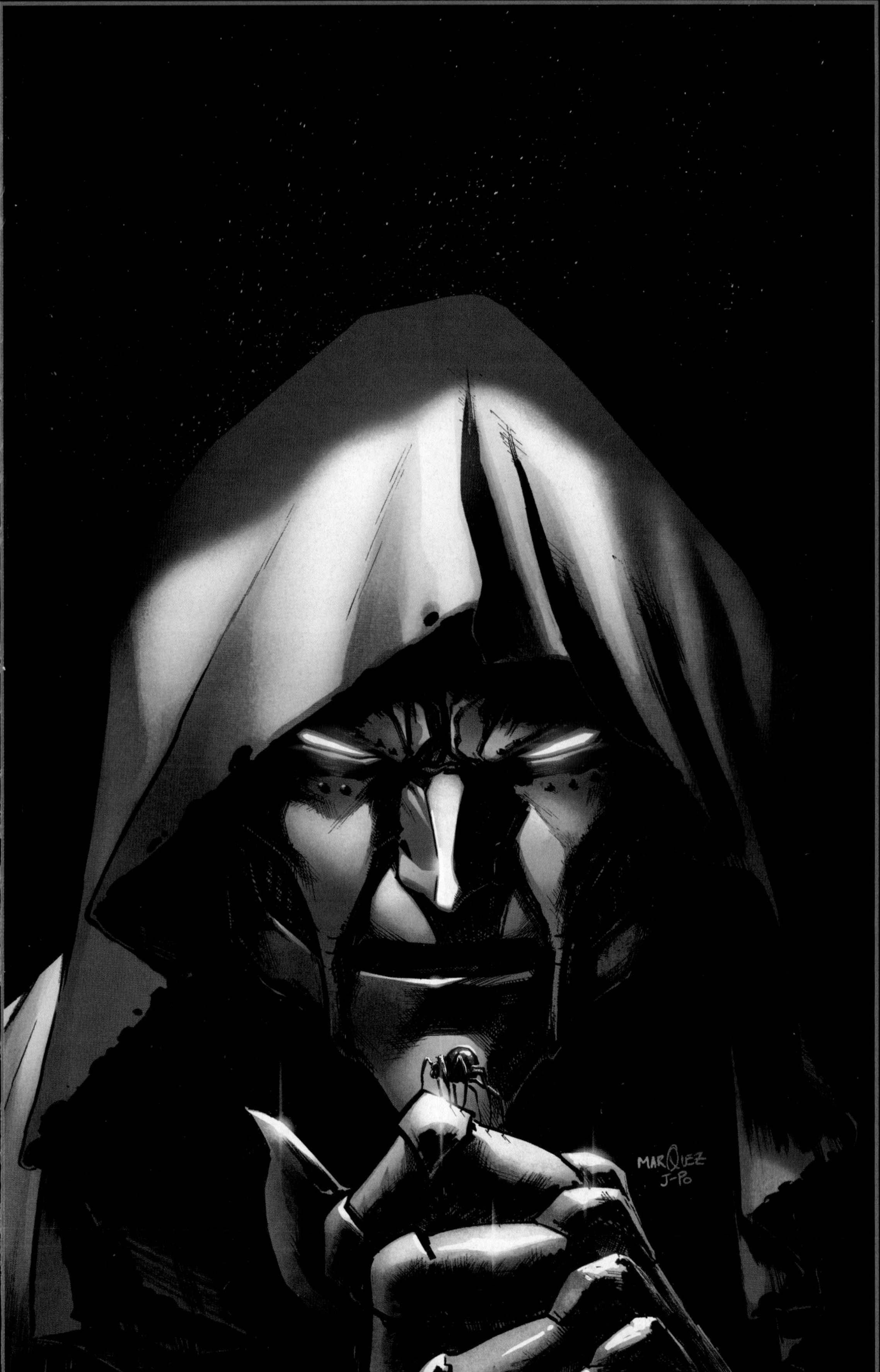
MARQUEZ
J-Po

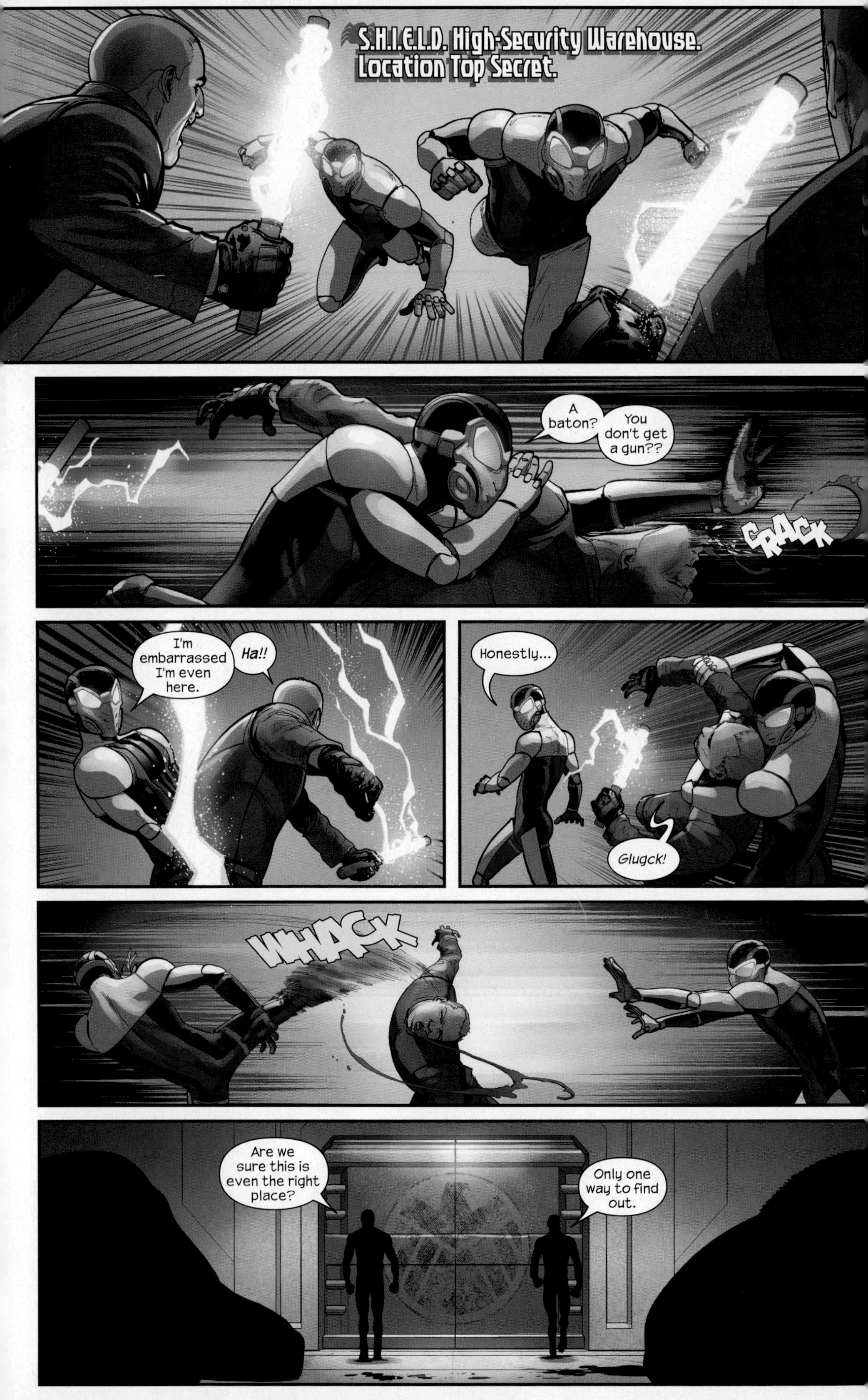
S.H.I.E.L.D. High-Security Warehouse.
Location Top Secret.
A baton?
You don't get a gun??
CRACK
I'm embarrassed I'm even here.
Ha!!
Honestly...
Glugck!
WHACK
Are we sure this is even the right place?
Only one way to find out.

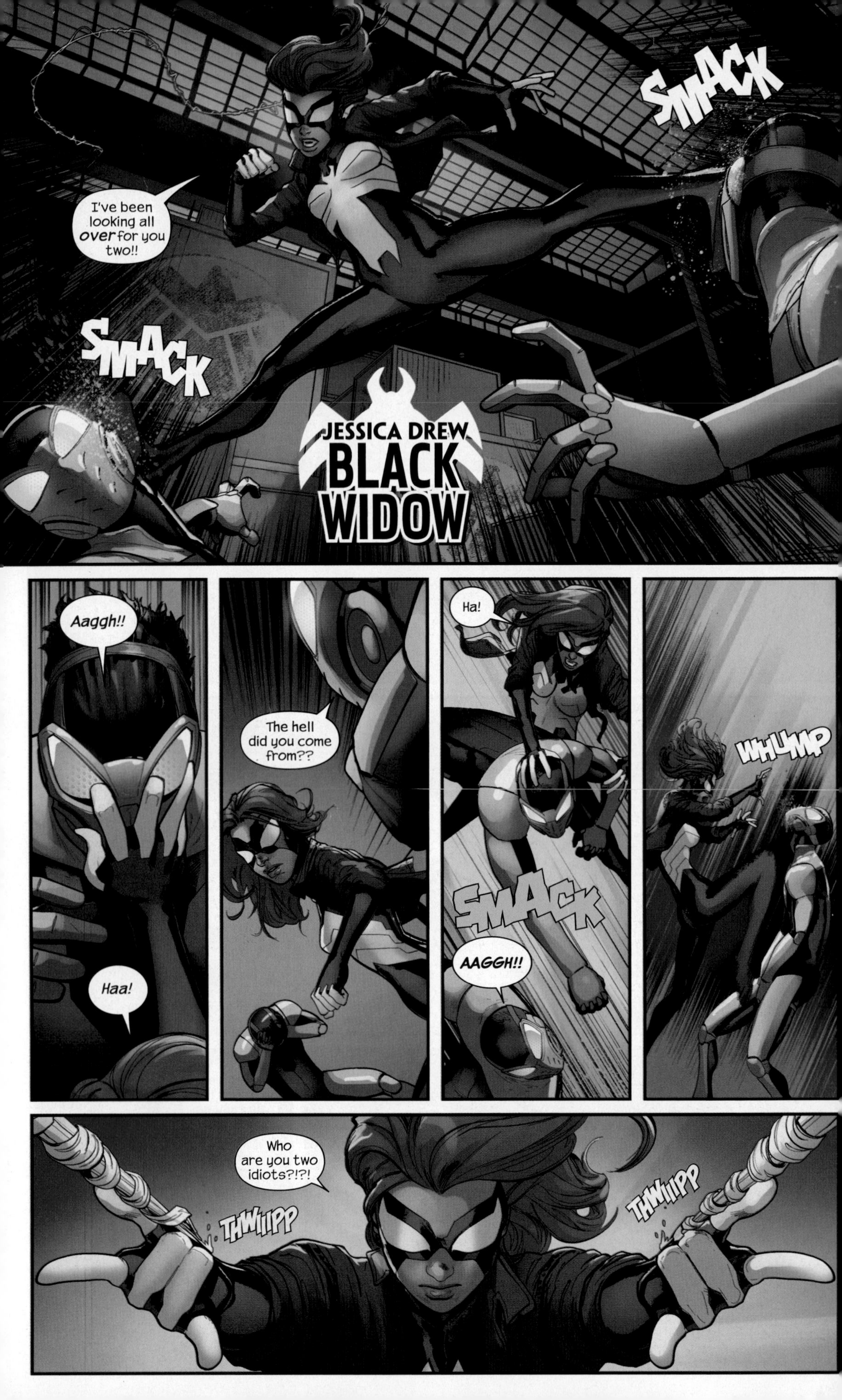
I've been looking all over for you two!!
SMACK
SMACK
JESSICA DREW
BLACK WIDOW
Aaggh!!
Haa!
The hell did you come from??
Ha!
SMACK
AAGGH!!
WHUMP
Who are you two idiots?!?!
THWIIIPP
THWIIIPP

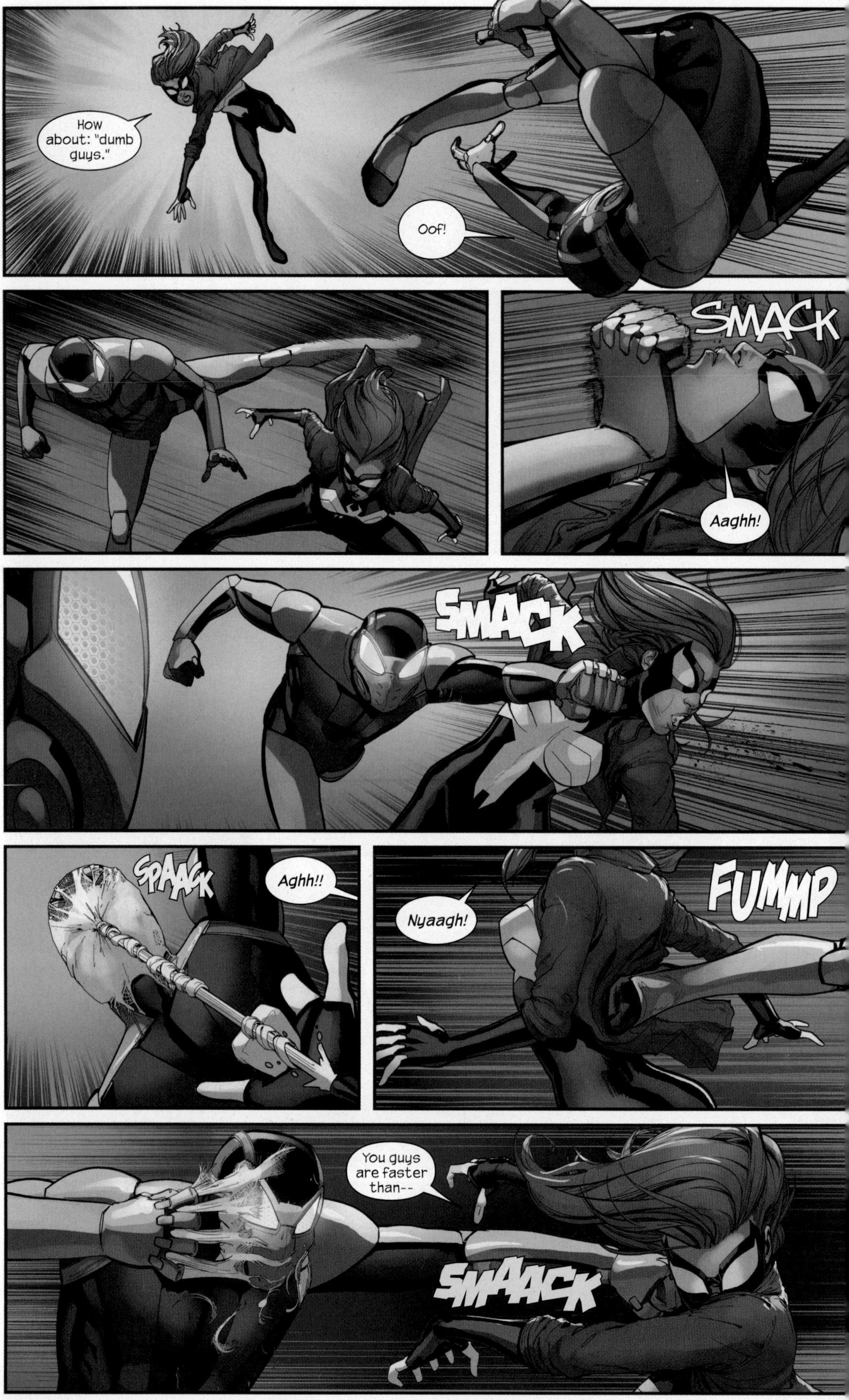
How about: "dumb guys."
Oof!
SMACK
Aaghh!
SMACK
SPAACK
Aghh!!
Nyaagh!
FUMMP
You guys are faster than--
SMAACK

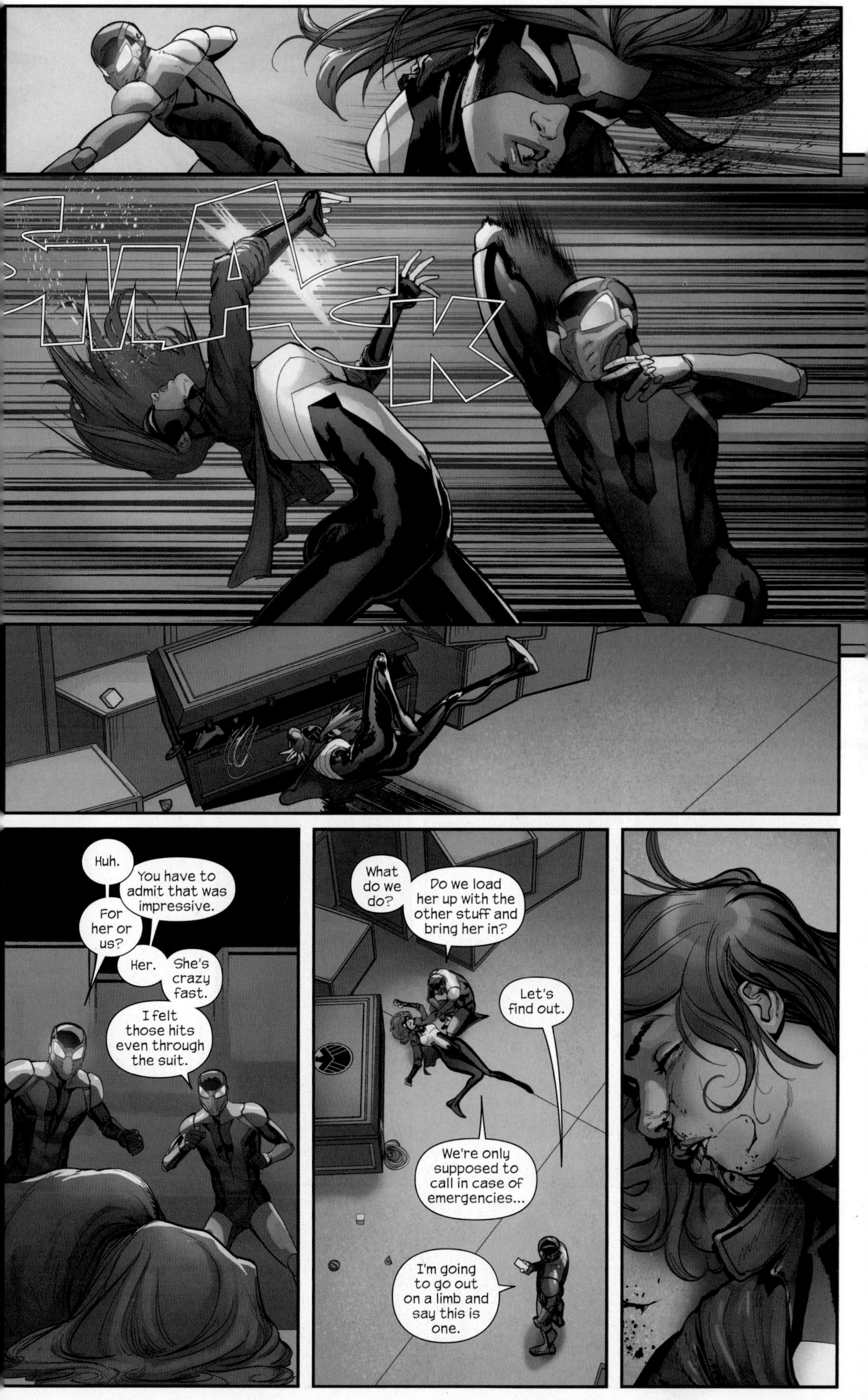
WHACK
Huh.
You have to admit that was impressive.
For her or us?
Her.
She's crazy fast.
I felt those hits even through the suit.
What do we do?
Do we load her up with the other stuff and bring her in?
Let's find out.
We're only supposed to call in case of emergencies...
I'm going to go out on a limb and say this is one.

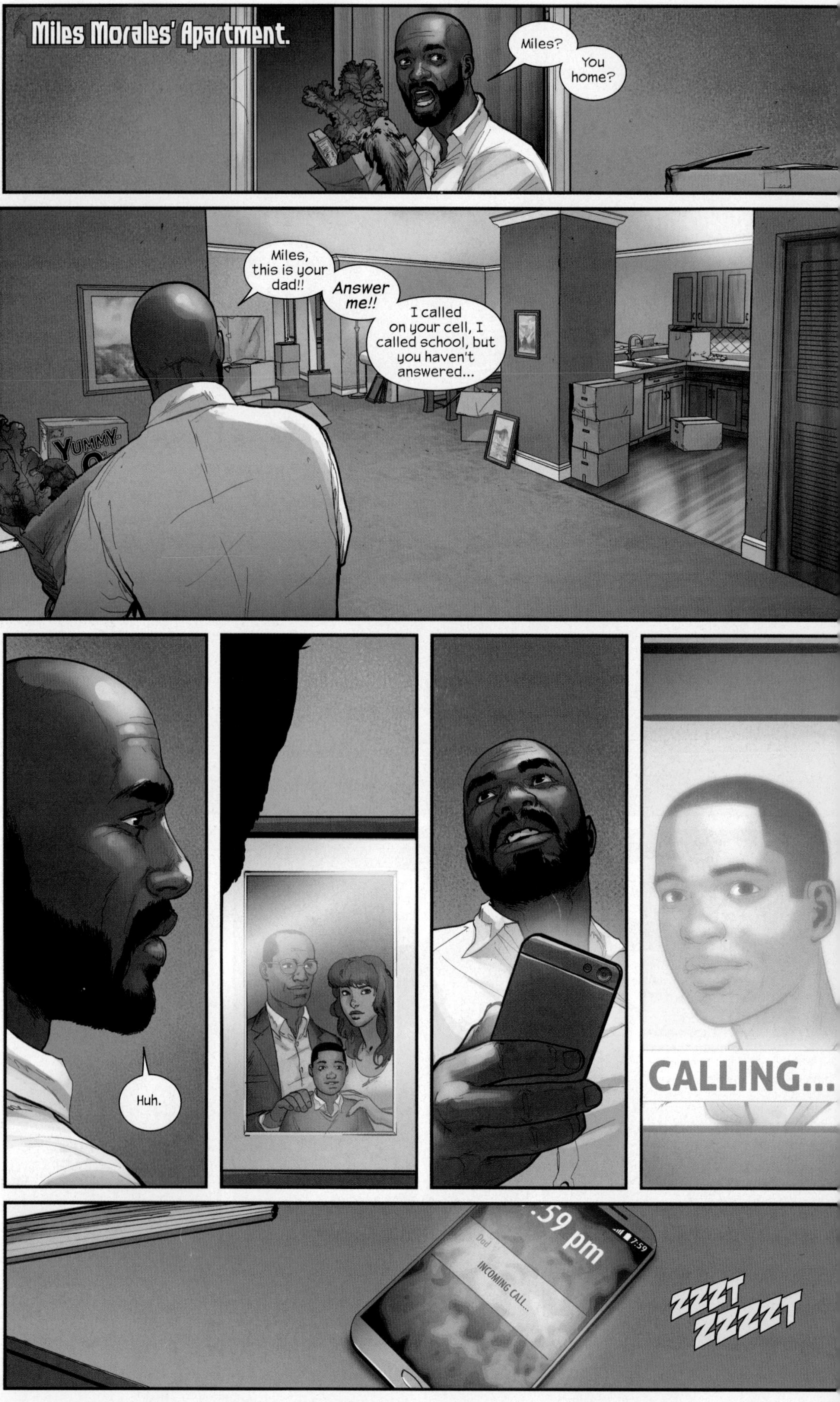
Miles Morales' Apartment.
Miles?
You home?
Miles, this is your dad!!
Answer me!!
I called on your cell, I called school, but you haven't answered...
Huh.
CALLING...
INCOMING CALL...
ZZZT ZZZZT

DINC

8:03 pm

Gankster (now)
Dude, your dad has
called like THREE TIMES

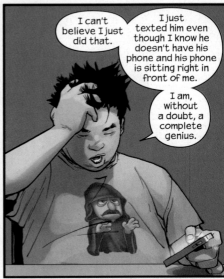

I can't believe I just did that.

I just texted him even though I know he doesn't have his phone and his phone is sitting right in front of me.

I am, without a doubt, a complete genius.

KNOCK KNOCK

Oh, uh, hey, Judge.

Here's your stick back.

Did it help?

Incredibly.

Hey, did you happen to see Katie Bishop walking around in the dorm hall?

No, I have to ask Katie something.

You're looking for Miles?

Isn't Katie always standing next to Miles?

Not always.

Oh, that's right.

Sometimes Miles is on a little mission.

Saving the world.

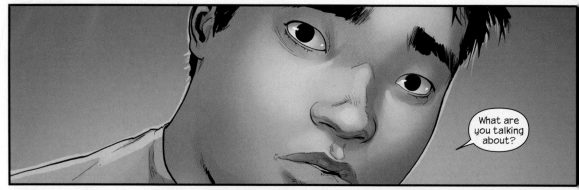

What are you talking about?

Please.

I roomed with you goofballs for a whole year.

Could you at least do me the favor of not acting like I'm stupid?

Um...

I don't know what you're talking about.

"Um..."

I'm sure Spider-Man does.

I'll let you know if I see his girlfriend walking around.

Uh-oh.

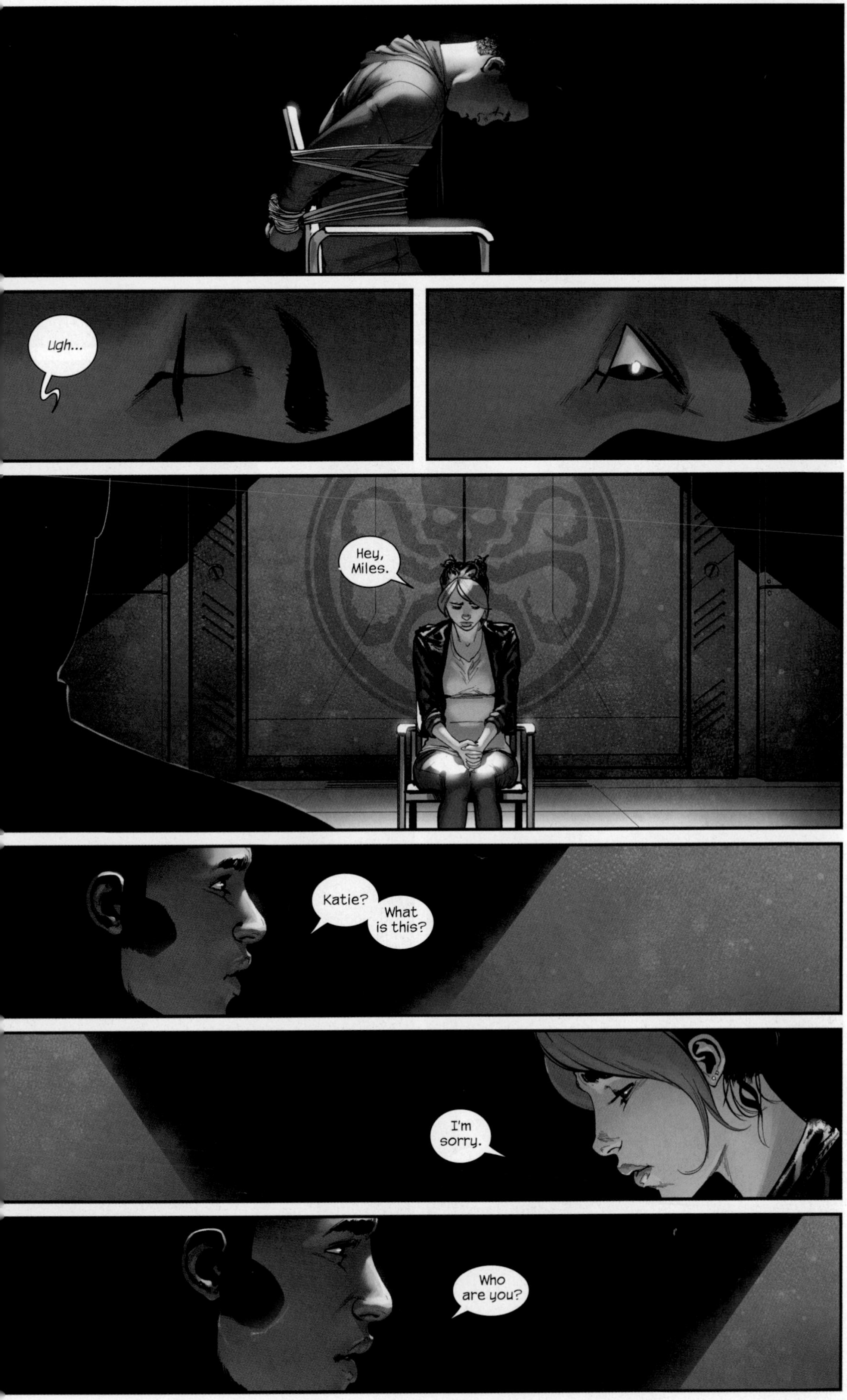
Ugh...
Hey, Miles.
Katie?
What is this?
I'm sorry.
Who are you?

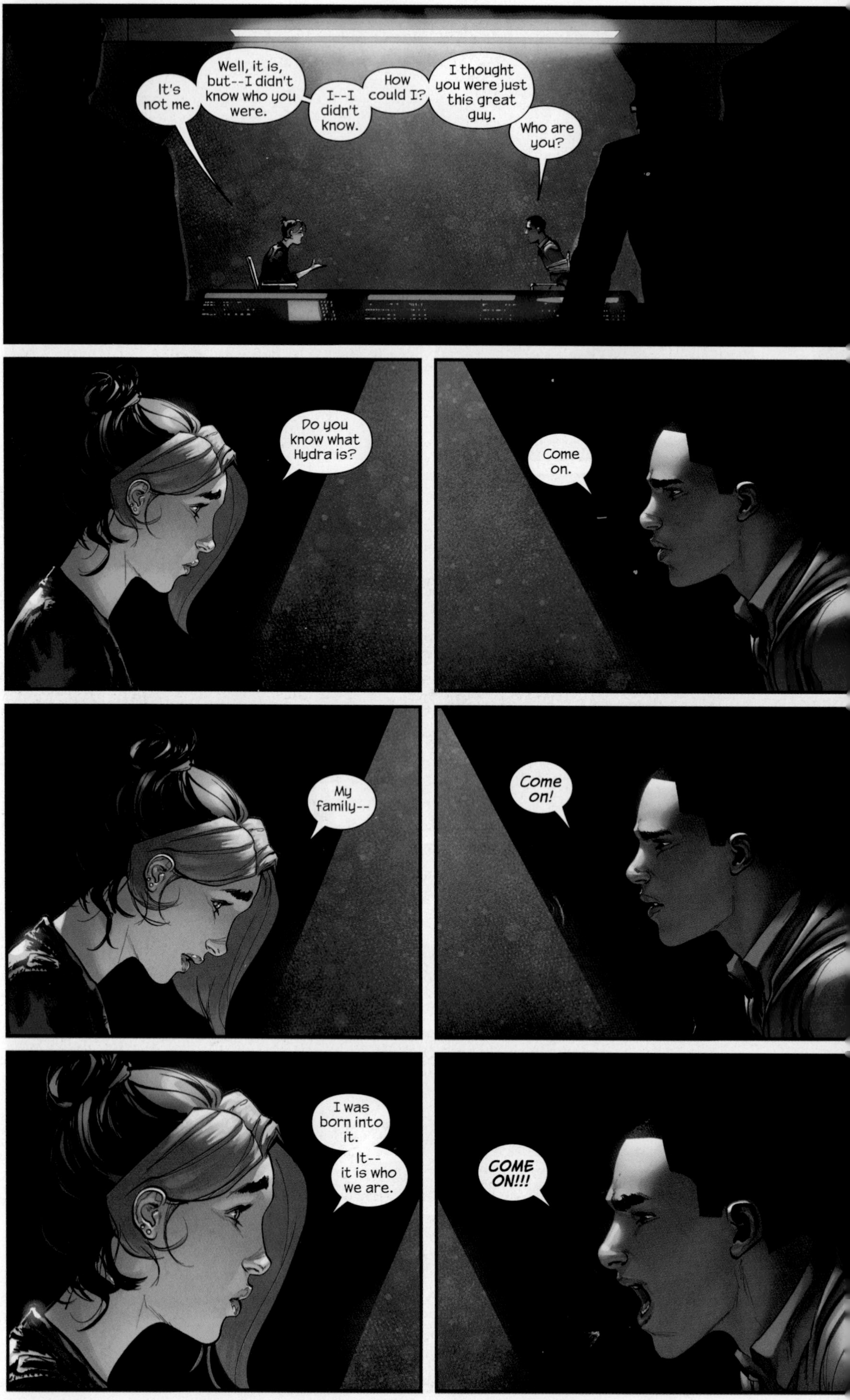

It's not me.
Well, it is, but--I didn't know who you were.
I--I didn't know.
How could I?
I thought you were just this great guy.
Who are you?
Do you know what Hydra is?
Come on.
My family--
Come on!
I was born into it.
It--it is who we are.
COME ON!!!

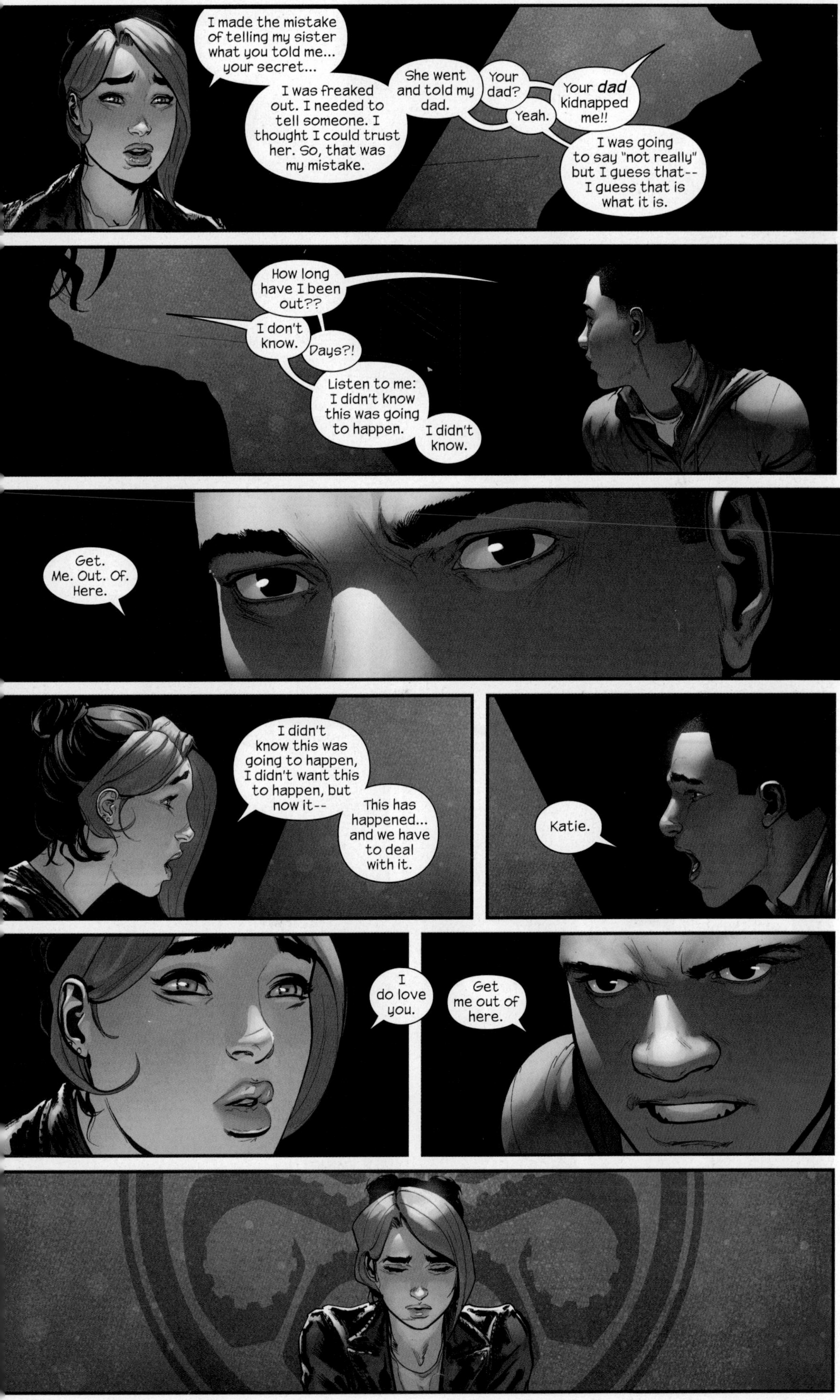

I made the mistake of telling my sister what you told me... your secret...
I was freaked out. I needed to tell someone. I thought I could trust her. So, that was my mistake.
She went and told my dad.
Your dad?
Yeah.
Your *dad* kidnapped me!!
I was going to say "not really" but I guess that-- I guess that is what it is.
How long have I been out??
I don't know.
Days?!
Listen to me: I didn't know this was going to happen.
I didn't know.
Get. Me. Out. Of. Here.
I didn't know this was going to happen, I didn't want this to happen, but now it--
This has happened... and we have to deal with it.
Katie.
I do love you.
Get me out of here.

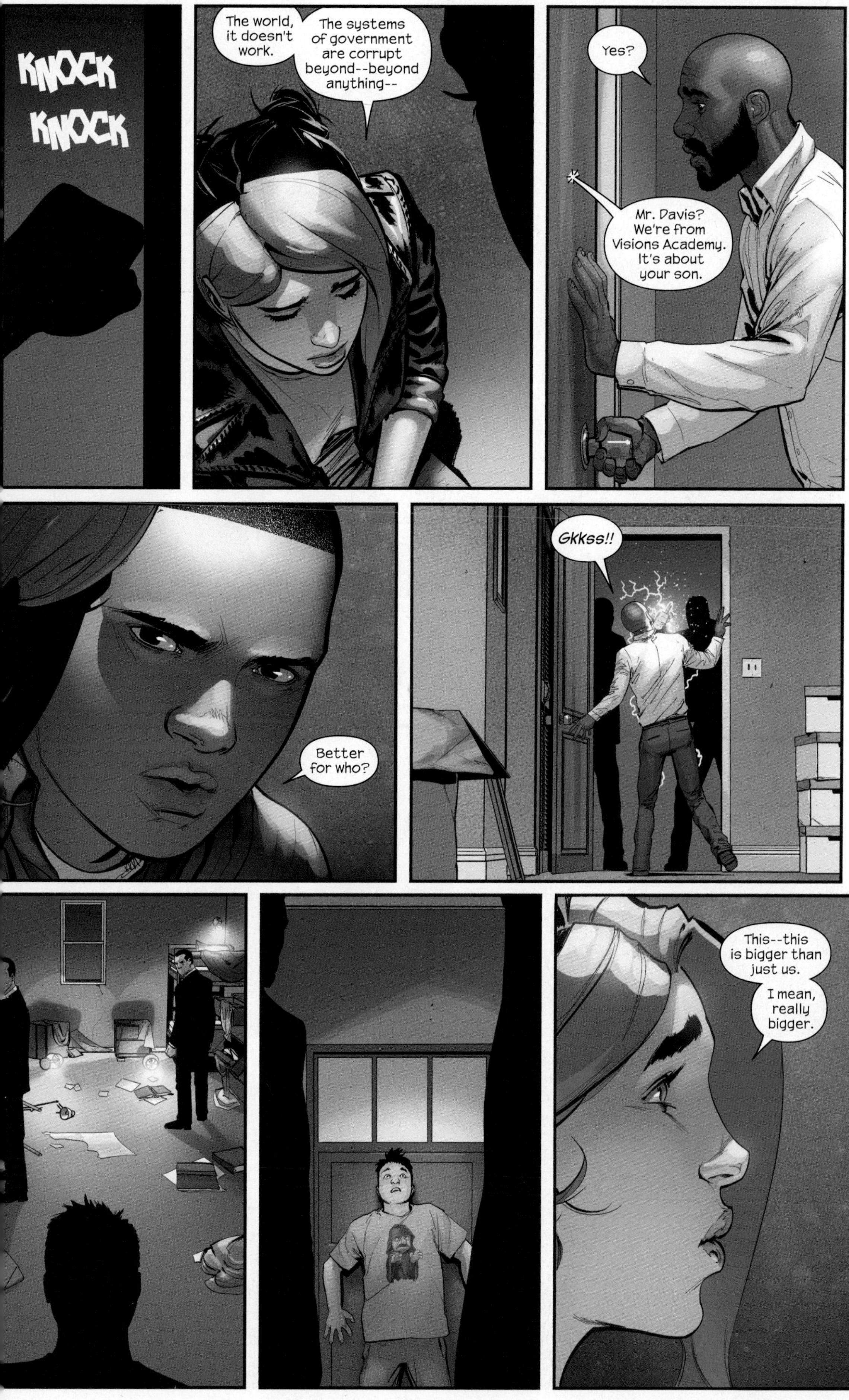

KNOCK
KNOCK
The world, it doesn't work.
The systems of government are corrupt beyond--beyond anything--
Yes?
Mr. Davis? We're from Visions Academy. It's about your son.
Better for who?
Gkkss!!
This--this is bigger than just us.
I mean, really bigger.

Miles, don't!

I know I'm going to have to fight my way out of here, but I'm going to!!

And I'm going to pull this entire thing down around your family's ears!!

Miles!

And if it's not clear, we're *broken up!*

Miles.

Behave.

Dad...

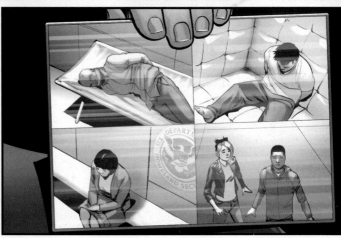

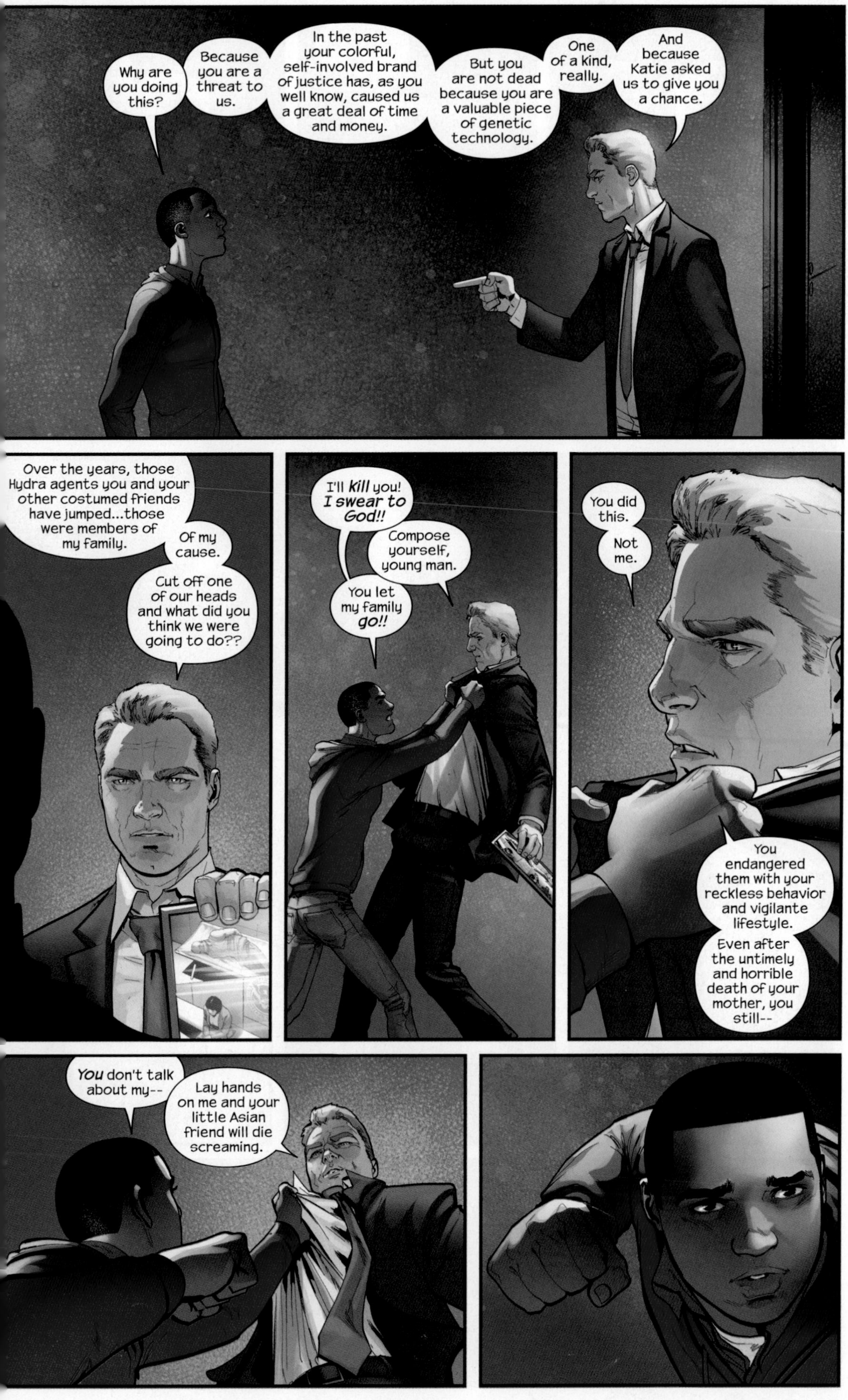

Why are you doing this?
Because you are a threat to us.
In the past your colorful, self-involved brand of justice has, as you well know, caused us a great deal of time and money.
But you are not dead because you are a valuable piece of genetic technology.
One of a kind, really.
And because Katie asked us to give you a chance.
Over the years, those Hydra agents you and your other costumed friends have jumped...those were members of my family.
Of my cause.
Cut off one of our heads and what did you think we were going to do??
I'll *kill* you! *I swear to God!!*
Compose yourself, young man.
You let my family *go!!*
You did this.
Not me.
You endangered them with your reckless behavior and vigilante lifestyle.
Even after the untimely and horrible death of your mother, you still--
*You* don't talk about my--
Lay hands on me and your little Asian friend will die screaming.

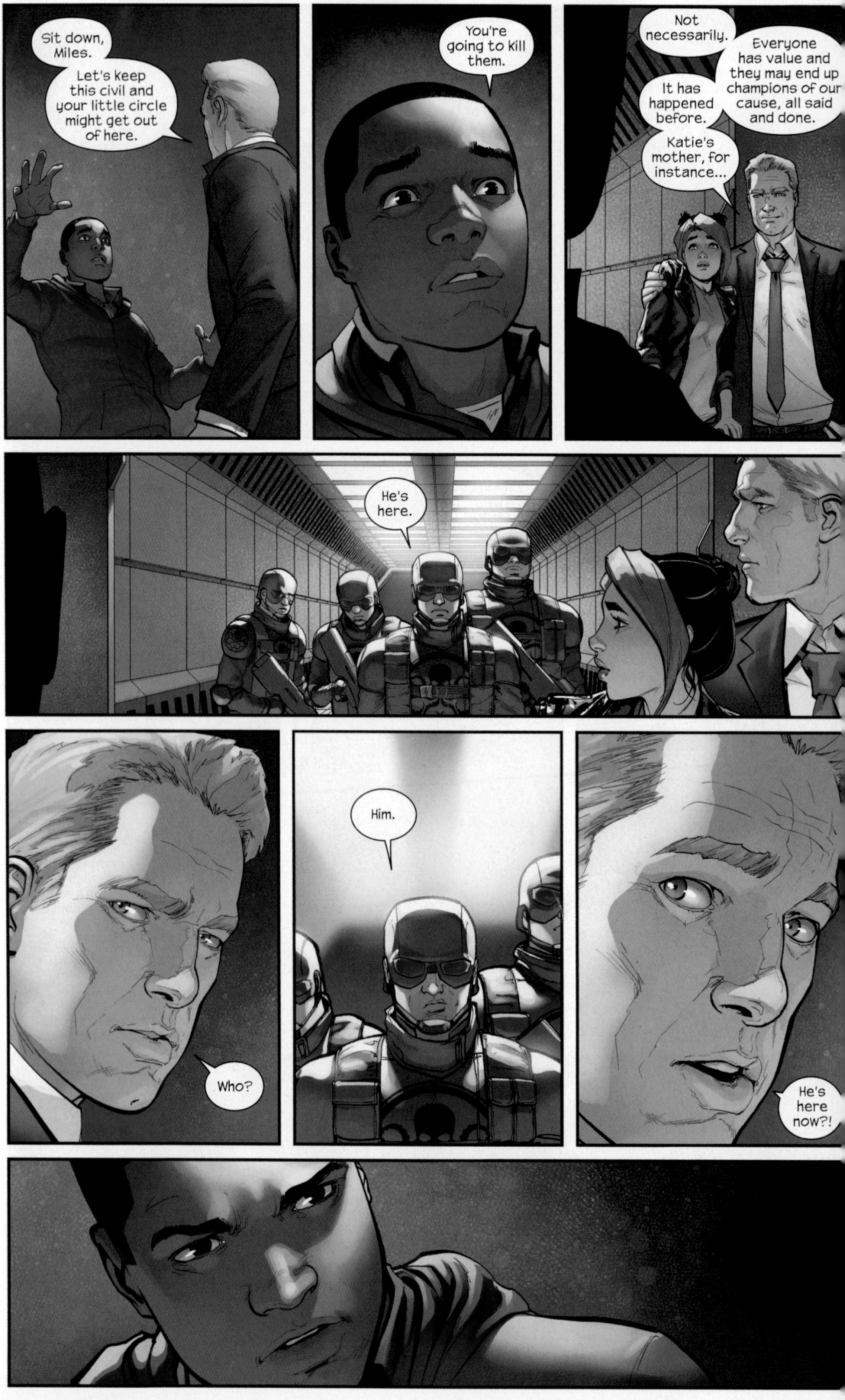
Sit down, Miles.
Let's keep this civil and your little circle might get out of here.
You're going to kill them.
Not necessarily.
Everyone has value and they may end up champions of our cause, all said and done.
It has happened before.
Katie's mother, for instance...
He's here.
Who?
Him.
He's here now?!

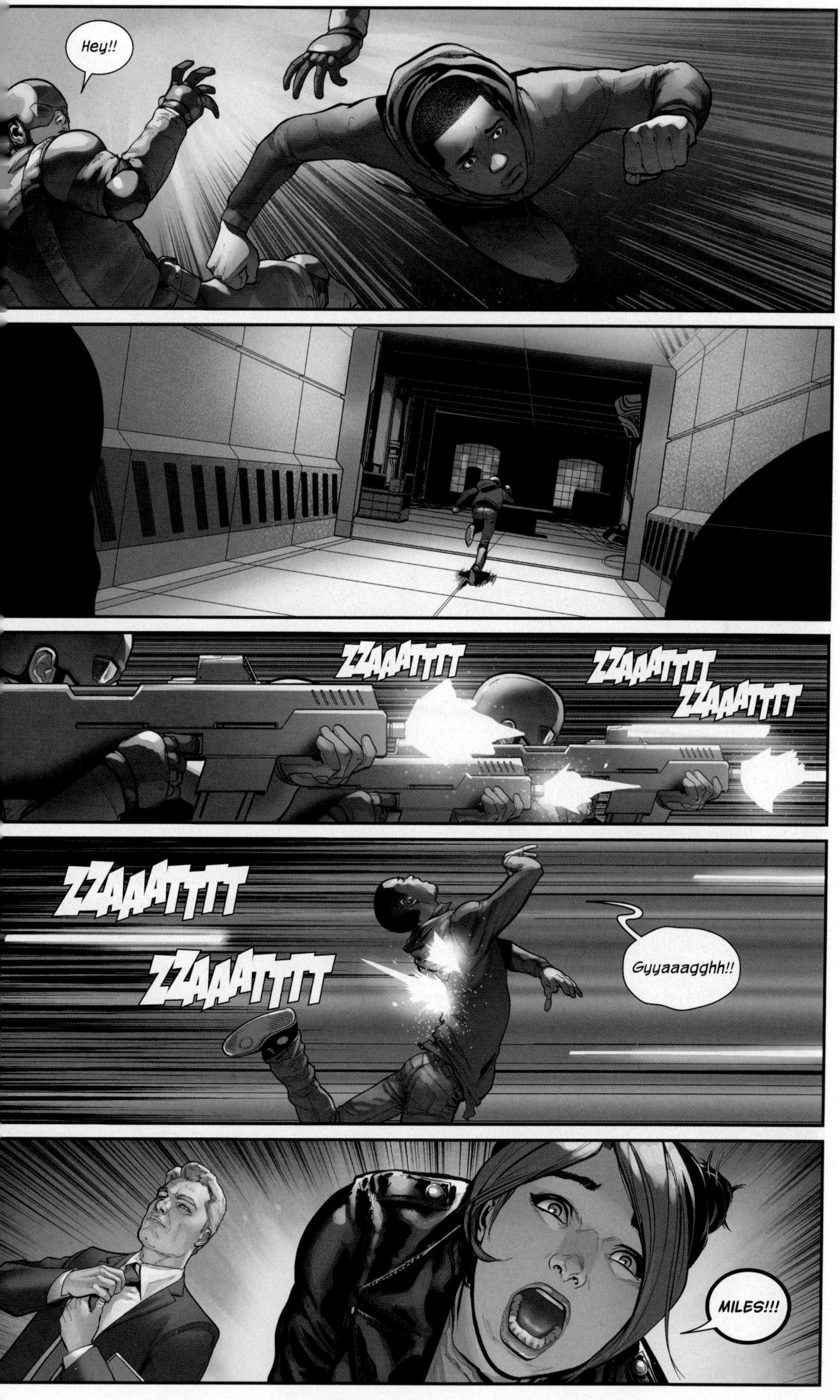
Hey!!
ZZAAATTTT
ZZAAATTTT
ZZAAATTTT
ZZAAATTTT
ZZAAATTTT
Gyyaaagghh!!
MILES!!!

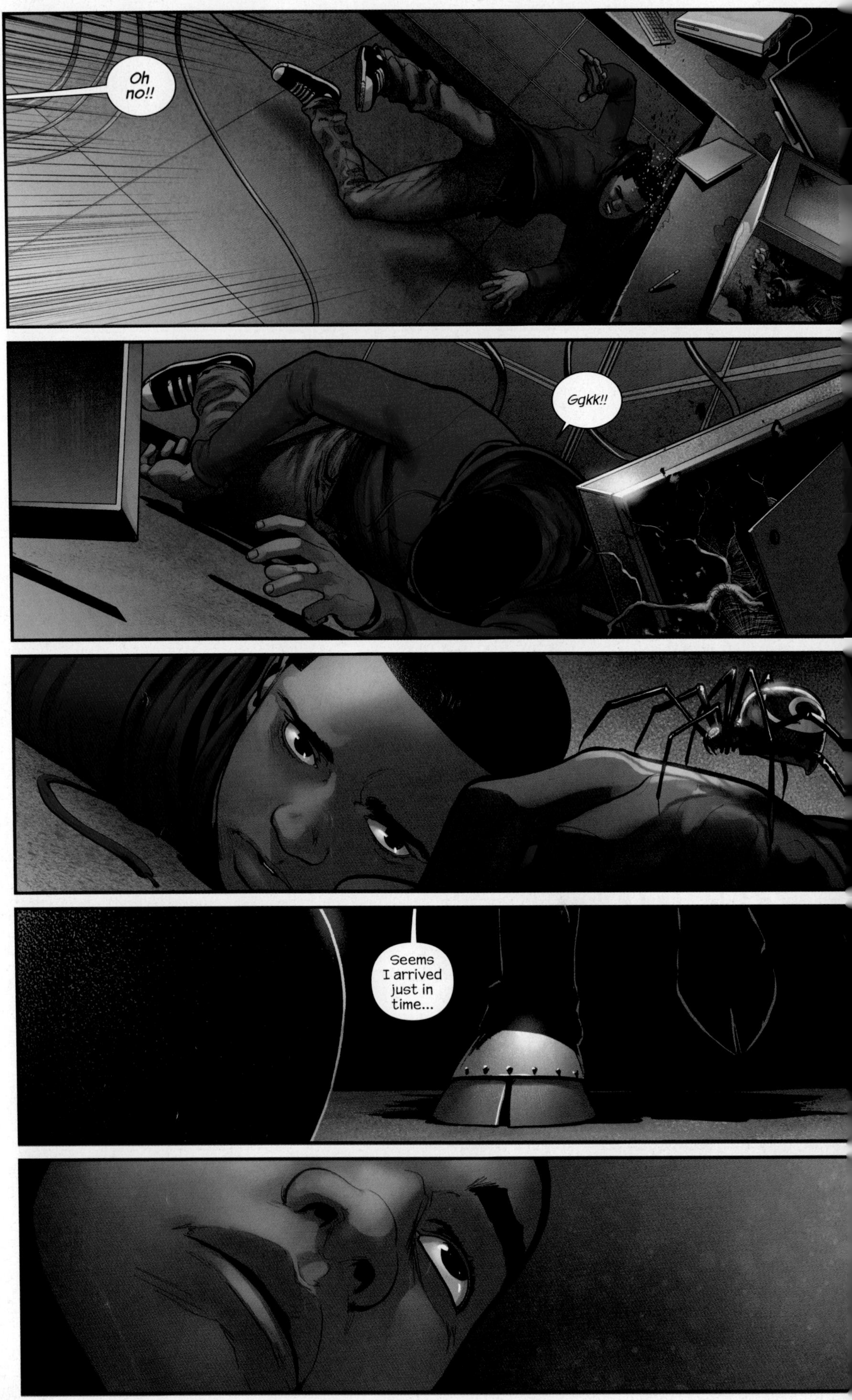
Oh no!!
Ggkk!!
Seems I arrived just in time...

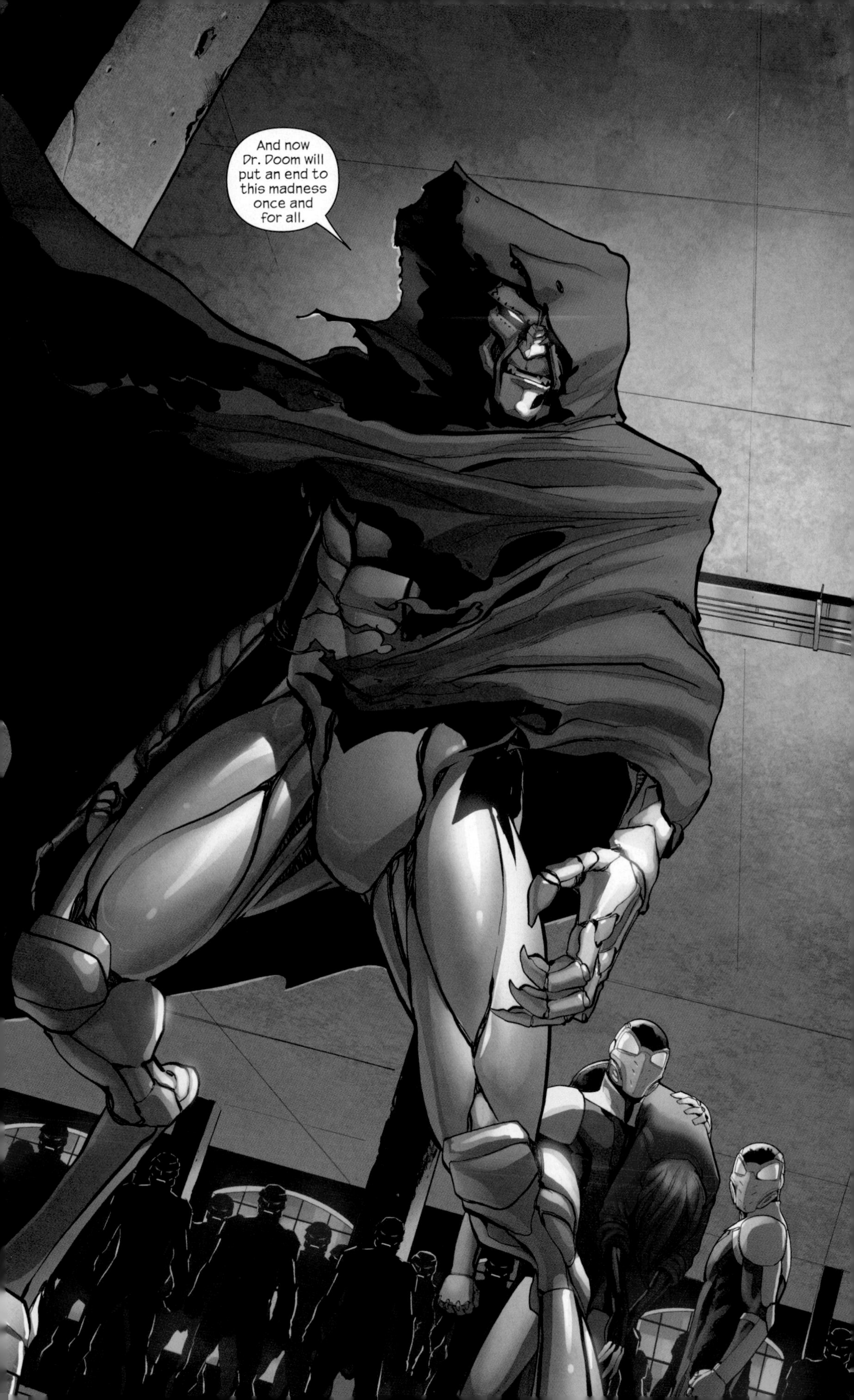
And now Dr. Doom will put an end to this madness once and for all.

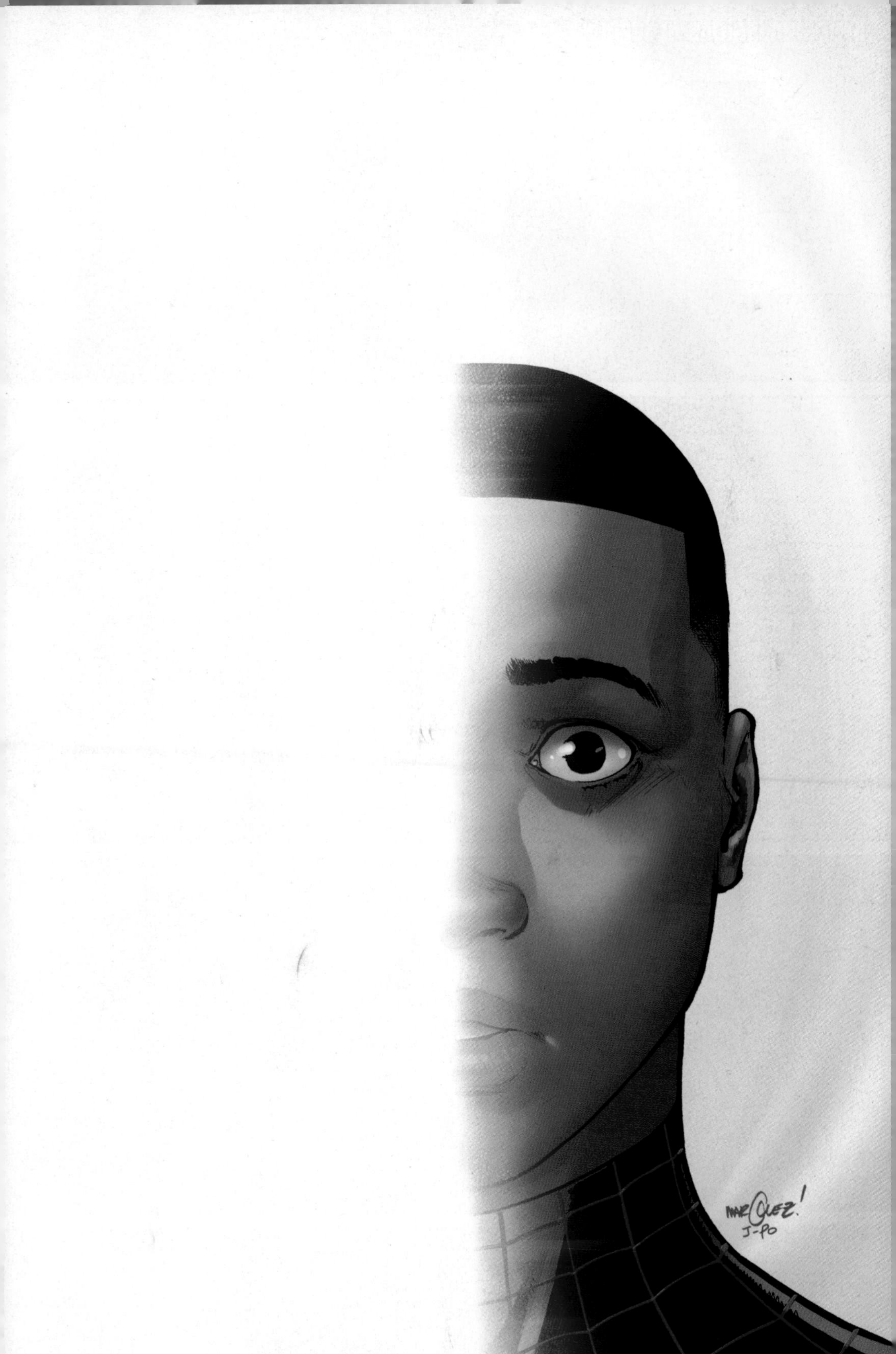
MARQUEZ!
J-PO

**Brooklyn Visions Academy.**

Has anyone seen Miles Morales, Ganke Lee or Katie Bishop?

Judge?

No.

No, I ain't seen them.

Well, I don't take kindly to absences.

Anyway, let's get back to our discussion of the creation of S.H.I.E.L.D.

It was the later days of World War II....

Yo, Gank!

Miles?

Ganke?

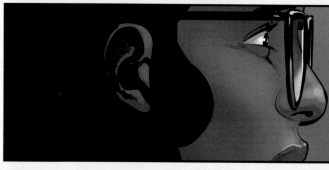

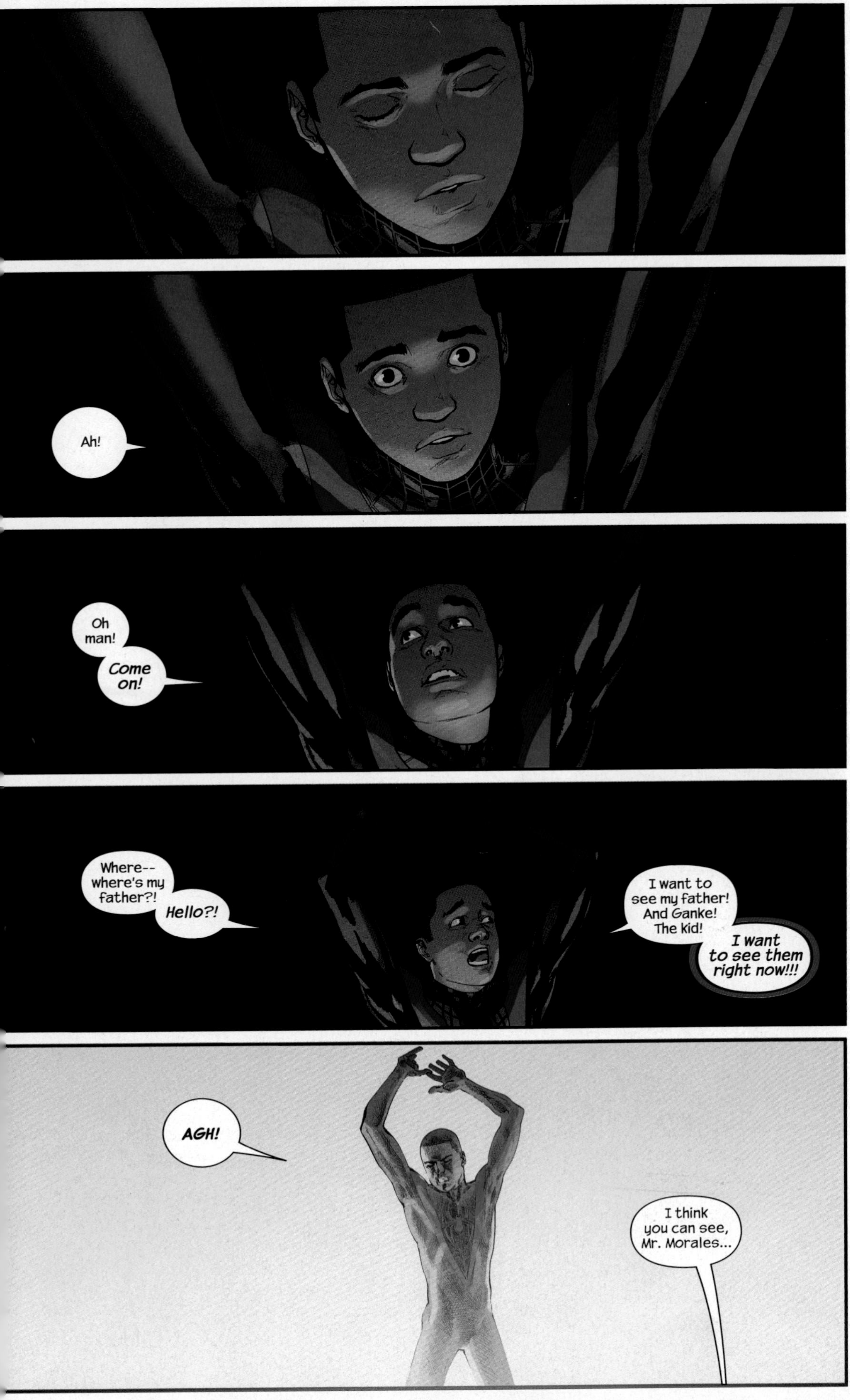
Ah!
Oh man!
Come on!
Where-- where's my father?!
Hello?!
I want to see my father! And Ganke! The kid!
I want to see them right now!!!
AGH!
I think you can see, Mr. Morales...

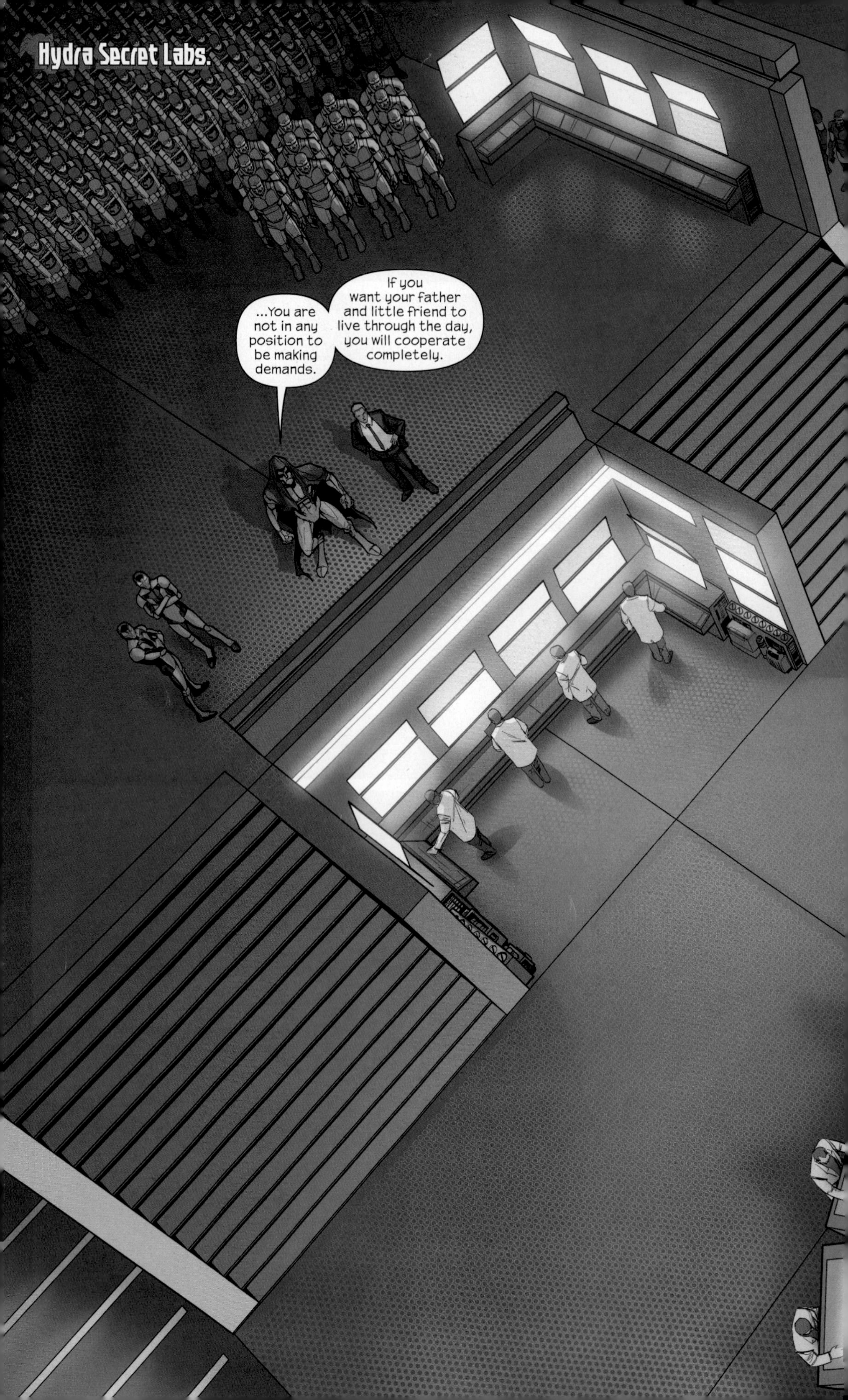
Hydra Secret Labs.
If you want your father and little friend to live through the day, you will cooperate completely.
...You are not in any position to be making demands.

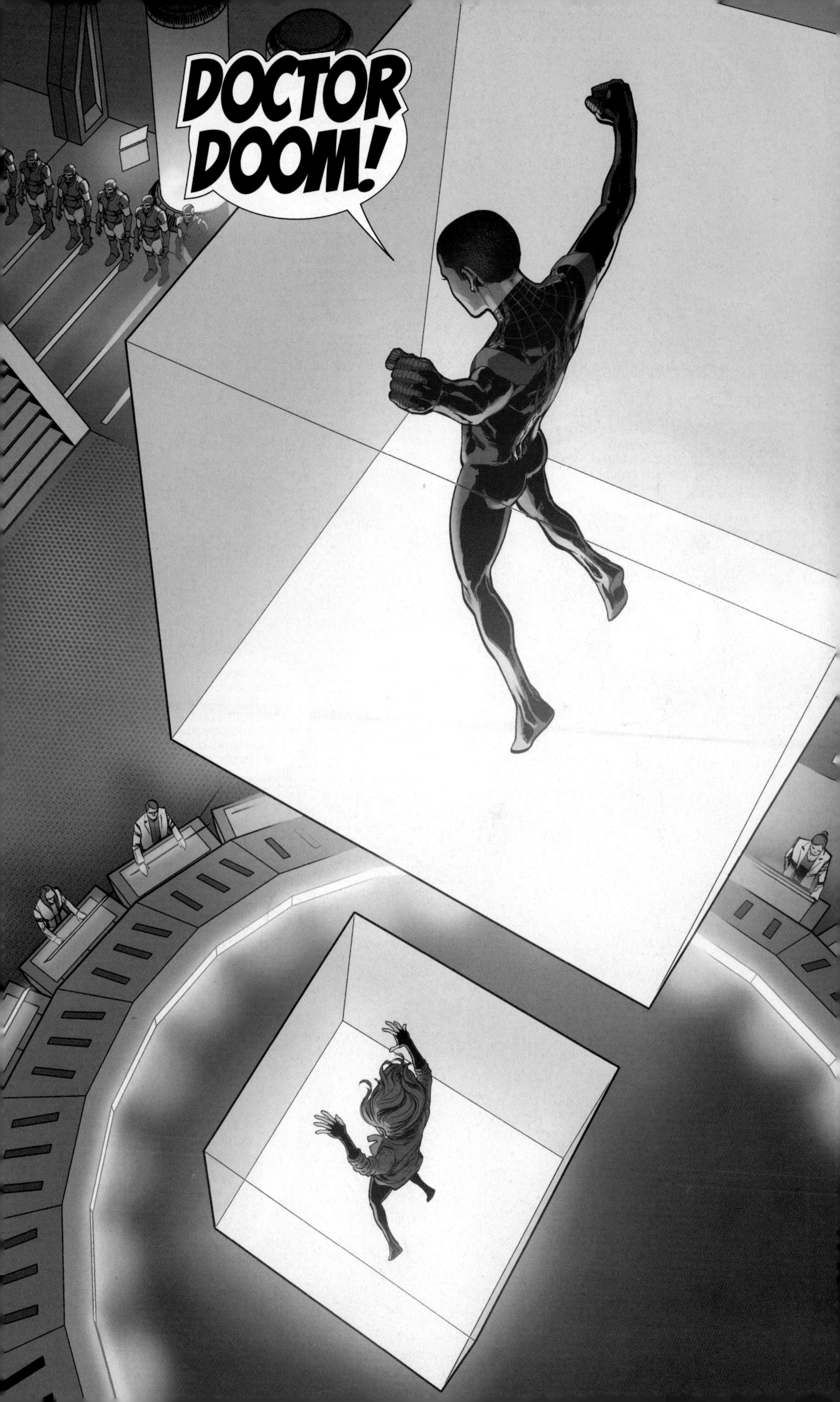
DOCTOR DOOM!

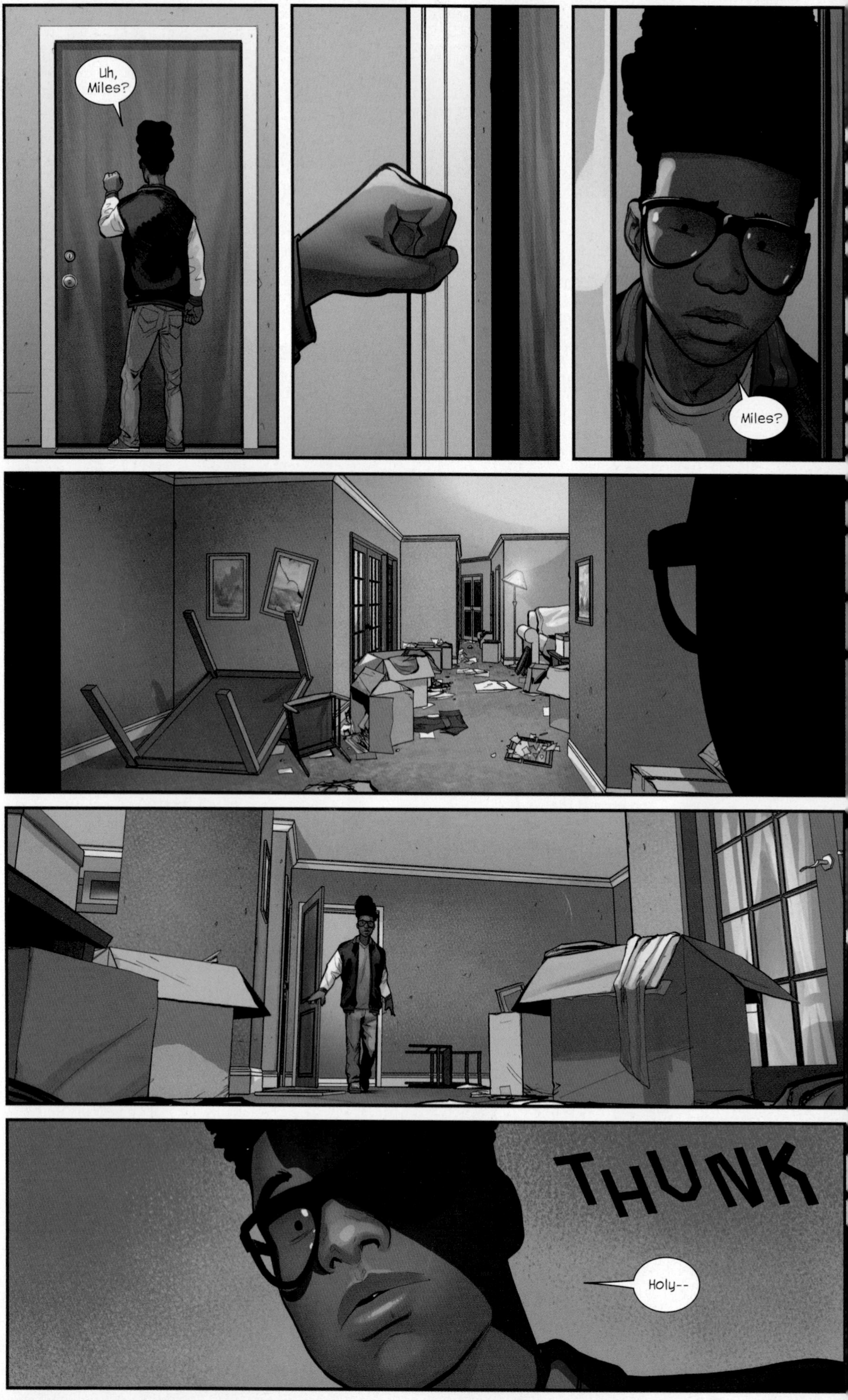
Uh, Miles?
Miles?
THUNK
Holy--

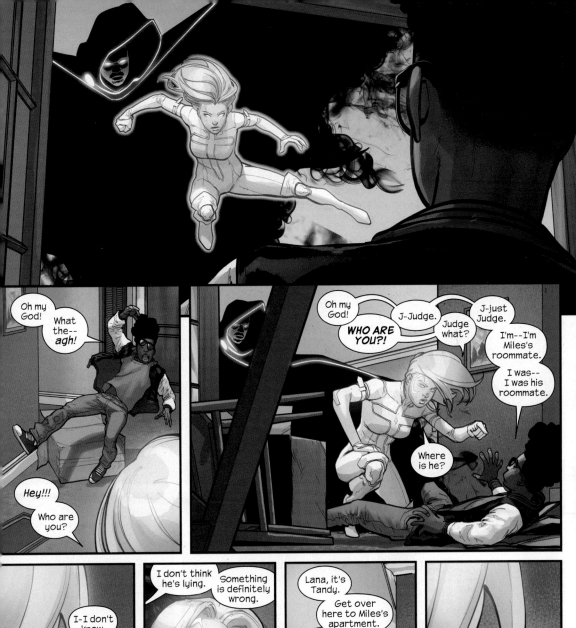

Oh my God! What the-- agh!

Hey!!!

Who are you?

Oh my God! WHO ARE YOU?!

J-Judge.

Judge what?

J-just Judge.

I'm--I'm Miles's roommate.

I was-- I was his roommate.

Where is he?

I-I don't know.

I came here because he wasn't at school.

And I walk in a-and his house looks like this!!!

I-I think something happened to him.

I don't think he's lying.

Something is definitely wrong.

Lana, it's Tandy.

Get over here to Miles's apartment.

Something's wrong.

Call the others.

If you know something, tell us now...

I-I know who Miles really is.

That's why I think something bad has happened.

**AAAGGHH!!**

This needleless sample process is entirely fascinating.

We developed a mix of zero-point energy and microscopic laser fields.

We get to take living tissue samples without any unnecessary interaction with the subject.

His vital signs are elevated, but within range.

It reduces sample contamination.

Why can't you get what you need from him when he's dead?

We'll do that too.

Comparing the living and dead tissues of both subjects will be very illuminating.

Bishop, this will make reverse-engineering what makes a Spider-Man a very simple task.

Your dream of an army of Hydra super-soldiers will finally be a reality.

I'd hug you, but you don't seem the type.

You are correct.

**YYAAGGHHH!!!**

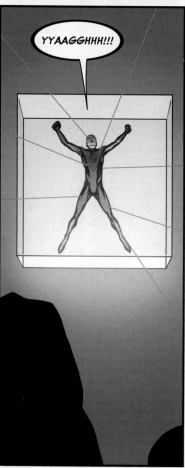

His vitals are rising!

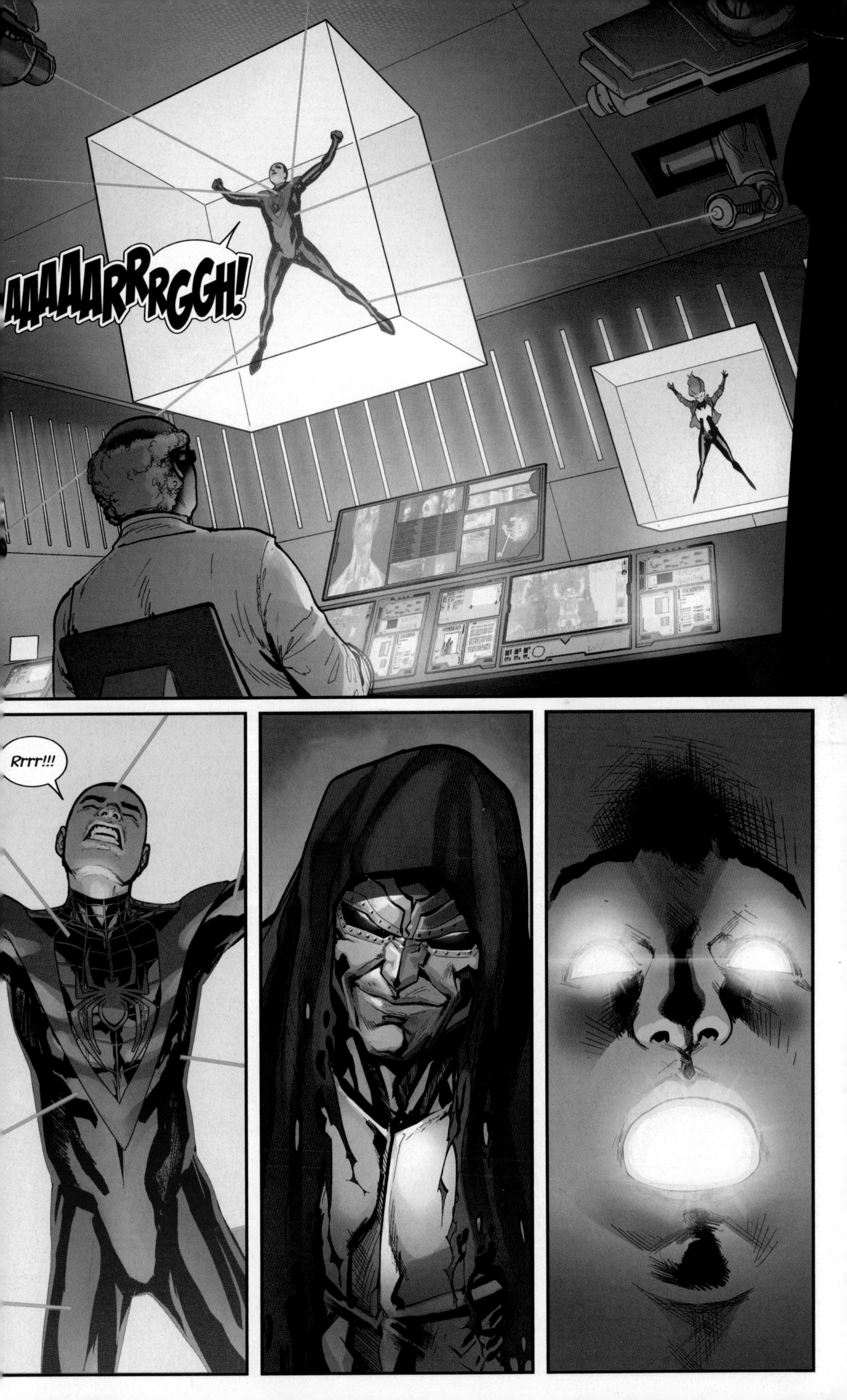
AAAAARRRGGH!
Rrrr!!!

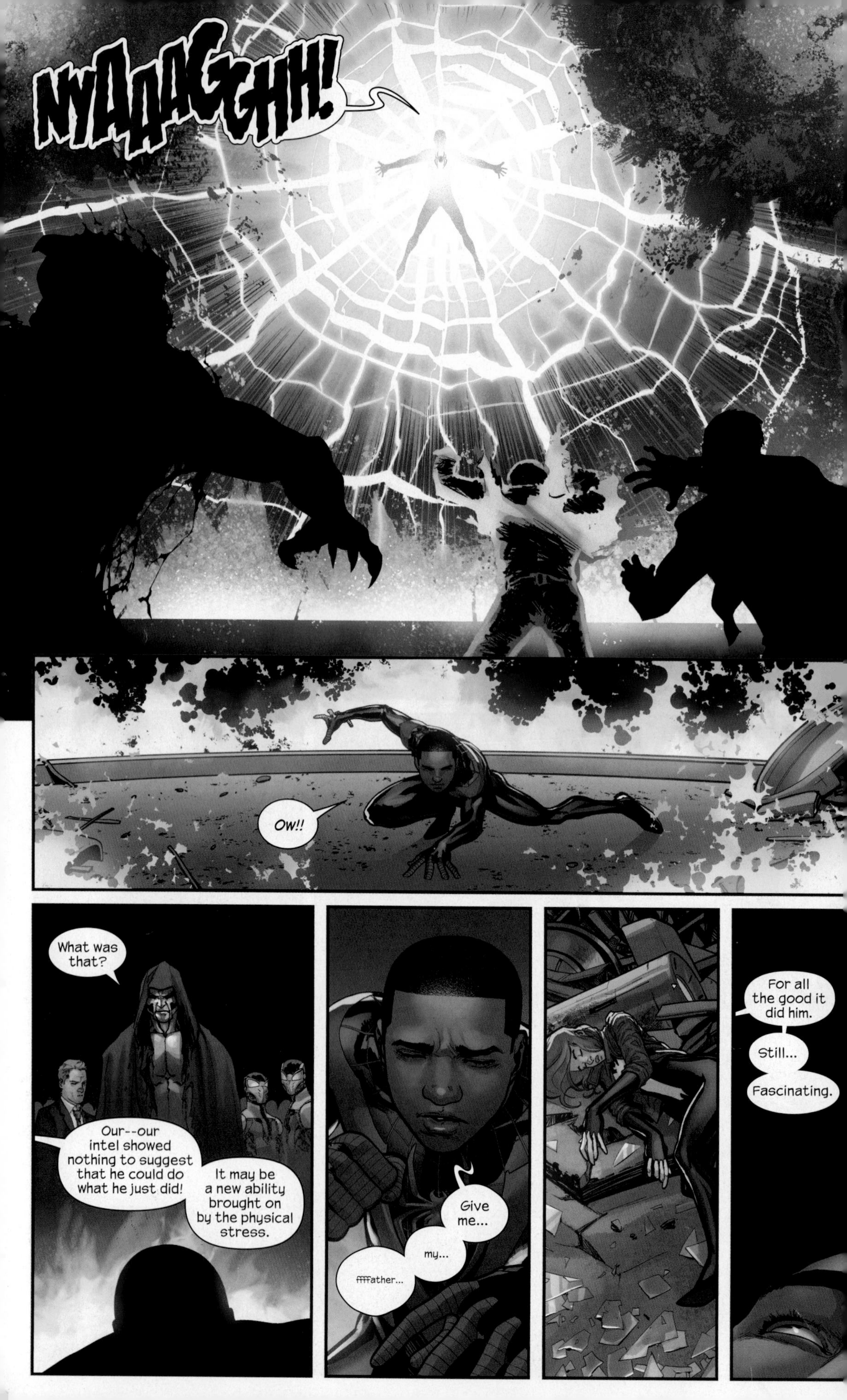
NYAAAGGHH!
Ow!!
What was that?
Our--our intel showed nothing to suggest that he could do what he just did!
It may be a new ability brought on by the physical stress.
Give me...
my...
ffffather...
For all the good it did him.
Still...
Fascinating.

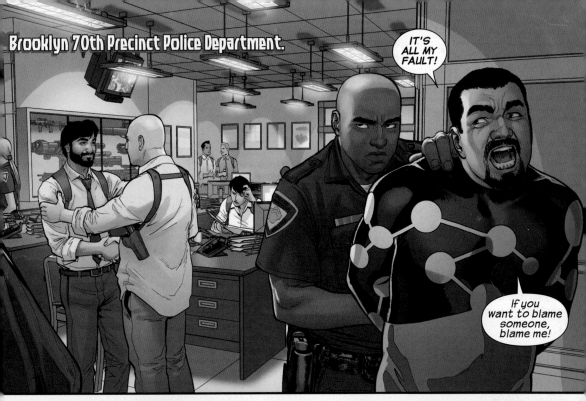

**Brooklyn 70th Precinct Police Department.**

IT'S ALL MY FAULT!

If you want to blame someone, blame me!

Oh my God!

Will all you derelicts just shut the--

Detective Hill?

What?!?!

I don't know if you remember us, but I'm Kitty Pryde... we're the Ultimates.

We need your help.

You used to be S.H.I.E.L.D.

You're a friend to Miles...

Well, Miles Morales needs our help.

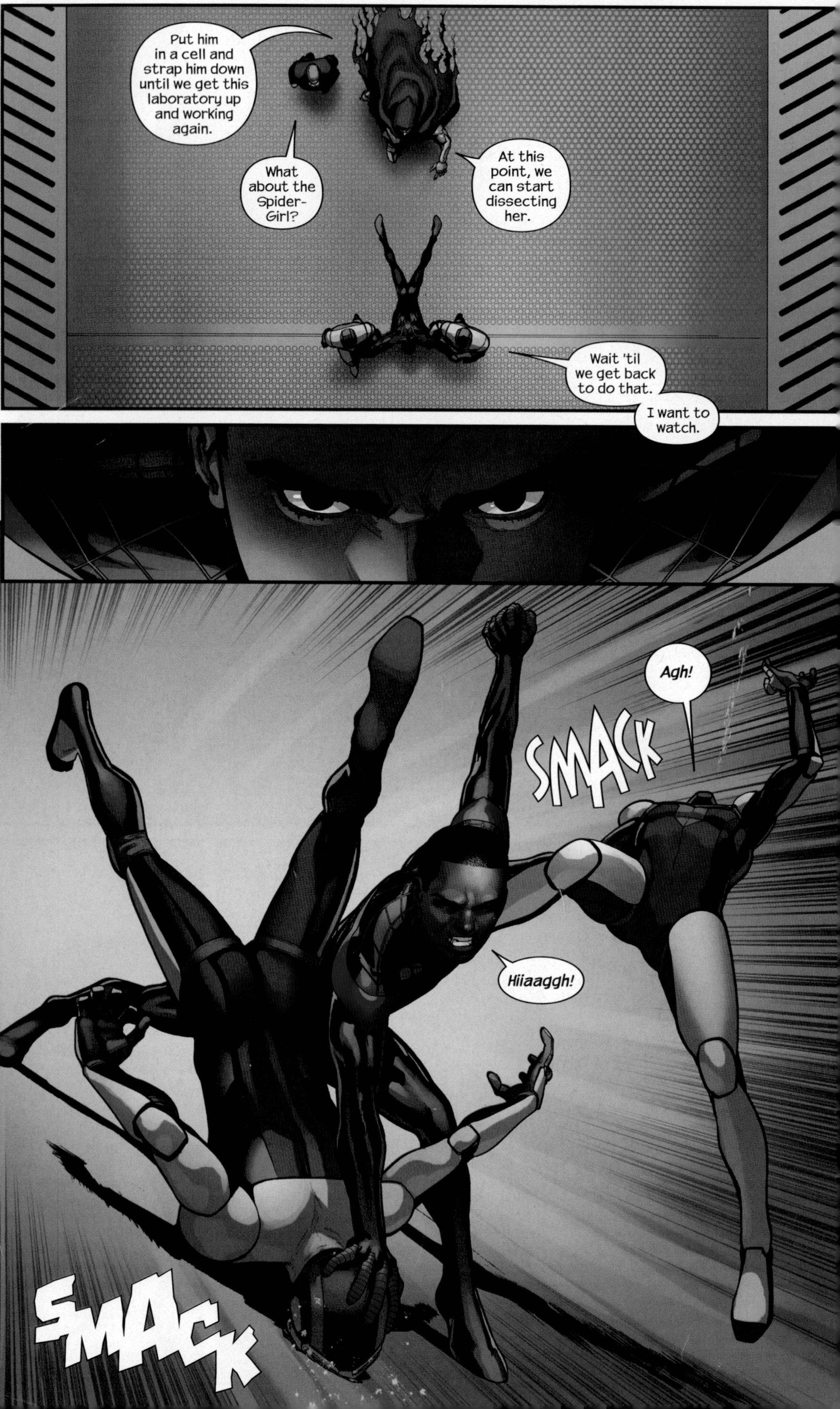
Put him in a cell and strap him down until we get this laboratory up and working again.
What about the Spider-Girl?
At this point, we can start dissecting her.
Wait 'til we get back to do that.
I want to watch.
Agh!
SMACK
Hiiaaggh!
SMACK

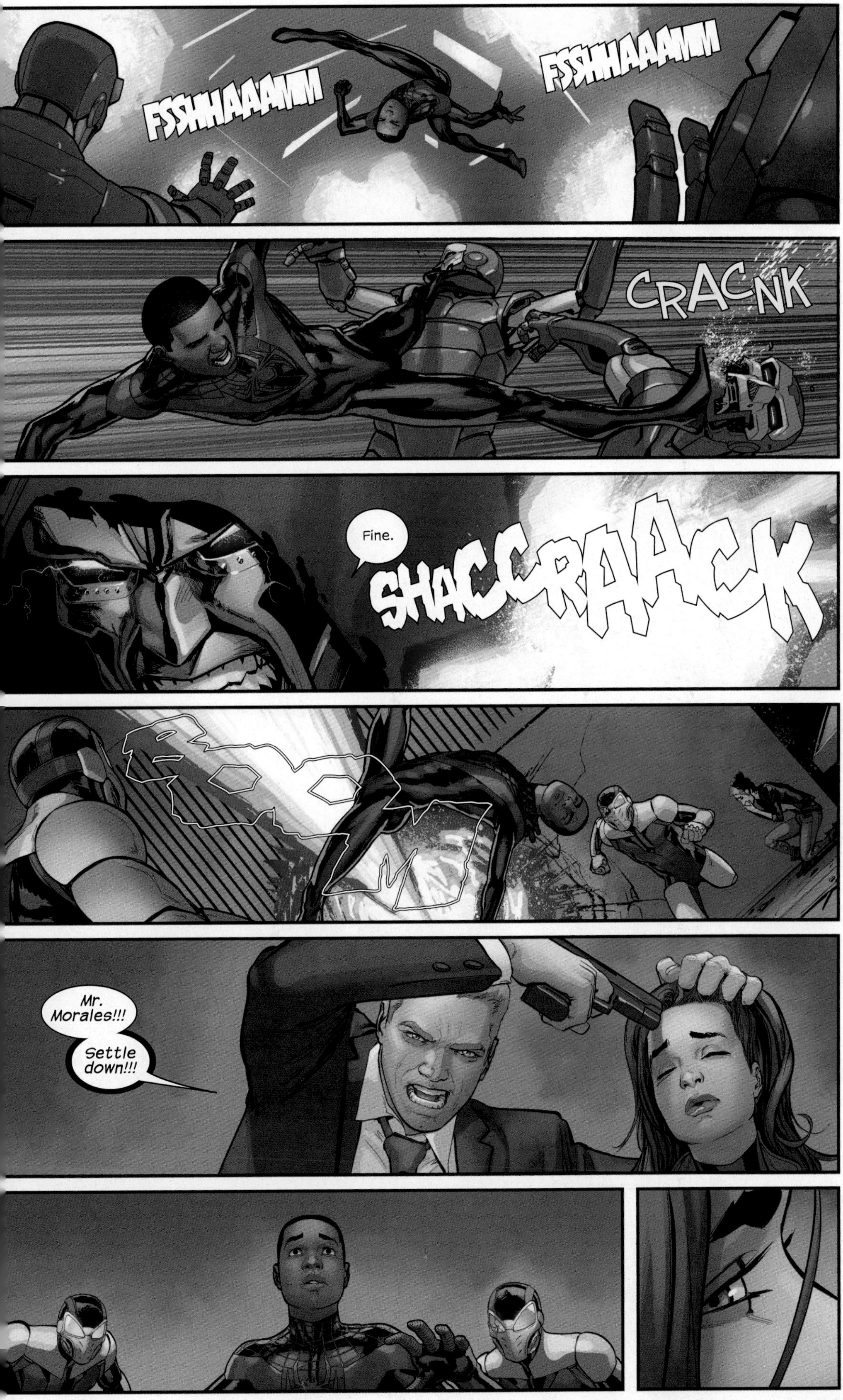
FSSHHAAAMM
FSSHHAAAMM
CRACNK
Fine.
SHACCRAACK
Mr. Morales!!!
Settle down!!!

Damn it!

Nothing?

Not a peep.

None of my old connections have heard of anything going on anywhere.

@#$@#!

Uh, Captain, you told us to keep an ear out for any unusual disturbances....

...we got some calls from Staten Island.

Yeah, but it's Staten Island. All they are is unusual--

Small explosions in the warehouse district. Flashing lights. Some movements.

They have cars on the way.

You have an address?

That does not mean it's Spider-Man related.

I can get us over there in a split second.

Can't hurt to try.

Okay, this might feel a little weird.

Hurry.

Come on...

I'm coming.

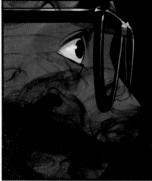

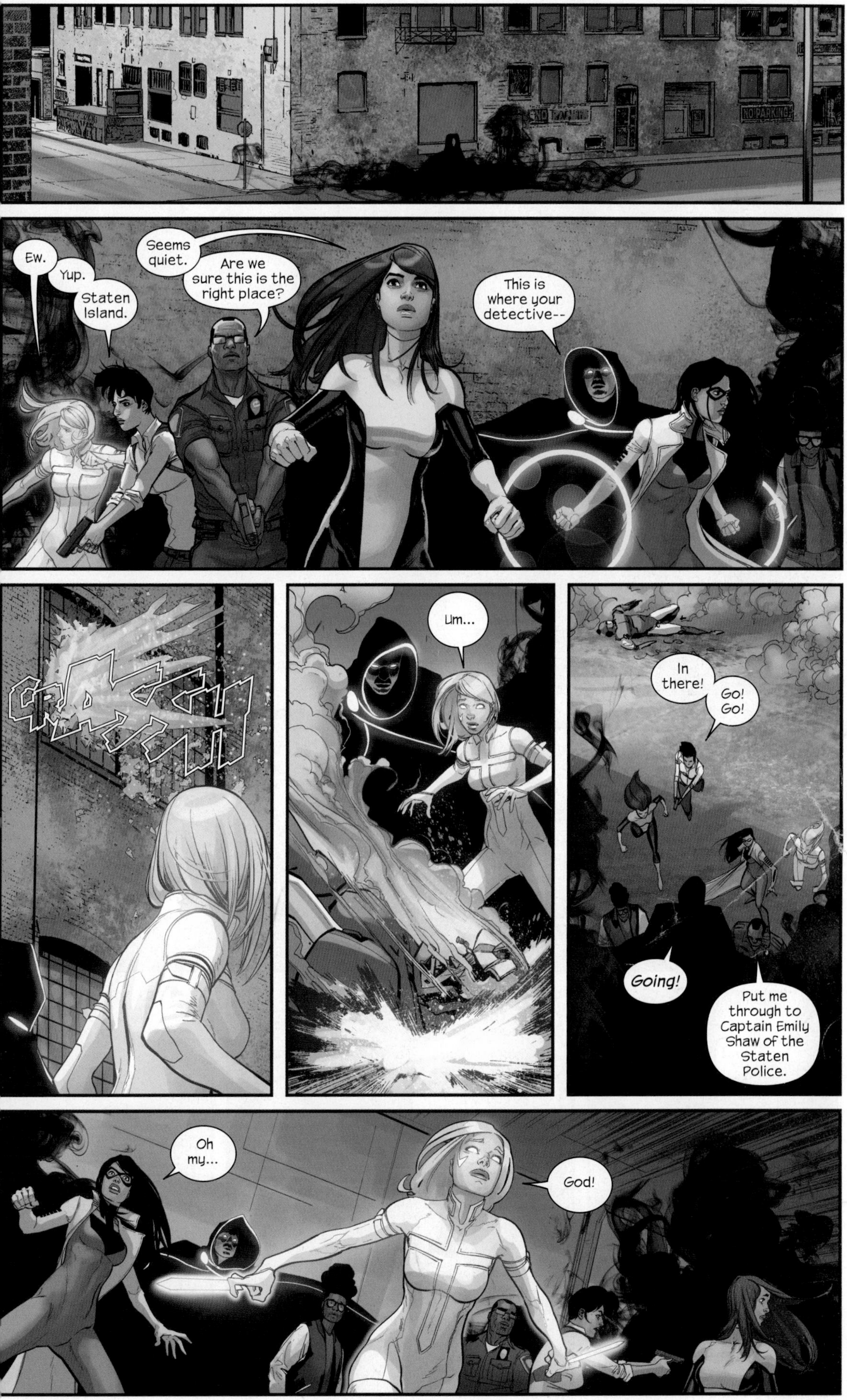

END TOWING
NO PARKING
Ew.
Yup.
Staten Island.
Seems quiet.
Are we sure this is the right place?
This is where your detective--
Um...
In there!
Go! Go!
Going!
Put me through to Captain Emily Shaw of the Staten Police.
Oh my...
God!

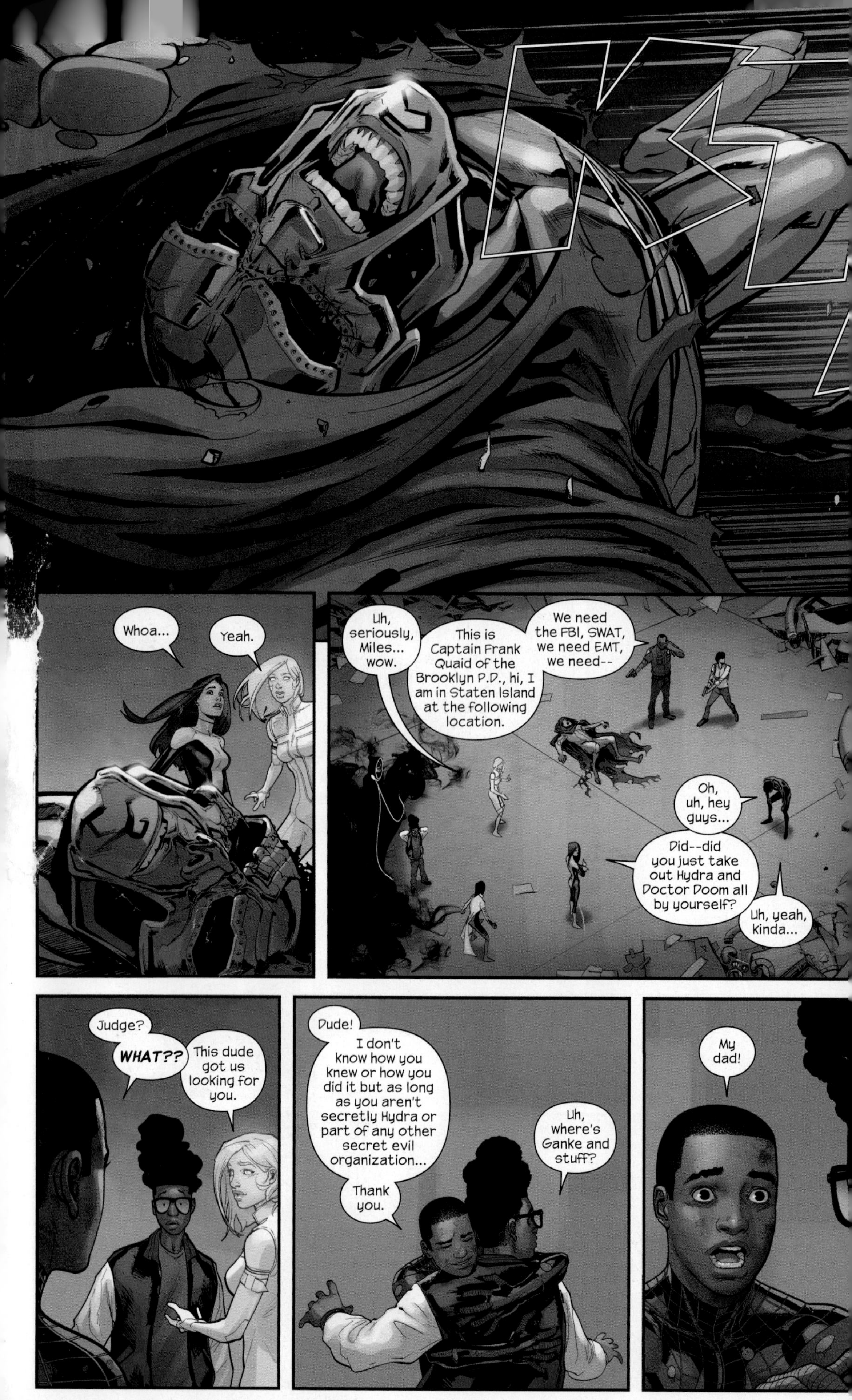

Whoa...
Yeah.
Uh, seriously, Miles... wow.
This is Captain Frank Quaid of the Brooklyn P.D., hi, I am in Staten Island at the following location.
We need the FBI, SWAT, we need EMT, we need--
Oh, uh, hey guys...
Did--did you just take out Hydra and Doctor Doom all by yourself?
Uh, yeah, kinda...
Judge?
WHAT??
This dude got us looking for you.
Dude!
I don't know how you knew or how you did it but as long as you aren't secretly Hydra or part of any other secret evil organization...
Thank you.
Uh, where's Ganke and stuff?
My dad!

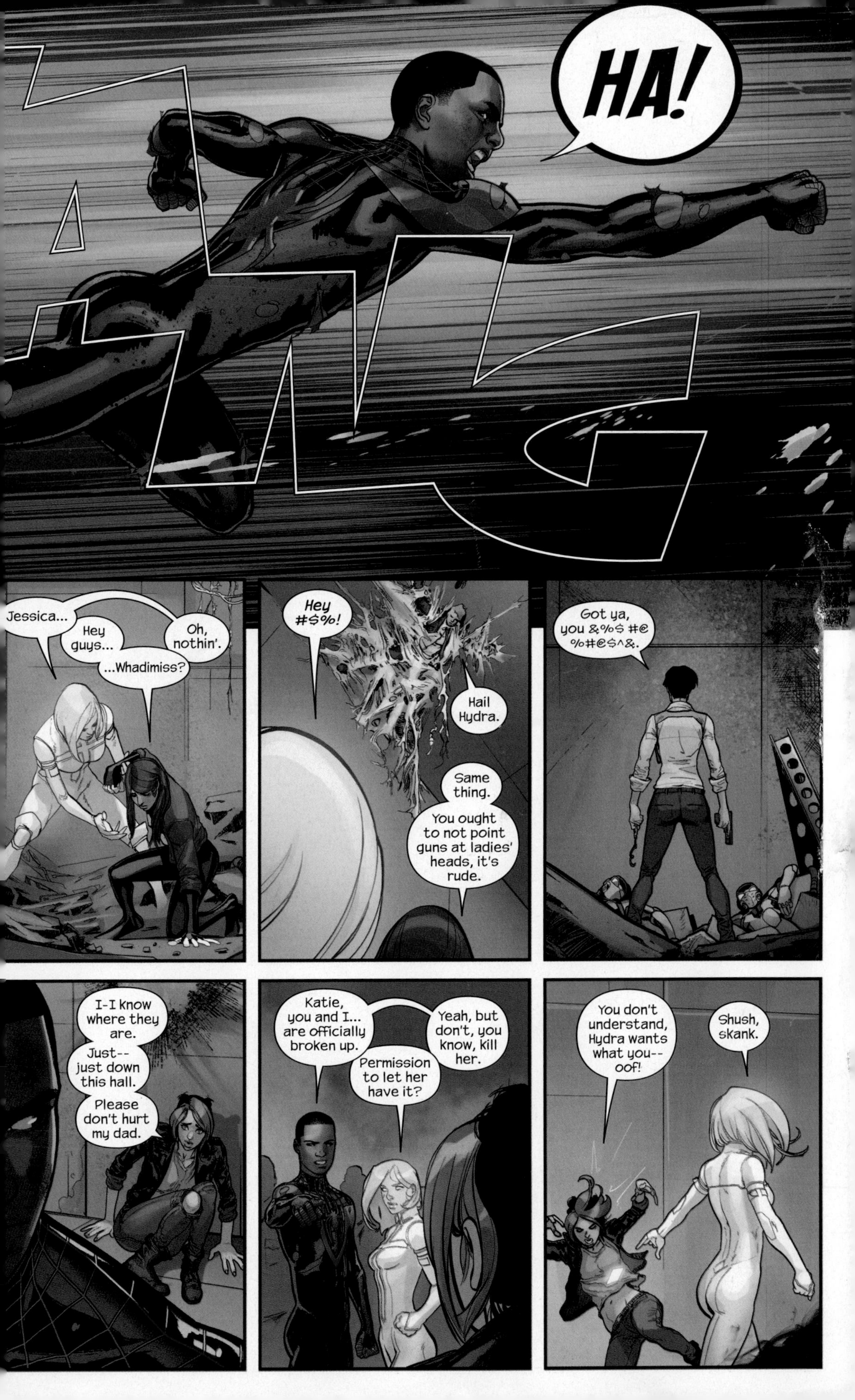
HA!
Jessica...
Hey guys...
...Whadimiss?
Oh, nothin'.
Hey #$%!
Hail Hydra.
Same thing.
You ought to not point guns at ladies' heads, it's rude.
Got ya, you &%$ #@ %#@$^&.
I-I know where they are.
Just-- just down this hall.
Please don't hurt my dad.
Katie, you and I... are officially broken up.
Yeah, but don't, you know, kill her.
Permission to let her have it?
You don't understand, Hydra wants what you-- oof!
Shush, skank.

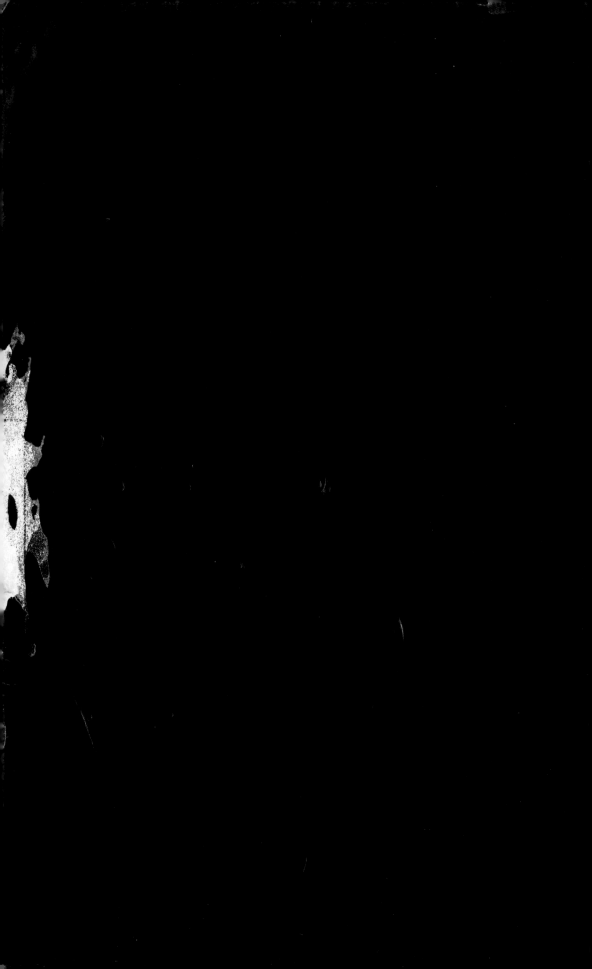

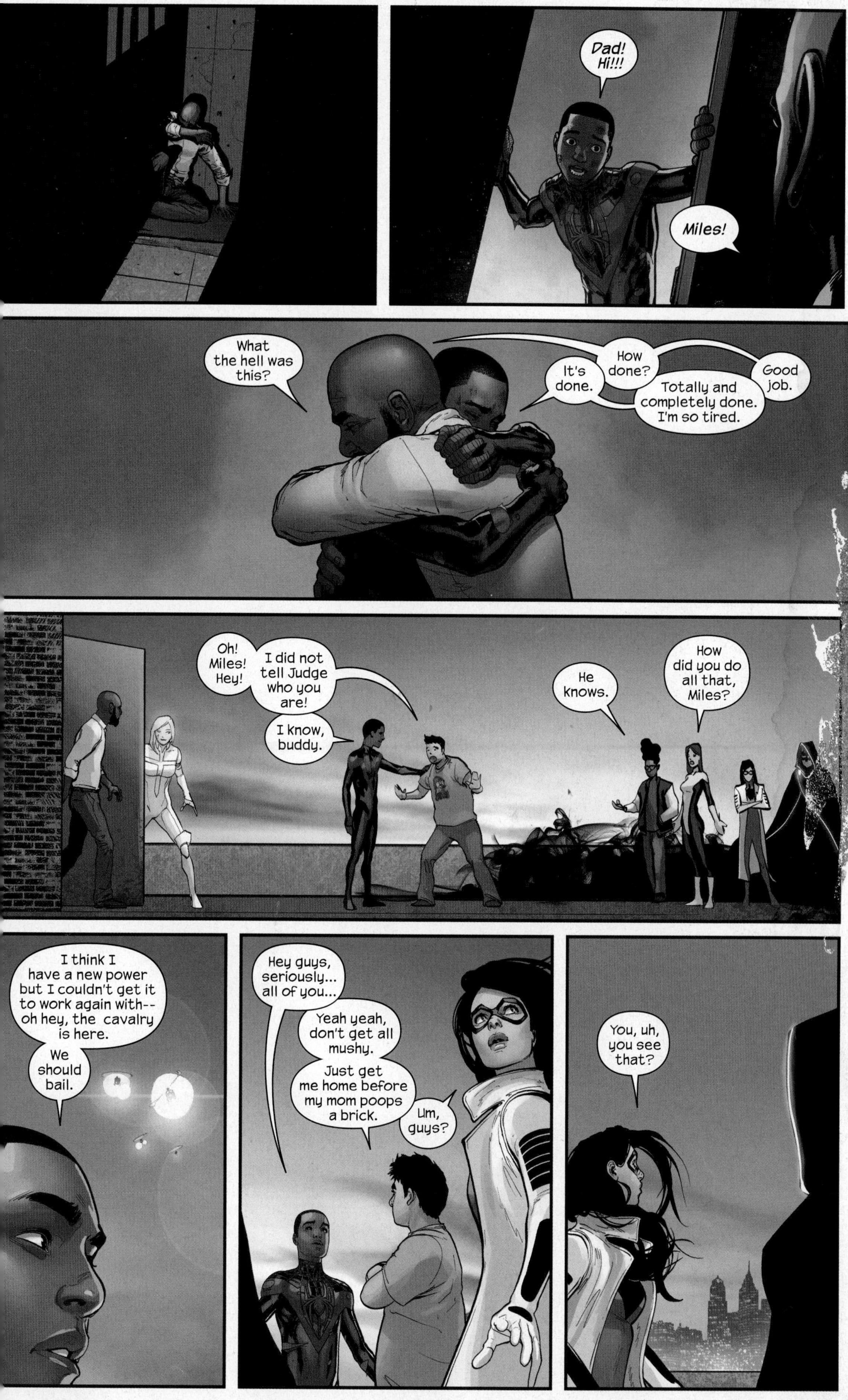
Dad! Hi!!!
Miles!
What the hell was this?
It's done.
How done?
Totally and completely done. I'm so tired.
Good job.
Oh! Miles! Hey!
I did not tell Judge who you are!
I know, buddy.
He knows.
How did you do all that, Miles?
I think I have a new power but I couldn't get it to work again with-- oh hey, the cavalry is here.
We should bail.
Hey guys, seriously... all of you...
Yeah yeah, don't get all mushy.
Just get me home before my mom poops a brick.
Um, guys?
You, uh, you see that?

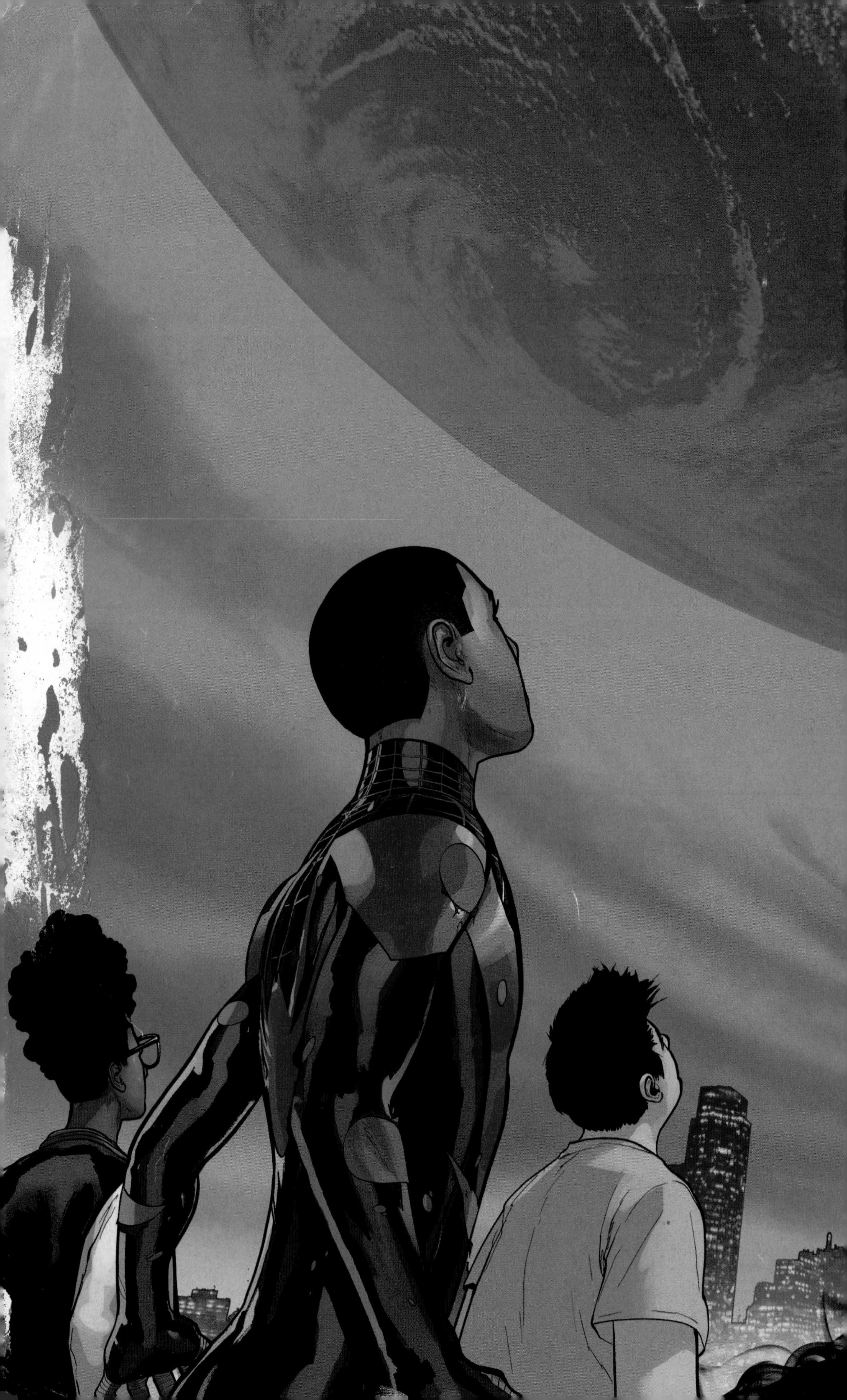